THE
COLLECTED WORKS

'OF

THEODORE PARKER,

MINISTER OF THE TWENTY-EIGHTH CONGREGATIONAL
SOCIETY AT BOSTON, U.S.

CONTAINING HIS

THEOLOGICAL, POLEMICAL, AND CRITICAL WRITINGS,
SERMONS, SPEECHES, AND ADDRESSES,
AND LITERARY MISCELLANIES.

EDITED BY

FRANCES POWER COBBE.

VOL. IV.

DISCOURSES OF POLITICS.

LONDON:
TRÜBNER & CO., 60, PATERNOSTER ROW.
1863.

DISCOURSES

OF

POLITICS.

BY

THEODORE PARKER,

MINISTER OF THE TWENTY-EIGHTH CONGREGATIONAL CHURCH IN BOSTON.

LONDON:

TRÜBNER & CO., 60, PATERNOSTER ROW.

1863.

CONTENTS.

I.

A SERMON OF WAR, PREACHED AT THE MELODEON, ON SUNDAY, JUNE 7, 1846.

"THE LORD IS A MAN OF WAR," Exodus xv. 3.—"GOD IS LOVE." 1 John iv. 8.

I ASK your attention to a Sermon of War. I have waited some time before treating this subject at length, till the present hostilities should assume a definite form, and the designs of the Government become more apparent. I wished to be able to speak coolly, and with knowledge of the facts, that we might understand the comparative merits of the present war. Besides, I have waited for others in the churches, of more experience to speak, before I ventured to offer my counsel; but I have thus far waited almost in vain! I did not wish to treat the matter last Sunday, for that was the end of our week of Pentecost, when cloven tongues of flame descend on the city, and some are thought to be full of new wine, and others of the Holy Spirit. The heat of the meetings, good and bad, of that week, could not wholly have passed away from you or me, and we ought to come coolly and consider a subject like this. So the last Sunday I only sketched the background of the picture, to-day intending to paint the horrors of war in front of that "Presence of Beauty in Nature," to which, with its "Meanings" and its "Lessons," I then asked you to attend.

It seems to me that an idea of God as the Infinite is given to us in our nature itself. But men create a more definite conception of God in their own image. Thus a rude savage man, who has learned only the presence of power in Nature, conceives of God mainly as a force, and speaks of Him as a God of power. Such, though not without beautiful exceptions, is the character ascribed to Jehovah in the Old Testament. "The Lord is a man of war." He is "the Lord of hosts." He kills men, and their cattle. If there is trouble in the enemies' city, it is the Lord who hath caused it. He will " whet his glittering sword, and render vengeance to his enemies. He will make his arrows drunk with blood, and his sword shall devour flesh !" It is with the sword that God pleads with all men. He encourages men to fight, and says, " Cursed be he that keepeth back his sword from blood." He sends blood into the streets ; he waters the land with blood, and in blood he dissolves the mountains. He brandishes his sword before kings, and they tremble at every moment. He treads nations as grapes in a wine-press, and his garments are stained with their life's blood.*

* Isaiah lxiii. 1—6.—*Noyes's* Version.

The People.

1. Who is this that cometh from Edom ?
   In scarlet garments from Bozrah ?
   This, that is glorious in his apparel,
   Proud in the greatness of his strength ?

Jehovah.

I, that proclaim deliverance,
And am mighty to save.

The People.

2. Wherefore is thine apparel red,
   And thy garments like those of one that treadeth the wine-vat ?

Jehovah.

3. I have trodden the wine-vat alone,
   And of the nations there was none with me.
   And I trod them in mine anger,
   And I trampled them in my fury,
   So that their life-blood was sprinkled upon my garments ;
   And I have stained all my apparel.
4. For the day of vengeance was in my heart,
   And the year of my deliverance was come.
5. And I looked and there was none to help,
   And I wondered that there was none to uphold,
   Therefore my own arm wrought salvation for me,
   And my fury, it sustained me.
6. I trod down the nations in my anger :
   I crushed them in my fury,
   And spilled their blood upon the ground.

A man who has grown up to read the Older Testament of God revealed in the beauty of the universe, and to feel the goodness of God therein set forth, sees Him not as force only, or in chief, but as love. He worships in love the God of goodness and of peace. Such is the prevalent character ascribed to God in the New Testament, except in the book of "Revelation." He is the "God of love and peace;" "our Father," "kind to the unthankful and the unmerciful." In one word, God is love. He loves us all, Jew and Gentile, bond and free. All are His children, each of priceless value in His sight. He is no God of battles; no Lord of hosts; no man of war. He has no sword nor arrows; He does not water the earth nor melt the mountains in blood, but "He maketh His sun to rise on the evil and on the good, and sendeth rain on the just and the unjust." He has no garments dyed in blood; curses no man for refusing to fight. He is spirit, to be worshipped in spirit and in truth! The commandment is: Love one another; resist not evil with evil; forgive seventy times seven; overcome evil with good; love your enemies; bless them that curse you; do good to them that hate you; pray for them that despitefully use you and persecute you.* There is no nation to shut its ports against another, all are men; no caste to curl its lip at inferiors; all are brothers, members of one body, united in the Christ, the ideal man and head of all. The most useful is the greatest. No man is to be master, for the Christ is our teacher. We are to fear no man, for God is our Father.

These precepts are undeniably the precepts of Christianity. Equally plain is it that they are the dictates of man's nature, only developed and active; a part of God's universal revelation; His law writ on the soul of man, established in the nature of things; true after all experience, and true before all experience. The man of real insight into spiritual things sees and knows them to be true.

Do not believe it the part of a coward to think so. I

* To show the differences between the Old and New Testament, and to serve as introduction to this discourse, the following passages were read as the morning lesson: Exodus xv. 1—6; 2 Sam. xxii. 32, 35—43, 48; xlv. 3—5; Isa. lxvi. 15, 16; Joel iii. 9—17; and Matt. v. 3—11, 38, 39, 43—45.

B 2

have known many cowards; yes, a great many; some very cowardly, pusillanimous, and faint-hearted cowards; but never one who thought so, or pretended to think so. It requires very little courage to fight with sword and musket, and that of a cheap kind. Men of that stamp are plenty as grass in June. Beat your drum, and they will follow; offer them but eight dollars a month, and they will come— fifty thousand of them, to smite and kill.* Every male animal, or reptile, will fight. It requires little courage to kill; but it takes much to resist evil with good, holding obstinately out, active or passive, till you overcome it. Call that non-resistance, if you will; it is the stoutest kind of combat, demanding all the manhood of a man.

I will not deny that war is inseparable from a low stage of civilization; so is polygamy, slavery, cannibalism. Taking men as they were, savage and violent, there have been times when war was unavoidable. I will not deny that it has helped forward the civilization of the race, for God often makes the folly and the sin of men contribute to the progress of mankind. It is none the less a folly or a sin. In a civilized nation like ourselves, it is far more heinous than in the Ojibeways or the Camanches.

War is in utter violation of Christianity. If war be right, then Christianity is wrong, false, a lie. But if Christianity be true, if reason, conscience, the religious sense, the highest faculties of man, are to be trusted, then war is the wrong, the falsehood, the lie. I maintain that aggressive war is a sin; that it is national infidelity, a denial of Christianity and of God. Every man who understands Christianity by heart, in its relations to man, to society, the nation, the world, knows that war is a wrong. At this day, with all the enlightenment of our age, after the long peace of the nations, war is easily avoided. Whenever it occurs, the very fact of its occurrence convicts the rulers of a nation either of entire incapacity as statesmen, or else of the worst form of treason: treason to the people, to mankind, to God! There is no other alternative. The very fact of an aggressive war shows that the men who cause it must be either fools or traitors. I think lightly of what is called treason against

* Such was the price offered, and such the number of soldiers then called for.

a government. That may be your duty to-day, or mine. Certainly it was our fathers' duty not long ago ; now it is our boast and their title to honour. But treason against the people, against mankind, against God, is a great sin, not lightly to be spoken of. The political authors of the war on this continent, and at this day, are either utterly incapable of a statesman's work, or else guilty of that sin. Fools they are, or traitors they must be.

Let me speak, and in detail, of the Evils of War. I wish this were not necessary. But we have found ourselves in a war ; the Congress has voted our money and our men to carry it on ; the Governors call for volunteers ; the volunteers come when they are called for. No voice of indignation goes forth from the heart of the eight hundred thousand souls of Massachusetts ; of the seventeen million freemen of the land how few complain ; only a man here and there ! The Press is well-nigh silent. And the Church, so far from protesting against this infidelity in the name of Christ, is little better than dead. The man of blood shelters himself behind its wall, silent, dark, dead, and emblematic. These facts show that it is necessary to speak of the evils of war. I am speaking in a city, whose fairest, firmest, most costly buildings are warehouses and banks ; a city whose most popular Idol is Mammon, the God of Gold ; whose Trinity is a Trinity of Coin ! I shall speak intelligibly, therefore, if I begin by considering war as a waste of property. It paralyzes industry. The very fear of it is a mildew upon commerce. Though the present war is but a skirmish, only a few random shots between a squad of regulars and some strolling battalions, a quarrel which in Europe would scarcely frighten even the Pope— yet see the effect of it upon trade. Though the fighting be thousands of miles from Boston, your stocks fall in the market ; the rate of insurance is altered ; your dealer in wood piles his boards and his timber on his wharf, not finding a market. There are few ships in the great Southern mart to take the freight of many ; exchange is disturbed. The clergyman is afraid to buy a book, lest his children want bread. It is so with all departments of industry and trade. In war the capitalist is uncertain and slow to venture, so the labourer's hand will be still, and his child ill-clad and hungry.

In the late war with England, many of you remember the condition of your fisheries, of your commerce; how the ships lay rotting at the wharf. The dearness of cloth, of provisions, flour, sugar, tea, coffee, salt; the comparative lowness of wages, the stagnation of business, the scarcity of money, the universal sullenness and gloom—all this is well remembered now. So is the ruin it brought on many a man.

Yet but few weeks ago some men talked boastingly of a war with England. There are some men who seem to have no eyes nor ears, only a mouth; whose chief function is talk. Of their talk I will say nothing; we look for dust in dry places. But some men thus talked of war, and seemed desirous to provoke it, who can scarce plead ignorance, and I fear not folly, for their excuse. I leave such to the just resentment sure to fall on them from sober, serious men, who dare to be so unpopular as to think before they speak, and then say what comes of thinking. Perhaps such a war was never likely to take place, and now, thanks to a few wise men, all danger thereof seems at an end. But suppose it had happened—what would become of your commerce, of your fishing-smacks on the banks or along the shore? what of your coasting vessels, doubling the headlands all the way from the St. John's to the Nueces? what of your whale-ships in the Pacific? what of your Indiamen, deep freighted with oriental wealth? what of that fleet which crowds across the Atlantic sea, trading with east and west, and north and south? I know some men care little for the rich, but when the owners keep their craft in port, where can the "hands" find work, or their mouths find bread? The shipping of the United States amounts nearly to 2,500,000 tons. At $40 a ton, its value is nearly $100,000,000. This is the value only of those sea-carriages; their cargoes I cannot compute. Allowing one sailor for every twenty tons burden, here will be 125,000 seamen. They and their families amount to 500,000 souls. In war, what will become of them? A capital of more than $13,000,000 is invested in the fisheries of Massachusetts alone. More than 19,000 men find profitable employment therein. If each man have but four others in his family, a small number for that class, here are more than 95,000 persons in this State alone, whose daily bread depends on this business. They cannot fish in troubled waters, for they are fishermen, not politicians. Where could they find bread or cloth in time of war? In Dartmoor prison? Ask that of your demagogues who courted war!

Then, too, the positive destruction of property in war is monstrous. A ship of the line costs from $500,000 to $1,000,000. The loss of a fleet by capture, by fire, or by decay, is a great loss. You know at what cost a fort is built, if you have counted the sums successively voted for Fort Adams in Rhode Island, or those in our own harbour. The destruction of forts is another item in the cost of war. The capture or destruction of merchant ships with their freight, creates a most formidable loss. In 1812 the whole tonnage of the United States was scarce half what it is now. Yet the loss of ships and their freight, in "the late war," brief as it was, is estimated at $100,000,000. Then the loss by plunder and military occupation is monstrous. The soldier, like the savage, cuts down the tree to gather its fruit. I cannot calculate the loss by burning towns and cities. But suppose Boston were bombarded and laid in ashes. Calculate the loss if you can. You may say, "This could not be," for it is as easy to say No, as Yes. But remember what befell us in the last war; remember how recently the best defended capitals of Europe, Vienna, Paris, Antwerp, have fallen into hostile hands. Consider how often a strong place, like Coblentz, Mentz, Malta, Gibraltar, St. Juan d'Ulloa, has been declared impregnable, and then been taken; calculate the force which might be brought against this town, and you will see that in eight and forty hours, or half that time, it might be left nothing but a heap of ruins smoking in the sun! I doubt not the valour of American soldiers, the skill of their engineers, nor the ability of their commanders. I am ready to believe all this is greater than we are told. Still, such are the contingencies of war. If some not very ignorant men had their way, this would be a probability and perhaps a fact. If we should burn every town from the Tweed to the Thames, it would not rebuild our own city.

But, on the supposition that nothing is destroyed, see the loss which comes from the misdirection of productive industry. Your fleets, forts, dockyards, arsenals, cannons, muskets, swords, and the like, are provided at great cost, and yet are unprofitable. They do not pay. They weave no cloth; they bake no bread; they produce nothing. Yet, from 1791 to 1832, in forty-two years, we expended in these things $303,242,576, namely, for the navy, &c., $112,703,933; for the army, &c., $190,538,643. For the same time, all other expenses of the nation came to but $37,158,047. More than eight-ninths of the whole revenue of the nation was spent for purposes of war. In four years, from 1812 to 1815, we paid in this way, $92,350,519·37. In six years, from 1835 to 1840, we paid annually on the average $21,328,903; in all, $127,973,418. Our Congress has just voted $17,000,000, as a special grant for the army alone. The 175,118 muskets at Springfield are valued at $3,000,000; we pay annually $200,000 to support that arsenal. The navy-yard at Charleston, with its stores, &c., has cost $4,741,000. And, for all profitable returns, this money might as well be sunk in the bottom of the sea. In some countries it is yet worse. There are towns and cities in which the fortifications have cost more than all the houses, churches, shops, and other property therein. This happens not among the Sacs and Foxes, but in " Christian" Europe.

Then your soldier is the most unprofitable animal you can keep. He makes no railroads; clears no land; raises no corn. No, he can make neither cloth nor clocks ! He does not raise his own bread, mend his own shoes, make his shoulder-knot of glory, nor hammer out his own sword. Yet he is a costly animal, though useless. If the President gets his fifty thousand volunteers, a thing likely to happen—for though Irish lumpers and hodmen want a dollar or a dollar and a half a day, your free American of Boston will enlist for twenty-seven cents, only having his livery, his feathers, and his " glory" thrown in—then at $8 a month, their wages amount to $400,000 a month. Suppose the present Government shall actually make advantageous contracts, and the subsistence of the soldier cost no more than in England, or $17 a month, this amounts to $850,000. Here are $1,250,000 a month to begin with. Then, if each man would be worth a dollar a day at any productive work, and there are 26 work-days in the month, here are $1,300,000 more to be added, making $2,550,000 a month for the new army of occupation. This is only for the rank and file of the army. The officers, the surgeons, and the chaplains, who teach the soldiers to *wad* their muskets with the leaves of the Bible, will perhaps cost as much more; or, in all, something more than $5,000,000 a month. This of course does not include the cost of their arms, tents, ammunition, baggage, horses, and hospital stores, nor the 65,000 gallons of whiskey which the Government has just advertised for! What do they give in return? They will give us three things, valour, glory, and—talk; which, as they are not in the price current, I must estimate as I can, and set them all down in one figure = 0; not worth the whiskey they cost.

New England is quite a new country. Seven generations ago it was a wilderness; now it contains about 2,500,000 souls. If you were to pay all the public debts of these States, and then, in fancy, divide all the property therein by the population, young as we are, I think you would find a larger amount of value for each man than in any other country in the world, not excepting England. The civilization of Europe is old; the nations old, England, France, Spain, Austria, Italy, Greece; but they have wasted their time, their labour, and their wealth in war, and so are poorer than we upstarts of a wilderness. We have fewer fleets, forts, cannon, and soldiers for the population, than any other " Christian" country in the world. This is one main reason why we have no national debt; why the women need not toil in the hardest labour of the fields, the quarries, and the mines; this is the reason that we are well fed, well clad, well housed; this is the reason that Massachusetts can afford to spend $1,000,000 a year for her public schools! War, wasting a nation's wealth, depresses the great mass of the people, but serves to elevate a few to opulence and power. Every despotism is established and sustained by war. This is the foundation of all the aristocracies of the old world, aristocracies of blood. Our famous men are often ashamed that their wealth was honestly got by working, or peddling, and foolishly copy the savage and bloody emblems of ancient heraldry in their assumed coats of arms—industrious men seeking to have a griffin on their seal! Nothing is so hostile to a true democracy as war. It elevates a few, often bold, bad men, at the expense of the many, who pay the money and furnish the blood for war.

War is a most expensive folly. The revolutionary war cost the general Government, directly and in specie, $135,000,000. It is safe to estimate the direct cost to the individual states also at the same sum, $135,000,000; making a total of $270,000,000. Considering the interruption of business, the waste of time, property and life, it is plain that this could not have been a fourth part of the whole. But suppose it was a third, then the whole pecuniary cost of the war would be $810,000,000. At the beginning of the Revolution the population was about $3,000,000; so that war, lasting about eight years, cost $270 for each person. To meet the expenses of the war each year there would have been required a tax of $33·75 on each man, woman, and child!

In the Florida war we spent between $30,000,000 and $40,000,000, as an eminent statesman once said, in fighting five hundred invisible Indians! It is estimated that the fortifications of the city of Paris, when completely furnished, will cost more than the whole taxable property of Massachusetts, with her 800,000 souls. Why this year our own grant for the army is $17,000,000. The estimate for the navy is $6,000,000 more; in all $23,000,000. Suppose, which is most unlikely, that we should pay no more, why, that sum alone would support public schools, as good and as costly as those of Massachusetts, all over the United States, offering each boy and girl, bond or free, as good a culture as they get here in Boston, and then leave a balance of $3,000,000 in our hands! We pay more for ignorance than we need for education! But $23,000,000 is not all we must pay this year. A great statesman has said, in the Senate, that our war expenses at present are nearly $500,000 a day, and the President informs your Congress that $22,952,904 more will be wanted for the army and navy before next June!

For several years we spent directly more than $21,000,000 for war purposes, though in time of peace. If a railroad cost $30,000 a mile, then we might build 700 miles a year for that sum, and in five years could build a railroad therewith from Boston to the further side of

Oregon. For the war money we paid in forty-two years, we could have had more than 10,000 miles of railroad, and, with dividends at seven per cent., a yearly income of $21,210,000. For military and naval affairs, in eight years, from 1835 to 1843, we paid $163,336,717. This alone would have made 5444 miles of railroad, and would produce, at seven per cent., an annual income of $11,433,569·19.

In Boston there are nineteen public grammar-schools, a Latin and English High school. The buildings for these schools, twenty in number, have cost $653,208. There are also 135 primary schools, in as many houses or rooms. I know not their value, as I think they are not all owned by the city. But suppose them to be worth $150,000, then all the school-houses of this city have cost $803,208. The cost of these 156 schools for this year is estimated at $172,000. The number of scholars in them is $16,479. Harvard University, the most expensive college in America, costs about $46,000 a year. Now the ship "Ohio," lying here in our harbour, has cost $834,845, and we pay for it each year $220,000 more. That is, it has cost $31,637 more than these 155 school-houses of this city, and costs every year $2000 more than Harvard University, and all the public schools of Boston!

The military academy at West Point contains two hundred and thirty-six cadets; the appropriation for it last year was $138,000, a sum greater, I think, than the cost of all the colleges in Maine, New Hampshire, Vermont, and Massachusetts, with their 1445 students.

The navy-yard at Charlestown, with its ordnance, stores, &c., cost $4,741,000. The cost of the 78 churches in Boston is $3,246,500; the whole property of Harvard University is $703,175; the 155 school-houses of Boston are worth $803,208; in all, $4,752,883. Thus the navy-yard at Charlestown has cost almost as much as the 78 churches and the 155 school-houses of Boston, with Harvard College, its halls, libraries, all its wealth, thrown in. Yet what does it teach?

Our country is singularly destitute of public libraries. You must go across the ocean to read the history of the Church or State; all the public libraries in America cannot furnish the books referred to in Gibbon's "Rome," or

Gieseler's "History of the Church." I think there is no public library in Europe which has cost three dollars a volume. There are six: the Vatican, at Rome; the Royal, at Paris; the British Museum, at London; the Bodleian, at Oxford; the University Libraries at Gottingen and Berlin—which contain, it is said, about 4,500,000 volumes. The recent grant of $17,000,000 for the army is 3,500,000 more than the cost of those magnificent collections!

There have been printed about 3,000,000 different volumes, great and little, within the last 400 years. If the Florida war cost but $30,000,000, it is ten times more than enough to have purchased one copy of each book ever printed, at one dollar a volume, which is more than the average cost.

Now all these sums are to be paid by the people, "the dear people," whom our republican demagogues love so well, and for whom they spend their lives,—rising early, toiling late; those self-denying heroes, those sainted martyrs of the Republic, eating the bread of carefulness for them alone! But how are they to be paid? By a direct tax levied on all the property of the nation, so that the poor man pays according to his little, and the rich man in proportion to his much, each knowing when he pays and what he pays for? No such thing; nothing like it. The people must pay, and not know it; must be deceived a little, or they would not pay after this fashion! You pay for it in every pound of sugar, copper, coal, in every yard of cloth; and if the counsel of some lovers of the people be followed, you will soon pay for it in each pound of coffee and tea. In this way the rich man always pays relatively less than the poor; often a positively smaller sum. Even here I think that three-fourths of all the property is owned by one-fourth of the people, yet that three-fourths by no means pays a third of the national revenue. The tax is laid on things men cannot do without, —sugar, cloth, and the like. The consumption of these articles is not in proportion to wealth, but persons. Now the poor man, as a general rule, has more children than the rich; and the tax being more in proportion to persons than property, the poor man pays more than the rich. So a tax is really laid on the poor man's children to pay for the war which makes him poor and keeps him poor. I think your captains and colonels, those sons of thunder and heirs of glory, will not tell you so. They tell you so! They know it! Poor brothers, how could they? I think your party newspapers, penny or pound, will not tell you so; nor the demagogues, all covered with glory and all forlorn, who tell the people when to hurrah, and for what! But if you cipher the matter out for yourself you will find it so, and not otherwise. Tell the demagogues, whig or democrat, that. It was an old Roman maxim, "The people wished to be deceived; let them." Now it is only practised on; not repeated—in public.

Let us deal justly even with war, giving that its due. There is one class of men who find their pecuniary advantage in it. I mean army contractors, when they chance to be favourites of the party in power; men who let steamboats to lie idle at $500 a-day. This class of men rejoice in a war. The country may become poor, they are sure to be rich. Yet another class turn war to account, get the "glory," and become important in song and sermon. I see it stated in a newspaper that the Duke of Wellington has received, as gratuities for his military services, $5,400,000, and $40,000 a-year in pensions!

But the waste of property is the smallest part of the evil. The waste of life in war is yet more terrible. Human life is a sacred thing. Go out into the lowest street of Boston; take the vilest and most squalid man in that miserable lane, and he is dear to some one. He is called brother; perhaps husband; it may be, father; at least, son. A human heart, sadly joyful, beat over him before he was born. He has been pressed fondly to his mother's arms. Her tears and her smiles have been for him; perhaps also her prayers. His blood may be counted mean and vile by the great men of the earth, who love nothing so well as the dear people, for he has no "coat of arms," no liveried servant to attend him, but it has run down from the same first man. His family is ancient as that of the most long-descended king. God made him; made this splendid universe to wait on him and teach him; sent His Christ to save him. He is an immortal soul. Needlessly to spill that man's blood is an awful sin. It

will cry against you out of the ground—Cain! where is
thy brother? Now in war you bring together 50,000 men
like him on one side, and 50,000 of a different nation on
the other. They have no natural quarrel with one another.
The earth is wide enough for both; neither hinders the
sun from the other. Many come unwillingly; many not
knowing what they fight for. It is but accident that determines on which side the man shall fight. The cannons
pour their shot—round, grape, canister; the howitzers
scatter their bursting shells; the muskets rain their leaden
death; the sword, the bayonet, the horse's iron hoof, the
wheels of the artillery, grind the men down into trodden
dust. There they lie, the two masses of burning valour,
extinguished, quenched, and grimly dead, each covering
with his body the spot he defended with his arms. They
had no quarrel: yet they lie there, slain by a brother's
hand. It is not old and decrepid men, but men of the
productive age, full of lusty life.

But it is only the smallest part that perish in battle.
Exposure to cold, wet, heat; unhealthy climates, unwhole-
some food, rum, and forced marches, bring on diseases
which mow down the poor soldiers worse than musketry
and grape. Others languish of wounds, and slowly pro-
crastinate a dreadful and a tenfold death. Far away,
there are widows, orphans, childless old fathers, who pore
over the daily news to learn at random the fate of a son, a
father, or a husband! They crowd disconsolate into the
churches, seeking of God the comfort men took from them,
praying in the bitterness of a broken heart, while the
priest gives thanks for " a famous victory," and hangs up
the bloody standard over his pulpit!

When ordinary disease cuts off a man, when he dies at
his duty, there is some comfort in that loss. " It was the
ordinance of God," you say. You minister to his wants;
you smooth down the pillow for the aching head; your
love beguiles the torment of disease, and your own bosom
gathers half the darts of death. He goes in his time, and
God takes him. But when he dies in such a war, in
battle, it is man who has robbed him of life. It is a
murderer that is butchered. Nothing alleviates that bitter,
burning smart!

Others not slain are maimed for life. This has no eyes;

that no hands; another no feet nor legs. This has been pierced by lances, and torn with the shot, till scarce anything human is left. The wreck of a body is crazed with pains God never meant for man. The mother that bore him would not know her child. Count the orphan asylums in Germany and Holland; go into the hospital at Greenwich, that of the invalids in Paris, you see the " trophies" of Napoleon and Wellington. Go to the arsenal at Toulon, see the wooden legs piled up there for men now active and whole, and you will think a little of the physical horrors of war.

In Boston there are perhaps about 25,000 able-bodied men between eighteen and forty-five. Suppose them all slain in battle, or mortally hurt, or mown down by the camp-fever, vomito, or other diseases of war; and then fancy the distress, the heart-sickness, amid wives, mothers, daughters, sons, and fathers, here! Yet 25,000 is a small number to be murdered in " a famous victory;" a trifle for a whole " glorious campaign" in a great war. The men of Boston are no better loved than the men of Tamaulipas. There is scarce an old family, of the middle class, in all New England, which did not thus smart in the Revolution; many, which have not, to this day, recovered from the bloody blow then falling on them. Think, wives, of the butchery of your husbands; think, mothers, of the murder of your sons!

Here, too, the burden of battle falls mainly on the humble class. They pay the great tribute of money; they pay also the horrid tax of blood. It was not your rich men who fought even the Revolution; not they. Your men of property and standing were leaguing with the British, or fitting out privateers when that offered a good investment, or buying up the estates of more consistent tories; making money out of the nation's dire distress. True, there were most honourable exceptions; but such, I think, was the general rule. Let this be distinctly remembered, that the burden of battle is borne by the humble classes of men; they pay the vast tribute of money; the awful tax of blood! The " glory" is got by a few; poverty, wounds, death, are for the people!

Military glory is the poorest kind of distinction, but the most dangerous passion. It is an honour to man to be able to mould iron; to be skilful at working in cloth, wood, clay, leather. It is man's vocation to raise corn, to subdue the rebellious fibre of cotton and convert it into beautiful robes, full of comfort for the body. They are the heroes of the race who abridge the time of human toil and multiply its results; they who win great truths from God, and send them to a people's heart; they who balance the many and the one into harmonious action, so that all are united and yet each left free. But the glory which comes of epaulets and feathers; that strutting glory which is dyed in blood—what shall we say of it? In this day it is not heroism; it is an imitation of barbarism long ago passed by. Yet it is marvellous how many men are taken with a red coat. You expect it in Europe, a land of soldiers and blood. You are disappointed to find that here the champions of force should be held in honour, and that even the lowest should voluntarily enrol themselves as butchers of men!

Yet more: aggressive war is a sin; a corruption of the public morals. It is a practical denial of Christianity; a violation of God's eternal law of love. This is so plain, that I shall say little upon it to-day. Your savagest and most vulgar captain would confess he does not fight as a Christian—but as a soldier; your magistrate calls for volunteers —not as a man loving Christianity, and loyal to God; only as governor, under oath to keep the constitution, the tradition of the elders; not under oath to keep the commandment of God. In war the laws are suspended, violence and cunning rule everywhere. The battle of Yorktown was gained by a lie, though a Washington told it. As a soldier it was his duty. Men "emulate the tiger;" the hand is bloody, and the heart hard. Robbery and murder are the rule, the glory of men. "Good men look sad, but ruffians dance and leap." Men are systematically trained to burn towns, to murder fathers and sons; taught to consider it "glory" to do so. The Government collects ruffians and cut-throats. It compels better men to serve with these and become cut-throats. It appoints chaplains to blaspheme Christianity; teaching the ruffians how to pray for the destruction of the enemy, the burning of his towns; to do this in the name of Christ and God.

I do not censure all the men who serve: some of them know no better; they have heard that a man would "perish everlastingly" if he did not believe the Athanasian creed; that if he questioned the story of Jonah, or the miraculous birth of Jesus, he was in danger of hell-fire, and if he doubted damnation was sure to be damned. They never heard that such a war was a sin; that to create a war was treason, and to fight in it wrong. They never thought of thinking for themselves; their thinking was to read a newspaper, or sleep through a sermon. They counted it their duty to obey the Government, without thinking if that Government be right or wrong. I deny not the noble, manly character of many a soldier—his heroism, self-denial, and personal sacrifice.

Still, after all proper allowance is made for a few individuals, the whole system of war is unchristian and sinful. It lives only by evil passions. It can be defended only by what is low, selfish, and animal. It absorbs the scum of the cities—pirates, robbers, murderers. It makes them worse, and better men like them. To take one man's life is murder; what is it to practise killing as an art, a trade; to do it by thousands? Yet I think better of the hands that do the butchering than of the ambitious heads, the cold, remorseless hearts, which plunge the nation into war.

In war the State teaches men to lie, to steal, to kill. It calls for privateers, who are commonly pirates with a national charter, and pirates are privateers with only a personal charter. Every camp is a school of profanity, violence, licentiousness, and crimes too foul to name. It is so without sixty-five thousand gallons of whisky. This is unavoidable. It was so with Washington's army, with Cornwallis's, with that of Gustavus Adolphus, perhaps the most moral army the world ever saw. The soldier's life generally unfits a man for the citizen's. When he returns from a camp, from a war, back to his native village, he becomes a curse to society and a shame to the mother that bore him. Even the soldiers of the Revolution, who survived the war, were mostly ruined for life— debauched, intemperate, vicious, and vile. What loathsome creatures so many of them were! They bore our burden: for such were the real martyrs of that war, not

the men who fell under the shot!   How many men of the
rank and file in the late war have since become respectable
citizens ?

To show how incompatible are War and Christianity,
suppose that he who is deemed the most Christian of
Christ's disciples, the well-beloved John, were made a
navy-chaplain, and some morning, when a battle is daily
looked for, should stand on the gun-deck, amid lockers of
shot, his Bible resting on a cannon, and expound Christianity to men with cutlasses by their side!   Let him read
for the morning lesson the Sermon on the Mount, and for
text take words from his own Epistle, so sweet, so beautiful, so true : " Every one that loveth is born of God, and
knoweth God, for God is love." Suppose he tells his
strange audience that all men are brothers; that God
is their common father ; that Christ loved us all, showing
us how to live the life of love ; and then, when he had
melted all those savage hearts by words so winsome and so
true, let him conclude, " Blessed are the men-slayers!
Seek first the glory which cometh of battle.   Be fierce as
tigers.   Mar God's image in which your brothers are
made.   Be not like Christ, but Cain who slew his brother!
When you meet the enemy, fire into their bosoms ; kill
them in the dear name of Christ; butcher them in the
spirit of God.   Give them no quarter, for we ought not
to lay down our lives for the brethren ; only the murderer
hath eternal life!"

Yet great as are these threefold evils, there are times
when the soberest men and the best men have welcomed war,
coolly and in their better moments.   Sometimes a people,
long oppressed, has " petitioned, remonstrated, cast itself
at the feet of the throne," with only insult for answer to
its prayer.   Sometimes there is a contest between a falsehood and a great truth; a self-protecting war for freedom
of mind, heart, and soul; yes, a war for a man's body, his
wife's and children's body, for what is dearer to men than
life itself, for the unalienable rights of man, for the idea
that all are born free and equal.   It was so in the American
Revolution ; in the English, in the French Revolution.   In
such cases men say, " Let it come."   They take down the
firelock in sorrow ; with a prayer they go forth to battle,

asking that the right may triumph. Much as I hate war, I cannot but honour such men. Were they better, yet more heroic, even war of that character might be avoided. Still, it is a colder heart than mine which does not honour such men, though it believes them mistaken. Especially do we honour them, when it is the few, the scattered, the feeble, contending with the many and the mighty; the noble fighting for a great idea, and against the base and tyrannical. Then most men think the gain, the triumph of a great idea, is worth the price it costs, the price of blood. I will not stop to touch that question, If man may ever shed the blood of man. But it is plain that an aggressive war like this is wholly unchristian, and a reproach to the nation and the age.

Now, to make the evils of war still clearer, and to bring them home to your door, let us suppose there was war between the counties of Suffolk, on the one side, and Middlesex on the other—this army at Boston, that at Cambridge. Suppose the subject in dispute was the boundary line between the two, Boston claiming a pitiful acre of flat land, which the ocean at low-tide disdained to cover. To make sure of this, Boston seizes whole miles of flats, unquestionably not its own. The rulers on one side are fools, and traitors on the other. The two commanders have issued their proclamations; the money is borrowed; the whisky provided; the soldiers—Americans, Negroes, Irishmen, all the able-bodied men—are enlisted. Prayers are offered in all the churches, and sermons preached, showing that God is a man of war, and Cain his first saint—an early Christian, a Christian before Christ. The Bostonians wish to seize Cambridge, burn the houses, churches, college-halls, and plunder the library. The men of Cambridge wish to seize Boston, burn its houses and ships, plundering its wares and its goods. Martial law is proclaimed on both sides. The men of Cambridge cut asunder the bridges, and make a huge breach in the mill-dam, planting cannon to enfilade all those avenues. Forts crown the hill-tops, else so green. Men, madder than lunatics, are crowded into the asylum. The Bostonians rebuild the old fortifications on the Neck; replace the forts on Beacon-hill, Fort-hill, Copps-hill, levelling houses to make room for redoubts and

bastions. The batteries are planted, the mortars got ready;
the furnaces and magazines are all prepared. The three
hills are grim with war. From Copps-hill men look
anxious to that memorable height the other side of the
water. Provisions are cut off in Boston; no man may
pass the lines; the aqueduct refuses its genial supply;
children cry for their expected food. The soldiers parade,
looking somewhat tremulous and pale; all the able-bodied
have come, the vilest most willingly; some are brought by
force of drink, some by force of arms. Some are in brilliant dresses, some in their working frocks. The banners
are consecrated by solemn words.* Your church-towers
are military posts of observation. There are Old Testament prayers to the "God of Hosts" in all the churches of
Boston; prayers that God would curse the men of Cambridge, make their wives widows, their children fatherless,
their houses a ruin, the men corpses, meat for the beast of
the field and the bird of the air. Last night the Bostonians made a feint of attacking Charlestown, raining bombs
and red-hot cannon-balls from Copps-hill, till they have
burnt a thousand houses, where the British burnt not half
so many. Women and children fled screaming from the
blazing rafters of their homes. The men of Middlesex
crowd into Charlestown.

In the meantime the Bostonians hastily repair a bridge
or two; some pass that way, some over the Neck; all
stealthily by night; and while the foe expect them at
Bunker's, amid the blazing town, they have stolen a march
and rush upon Cambridge itself. The Cambridge men
turn back. The battle is fiercely joined. You hear the
cannon, the sharp report of musketry. You crowd the
hills, the housetops; you line the Common, you cover the
shore, yet you see but little in the sulphurous cloud. Now
the Bostonians yield a little, a reinforcement goes over.
All the men are gone; even the grey-headed who can
shoulder a firelock. They plunge into battle, mad with
rage, madder with rum. The chaplains loiter behind.

> "Pious men, whom duty brought,
> To dubious verge of battle fought,
> To shrive the dying, bless the dead!"

* See the appropriate forms of prayer for that service by the present
Bishop of Oxford, in Jay's Address before the American Peace Society, in
1845.

The battle hangs long in even scale. At length it turns. The Cambridge men retreat, they run, they fly. The houses burn. You see the churches and the colleges go up, a stream of fire. That library—founded amid want and war, and sad sectarian strife, slowly gathered by the saving of two centuries; the hope of the poor scholar, the boast of the rich one—is scattered to the winds and burnt with fire, for the solid granite is blasted by powder, and the turrets fall. Victory is ours. Ten thousand men of Cambridge lie dead; eight thousand of Boston. There writhe the wounded; men who but few hours before were poured over the battle-field a lava flood of fiery valour—fathers, brothers, husbands, sons. There they lie, torn and mangled; black with powder; red with blood; parched with thirst; cursing the load of life they now must bear with bruised frames and mutilated limbs. Gather them into hasty hospitals—let this man's daughter come to-morrow and sit by him, fanning away the flies; he shall linger out a life of wretched anguish, unspoken and unspeakable, and when he dies his wife religiously will keep the shot which tore his limbs. There is the battle-field! Here the horse charged; there the howitzers scattered their shells, pregnant with death; here the murderous canister and grape mowed down the crowded ranks; there the huge artillery, teeming with murder, was dragged o'er heaps of men—wounded friends, who just now held its ropes, men yet curling with anguish, like worms in the fire. Hostile and friendly, head and trunk are crushed beneath those dreadful wheels. Here the infantry showered their murdering shot. That ghastly face was beautiful the day before—a sabre hewed its half away.

> "The earth is covered thick with other clay,
> Which her own clay must cover; heaped and pent,
> Rider and horse, friend, foe, in one red burial blent."

Again it is night. Oh, what a night, and after what a day! Yet the pure tide of woman's love, which never ebbs since earth began, flows on in spite of war and battle. Stealthily, by the pale moonlight, a mother of Boston treads the weary miles to reach that bloody spot; a widow she—seeking among the slain her only son. The arm of power drove him forth reluctant to the fight. A friendly

soldier guides her way.   Now she turns over this face,
whose mouth is full of purple dust, bit out of the ground
in his extremest agony, the last sacrament offered him by
earth herself; now she raises that form, cold, stiff, stony,
and ghastly as a dream of hell.   But, lo! another comes;
she too a woman, younger and fairer, yet not less bold, a
maiden from the hostile town to seek her lover.   They
meet, two women among the corpses; two angels come to
Golgotha, seeking to raise a man.   There he lies before
them; they look.   Yes, it is he you seek; the same dress,
form, features, too; it is he, the son, the lover.   Maid and
mother could tell that face in any light.   The grass is wet
with his blood.   The ground is muddy with the life of
men.   The mother's innocent robe is drabbled in the blood
her bosom bore.   Their kisses, groans, and tears recall the
wounded man.   He knows the mother's voice; that voice
yet more beloved.   His lips move only, for they cannot
speak.   He dies!   The waxing moon moves high in
heaven, walking in beauty amid the clouds, and murmurs
soft her cradle-song unto the slumbering earth.   The
broken sword reflects her placid beams.   A star looks
down, and is imaged back in a pool of blood.   The cool
night wind plays in the branches of the trees shivered
with shot.   Nature is beautiful—that lovely grass underneath their feet; those pendulous branches of the leafy
elm; the stars, and that romantic moon lining the clouds
with silver light!   A groan of agony, hopeless and prolonged, wails out from that bloody ground.   But in yonder
farm the whippoorwill sings to her lover all night long;
the rising tide ripples melodious against the shores.   So
wears the night away,—Nature, all sinless, round that field
of woe.

> " The morn is up again, the dewy morn,
>   With breath all incense and with cheek all bloom,
>   Laughing the clouds away with playful scorn,
>   And living as if earth contained no tomb,
>   And glowing into day."

What a scene that morning looks upon!   I will not
turn again.   Let the dead bury their dead.   But their
blood cries out of the ground against the rulers who shed
it,—"Cain! where are thy brothers?"   What shall the
fool answer; what the traitor say?

Then comes thanksgiving in all the churches of Boston.

The consecrated banners, stiff with blood and "glory," are hung over the altar. The minister preaches and the singer sings: "The Lord hath been on our side. He treadeth the people under me. He teacheth my hands to war, my fingers to fight. Yea, He giveth me the necks of mine enemies; for the Lord is His name;" and "It was a famous victory!" Boston seizes miles square of land; but her houses are empty; her wives widows; her children fatherless. Rachel weeps for the murder of her innocents, yet dares not rebuke the rod.

I know there is no fighting across Charles River, as in this poor fiction; but there was once, and instead of Charles say Rio Grande; for Cambridge read Metamoras, and it is what your President recommended; what your Congress enacted; what your Governor issued his proclamation for; what your volunteers go to accomplish: yes, what they fired cannon for on Boston Common the other day. I wish that were a fiction of mine!

We are waging a most iniquitous war—so it seems to me. I know I may be wrong, but I am no partisan; and if I err, it is not wilfully, not rashly. I know the Mexicans are a wretched people; wretched in their origin, history, and character. I know but two good things of them as a people—they abolished negro slavery, not long ago; they do not covet the lands of their neighbours. True, they have not paid all their debts; but it is scarcely decent in a nation, with any repudiating States, to throw the first stone at Mexico for that!

I know the Mexicans cannot stand before this terrible Anglo-Saxon race, the most formidable and powerful the world ever saw; a race which has never turned back; which, though it number less than forty millions, yet holds the Indies, almost the whole of North America; which rules the commerce of the world; clutches at New Holland, China, New Zealand, Borneo, and seizes island after island in the furthest seas; the race which invented steam as its awful type. The poor, wretched Mexicans can never stand before us. How they perished in battle! They must melt away as the Indians before the white man. Considering how we acquired Louisiana, Florida, Oregon, I cannot forbear thinking that this people will possess the whole of the continent before many years; perhaps before the century ends. But this may be had fairly; with no injustice to any one; by the steady advance of a superior race, with superior ideas and a better civilization; by commerce, trade, arts; by being better than Mexico, wiser, humaner, more free and manly. Is it not better to acquire it by the schoolmaster than the cannon? by peddling cloth, tin, anything rather than bullets? It may not all belong to this Government, and yet to this race. It would be a gain to mankind if we could spread over that country the idea of America—that all men are born free and equal in rights, and establish there political, social, and individual freedom. But to do that, we must first make real these ideas at home.

In the general issue between this race and that, we are in the right. But in this special issue, and this particular war, it seems to me that we are wholly in the wrong; that our invasion of Mexico is as bad as the partition of Poland in the last century and in this. If I understand the matter, the whole movement, the settlement of Texas, the Texan revolution, the annexation of Texas, the invasion of Mexico, has been a movement hostile to the American idea, a movement to extend slavery. I do not say such was the design on the part of the people, but on the part of the politicians who pulled the strings. I think the papers of the Government and the debates of Congress prove that. The annexation has been declared unconstitutional in its mode, a virtual dissolution of the Union, and that by very high and well-known authority. It was expressly brought about for the purpose of extending slavery. An attempt is now made to throw the shame of this on the democrats. I think the democrats deserve the shame; but I could never see that the whigs, on the whole, deserved it any less; only they were not quite so open. Certainly, their leaders did not take ground against it, never as against a modification of the tariff! When we annexed Texas, we of course took her for better or worse, debts and all, and annexed her war along with her. I take it everybody knew that; though now some seem to pretend a decent astonishment at the result. Now one party is ready to fight for it as the other! The North did not oppose the annexation of Texas. Why not? They knew they could make money by it. The eyes of the North are full of cotton; they see nothing else, for a web is before them; their ears are full of cotton, and they hear nothing but the buzz of their mills; their mouth is full of cotton, and they can speak audibly but two words—Tariff, Tariff, Dividends, Dividends. The talent of the North is blinded, deafened, gagged with its own cotton. The North clamoured loudly when the nation's treasure was removed from the United States Bank; it is almost silent at the annexation of a slave territory big as the kingdom of France, encumbered with debts, loaded with the entailment of war! Northern governors call for soldiers; our men volunteer to fight in a most infamous war for the extension of slavery! Tell it not in Boston, whisper it not in Faneuil Hall, lest you waken the slumbers of your fathers, and they curse you as cowards and traitors unto men! Not satisfied with annexing Texas and a war, we next invaded a territory which did not belong to Texas, and built a fort on the Rio Grande, where, I take it, we had no more right than the British, in 1841, had on the Penobscot or the Saco. Now the Government and its Congress would throw the blame on the innocent, and say war exists "by the act of Mexico!" If a lie was ever told, I think this is one. Then the "dear people" must be called on for money and men, for "the soil of this free republic is invaded;" and the Governor of Massachusetts, one of the men who declared the annexation of Texas unconstitutional, recommends the war he just now told us to pray against, and appeals to our "patriotism," and "humanity," as arguments for butchering the Mexicans, when they are in the right and we in the wrong! The maxim is held up, "Our country, right or wrong;" "Our country, howsoever bounded;" and it might as well be, "Our country, howsoever governed." It seems popularly and politically forgotten that there is such a thing as Right. The nation's neck invites a tyrant. I am not at all astonished that northern representatives voted for all this work of crime. They are no better than Southern representatives; scarcely less in favour of slavery, and not half so open. They say: Let the North make money, and you may do what you please with the nation; and we will choose governors that dare not oppose you, for, though we are descended from the Puritans, we have but one

article in our creed we never flinch from following, and
that is—to make money; honestly, if we can; if not, as
we can!

Look through the action of your Government, and your
Congress. You see that no reference has been had in this
affair to Christian ideas; none to justice and the eternal
right. Nay, none at all! In the churches, and among
the people, how feeble has been the protest against this
great wrong. How tamely the people yield their necks—
and say: "Take our sons for the war—we care not, right
or wrong." England butchers the Sikhs in India—her
generals are elevated to the peerage, and the head of her
church writes a form of thanksgiving for the victory, to
be read in all the churches of that Christian land.* To

* *Form of Prayer and Thanksgiving to Almighty God.*

"O Lord God of Hosts, in whose hand is power and might irresistible,
we, Thine unworthy servants, most humbly acknowledge Thy goodness in
the victories lately vouchsafed to the armies of our Sovereign over a host
of barbarous invaders, who sought to spread desolation over fruitful and
populous provinces, enjoying the blessings of peace, under the protection
of the British Crown. We bless Thee, O merciful Lord, for having brought
to a speedy and prosperous issue a war to which no occasion had been
given by injustice on our part, or apprehension of injury at our hands!
To Thee, O Lord, we ascribe the glory! It was Thy wisdom which guided
the counsel! Thy power which strengthened the hands of those whom
it pleased Thee to use as Thy instruments in the discomfiture of the lawless aggressor, and the frustration of his ambitious designs! From Thee
alone cometh the victory, and the spirit of moderation and mercy in the
day of success. Continue, we beseech Thee, to go forth with our armies,
whensoever they are called into battle in a righteous cause; and dispose
the hearts of their leaders to exact nothing more from the vanquished
than is necessary for the maintenance of peace and security against violence and rapine.

"Above all, give Thy grace to those who preside in the councils of our
Sovereign, and administer the concerns of her widely-extended domi-
nions, that they may apply all their endeavours to the purposes designed
by Thy good Providence, in committing such power to their hands, the
temporal and spiritual benefit of the nations intrusted to their care.

"And whilst Thou preservest our distant possessions from the horrors
of war, give us peace and plenty at home, that the earth may yield her
increase, and that we, Thy servants, receiving Thy blessings with thankfulness and gladness of heart, may dwell together in unity, and faithfully
serve Thee, to Thy honour and glory, through Jesus Christ our Lord, to
whom, with Thee and the Holy Ghost, belong all dominion and power,
both in heaven and earth, now and for ever. Amen."—See a defence of
this prayer in the London *Christian Observer* for May, p. 319, *et seq.,*
and for June, p. 346, *et seq.*

Would you know what he gave thanks for on Easter Sunday? Here is
the history of the battle:—

"This battle had begun at six, and was over at eleven o'clock; the make it still more abominable, the blasphemy is enacted on Easter Sunday, the great holiday of men who serve the Prince of Peace. We have not had prayers in the churches, for we have no political Archbishop. But we fired cannon in joy that we had butchered a few wretched men—half-starved, and forced into the ranks by fear of death! Your peace-societies, and your churches, what can they do? What dare they? Verily, we are a faithless and perverse generation. God be merciful to us, sinners as we are!

But why talk for ever? What shall we do? In regard to this present war, we can refuse to take any part in it; we can encourage others to do the same; we can aid men, if need be, who suffer because they refuse. Men will call us traitors: what then? That hurt nobody in '76! We are a rebellious nation; our whole history is treason; our blood was attainted before we were born; our creeds are infidelity to the mother-church; our Constitution treason to our fatherland. What of that? Though all the governors in the world bid us commit treason against man, and set the example, let us never submit. Let God only be a master to control our conscience!

We can hold public meetings in favour of peace, in which what is wrong shall be exposed and condemned. It is proof of our cowardice that this has not been done before now. We can show in what the infamy of a nation consists; in what its real glory. One of your own men, the last summer, startled the churches out of their sleep,* by his manly trumpet, talking with us, and telling that the true grandeur of a nation was justice, not glory; peace, not war.

We can work now for future times, by taking pains to spread abroad the sentiments of peace, the ideas of peace, among the people in schools, churches—everywhere. At

hand-to-hand combat commenced at nine, and lasted scarcely two hours. The river was full of sinking men. For two hours, volley after volley was poured in upon the human mass—the stream being literally red with blood, and covered with the bodies of the slain. At last, the musket ammunition becoming exhausted, the infantry fell to the rear, the horse artillery plying grape till not a man was visible within range. No compassion was felt or mercy shown." But, " 'Twas a famous victory!"

* Mr. Charles Sumner.

length we can diminish the power of the national Government, so that the people alone shall have the power to declare war, by a direct vote, the Congress only to recommend it. We can take from the Government the means of war, by raising only revenue enough for the nation's actual wants, and raising that directly, so that each man knows what he pays, and when he pays it, and then he will take care that it is not paid to make him poor and keep him so. We can diffuse a real practical Christianity among the people, till the mass of men have courage enough to overcome evil with good, and look at aggressive war as the worst of treason and the foulest infidelity !

Now is the time to push and be active. War itself gives weight to words of peace. There will never be a better time till we make the times better. It is not a day for cowardice, but for heroism. Fear not that the " honour of the nation" will suffer from Christian movements for peace. What if your men of low degree are a vanity, and your men of high degree are a lie? That is no new thing. Let true men do their duty, and the lie and the vanity will pass each to its reward. Wait not for the churches to move, or the State to become Christian. Let us bear our testimony like men, not fearing to be called traitors, infidels ; fearing only to be such.

I would call on Americans, by their love of our country, its great ideas, its real grandeur, its hopes, and the memory of its fathers—to come and help to save that country from infamy and ruin. I would call on Christians, who believe that Christianity is a truth, to lift up their voice, public and private, against the foulest violation of God's law, this blasphemy of the Holy Spirit of Christ, this worst form of infidelity to man and God. I would call on all men, by the one nature that is in you, by the great human heart beating alike in all your bosoms, to protest manfully against this desecration of the earth, this high treason against both man and God. Teach your rulers that you are Americans, not slaves ; Christians, not heathen ; men, not murderers, to kill for hire ! You may effect little in this generation, for its head seems crazed and its heart rotten. But there will be a day after today. It is for you and me to make it better : a day of peace, when nation shall no longer lift up sword against nation; when all shall indeed be brothers, and all blest. Do this, you shall be worthy to dwell in this beautiful land; Christ will be near you; God work with you, and bless you for ever!

This present trouble with Mexico may be very brief; surely it might be even now brought to an end with no unusual manhood in your rulers. Can we say we have not deserved it? Let it end; but let us remember that war, horrid as it is, is not the worst calamity which ever befalls a people. It is far worse for a people to lose all reverence for right, for truth, all respect for man and God; to care more for the freedom of trade than the freedom of men; more for a tariff than millions of souls. This calamity came upon us gradually, long before the present war, and will last long after that has died away. Like people like ruler, is a true word. Look at your rulers, representatives, and see our own likeness! We reverence force, and have forgot there is any right beyond the vote of a Congress or a people; any good beside dollars; any God but majorities and force. I think the present war, though it should cost 50,000 men and $50,000,000, the smallest part of our misfortune. Abroad we are looked on as a nation of swindlers and men-stealers! What can we say in our defence? Alas! the nation is a traitor to its great idea,—that all men are born equal, each with the same unalienable rights. We are infidels to Christianity. We have paid the price of our shame.

There have been dark days in this nation before now. It was gloomy when Washington with his little army fled through the Jerseys. It was a long dark day from '83 to '89. It was not so dark as now; the nation never so false. There was never a time when resistance to tyrants was so rare a virtue; when the people so tamely submitted to a wrong. Now you can feel the darkness. The sack of this city and the butchery of its people were a far less evil than the moral deadness of the nation. Men spring up again like the mown grass; but to raise up saints and heroes in a dead nation corrupting beside its golden tomb, what shall do that for us? We must look not to the many for that, but to the few who are faithful unto God and man.

I know the hardy vigour of our men, the stalwart

intellect of this people. Would to God they could learn to love the right and true. Then what a people should we be, spreading from the Madawaska to the Sacramento, diffusing our great idea, and living our religion, the Christianity of Christ! O Lord! make the vision true; waken thy prophets and stir thy people till righteousness exalt us! No wonders will be wrought for that. But the voice of conscience speaks to you and me, and all of us: the right shall prosper; the wicked States shall die; and History responds her long amen.

What lessons come to us from the past! The Genius of the old civilization, solemn and sad, sits there on the Alps, his classic beard descending o'er his breast. Behind him arise the new nations, bustling with romantic life. He bends down over the midland sea, and counts up his children—Assyria, Egypt, Tyre, Carthage, Troy, Etruria, Corinth, Athens, Rome—once so renowned, now gathered with the dead, their giant ghosts still lingering pensive o'er the spot. He turns westward his face, too sad to weep, and raising from his palsied knee his trembling hand, looks on his brother genius of the new civilization. That young giant, strong and mocking, sits there on the Alleghanies. Before him lie the waters, covered with ships; behind him he hears the roar of the Mississippi and the far distant Oregon—rolling their riches to the sea. He bends down, and that far ocean murmurs pacific in his ear. On his left are the harbours, shops, and mills of the East, and a fivefold gleam of light goes up from Northern lakes. On his right spread out the broad savannahs of the South, waiting to be blessed; and far off that Mexique bay bends round her tropic shores. A crown of stars is on that giant's head, some glorious with flashing, many-coloured light; some bloody red; some pale and faint, of most uncertain hue. His right hand lies folded in his robe; the left rests on the Bible's opened page, and holds these sacred words—All men are equal, born with equal rights from God. The old says to the young, "Brother, beware!" and Alps and Rocky Mountains say, "Beware!" That stripling giant, ill-bred and scoffing, shouts amain: "My feet are red with the Indian's blood; my hand has forged the negro's chain. I am strong; who dares assail me? I will drink his blood, for I have made my covenant of lies, and leagued with hell for my support. There is no right, no truth; Christianity is false, and God a name." His left hand rends those sacred scrolls, casting his Bibles underneath his feet, and in his right he brandishes the negro-driver's whip, crying again—"Say, who is God, and what is Right!" And all his mountains echo—Right. But the old genius sadly says again: "Though hand join in hand, the wicked shall not prosper." The hollow tomb of Egypt, Athens, Rome, of every ancient State, with all their wandering ghosts, replies, "AMEN."

II.

SPEECH DELIVERED AT THE ANTI-WAR MEETING, IN FANEUIL HALL, FEBRUARY 4, 1847.

Mr. Chairman,—We have come here to consult for the honour of our country. The honour and dignity of the United States are in danger. I love my country; I love her honour. It is dear to me almost as my own. I have seen stormy meetings in Faneuil Hall before now, and am not easily disturbed by a popular tumult. But never before did I see a body of armed soldiers attempting to overawe the majesty of the people, when met to deliberate on the people's affairs. Yet the meetings of the people of Boston have been disturbed by soldiers before now, by British bayonets; but never since the Boston massacre on the 5th of March, 1770! Our fathers hated a standing army. This is a new one, but behold the effect! Here are soldiers with bayonets to overawe the majesty of the people! They went to our meeting last Monday night, the hireling soldiers of President Polk, to overawe and disturb the meetings of honest men. Here they are now, and in arms!

We are in a war; the signs of war are seen here in Boston. Men, needed to hew wood and honestly serve society, are marching about your streets; they are learning to kill men, men who never harmed us nor them; learning to kill their brothers. It is a mean and infamous war we are fighting. It is a great boy fighting a little one, and that little one feeble and sick. What makes it worse is, the little boy is in the right, and the big boy is in the wrong, and tells solemn lies to make his side seem right. He wants, besides, to make the small boy pay the expenses of the quarrel.

The friends of the war say, " Mexico has invaded our

territory!" When it is shown that it is we who have invaded hers, then it is said, "Ay, but she owes us money." Better say outright, "Mexico has land, and we want to steal it!"

This war is waged for a mean and infamous purpose, for the extension of slavery. It is not enough that there are fifteen Slave States, and 3,000,000 men here who have no legal rights—not so much as the horse and the ox have in Boston; it is not enough that the slaveholders annexed Texas, and made slavery perpetual therein, extending even north of Mason and Dixon's line, covering a territory forty-five times as large as the State of Massachusetts. Oh, no; we must have yet more land to whip negroes in!

The war had a mean and infamous beginning. It began illegally, unconstitutionally. The whigs say, "The President made the war." Mr. Webster says so! It went on meanly and infamously. Your Congress lied about it. Do not lay the blame on the democrats; the whigs lied just as badly. Your Congress has seldom been so single-mouthed before. Why, only sixteen voted against the war, or the lie. I say this war is mean and infamous, all the more, because waged by a people calling itself democratic and Christian. I know but one war so bad in modern times, between civilized nations, and that was the war for the partition of Poland. Even for that there was more excuse.

We have come to Faneuil Hall to talk about the war; to work against the war. It is rather late, but "better late than never." We have let two opportunities for work pass unemployed. One came while the annexation of Texas was pending. Then was the time to push and be active. Then was the time for Massachusetts and all the North, to protest as one man against the extension of slavery. Everybody knew all about the matter, the democrats and the whigs. But how few worked against that gross mischief! One noble man lifted up his warning voice;* a man noble in his father—and there he stands in marble; noble in himself—and there he stands yet higher up;—and I hope time will show him yet

* John Quincy Adams.

nobler in his son—and there he stands, not in marble, but in man! He talked against it, worked against it, fought against it. But Massachusetts did little. Her tonguey men said little; her handy men did little. Too little could not be done or said. True, we came here to Faneuil Hall and passed resolutions; good resolutions they were, too. Daniel Webster wrote them, it is said. They did the same in the State House; but nothing came of them. They say "Hell is paved with resolutions;" these were of that sort of resolutions, which resolve nothing, because they are of words, not works!

Well, we passed the resolutions; you know who opposed them; who hung back and did nothing—nothing good I mean; quite enough not good. Then we thought all the danger was over; that the resolutions settled the matter. But then was the time to confound at once the enemies of your country; to show an even front hostile to slavery.

But the chosen time passed over, and nothing was done. Do not lay the blame on the democrats; a Whig Senate annexed Texas, and so annexed a war. We ought to have told our delegation in Congress, if Texas were annexed, to come home, and we would breathe upon it and sleep upon it, and then see what to do next. Had our resolutions, taken so warmly here in Faneuil Hall in 1845, been but as warmly worked out, we had now been as terrible to the slave power as the slave power, since extended, now is to us!

Why was it that we did nothing? That is a public secret. Perhaps I ought not to tell it to the people. (Cries of "Tell it.")

The annexation of Texas, a slave territory big as the kingdom of France, would not furl a sail on the ocean; would not stop a mill-wheel at Lowell! Men thought so.

That time passed by, and there came another. The Government had made war; the Congress voted the dollars, voted the men, voted a lie. Your representative, men of Boston, voted for all three—the lie, the dollars, and the men; all three, in obedience to the slave power! Let him excuse that to the conscience of his party; it is an easy matter. I do not believe he can excuse it to his own conscience. To the conscience of the world it admits of no excuse. Your President called for volunteers, 50,000 of them. Then came an opportunity such as offers not once in one hundred years, an opportunity to speak for freedom and the rights of mankind! Then was the time for Massachusetts to stand up in the spirit of '76, and say, "We won't send a man, from Cape Ann to Williamstown —not one Yankee man, for this wicked war." Then was the time for your Governor to say, "Not a volunteer for this wicked war." Then was the time for your merchants to say, "Not a ship, not a dollar, for this wicked war;" for your manufacturers to say, "We will not make you a cannon, nor a sword, nor a kernel of powder, nor a soldier's shirt, for this wicked war." Then was the time for all good men to say, "This is a war for slavery, a mean and infamous war; an aristocratic war, a war against the best interests of mankind. If God please, we will die a thousand times, but never draw blade in this wicked war." (Cries of "Throw him over," &c.) Throw him over, what good would that do? What would you do next, after you have thrown him over? ("Drag you out of the hall!") What good would that do? It would not wipe off the infamy of this war! would not make it less wicked!

That is what a democratic nation, a Christian people ought to have said, ought to have done. But we did not say so; the Bay State did not say so, nor your Governor, nor your merchants, nor your manufacturers, nor your good men; the Governor accepted the President's decree, issued his proclamation calling for soldiers, recommended men to enlist, appealing to their "patriotism" and "humanity."

Governor Briggs is a good man; and so far I honour him. He is a temperance man, strong and consistent; I honour him for that. He is a friend of education; a friend of the people. I wish there were more such. Like many other New England men, he started from humble beginnings; but unlike many such successful men of New England, he is not ashamed of the lowest round he ever trod on. I honour him for all this. But that was a time which tried men's souls, and his soul could not stand the rack. I am sorry for him. He did as the President told him.

What was the reason for all this? Massachusetts did

not like the war, even then; yet she gave her consent to it. Why so? There are two words which can drive the blood out of the cheeks of cowardly men in Massachusetts any time. They are "Federalism" and "Hartford Convention!" The fear of those words palsied the conscience of Massachusetts, and so her Governor did as he was told. I feel no fear of either. The Federalists did not see all things; who ever did? They had not the ideas which were destined to rule this nation; they looked back when the age looked forward. But to their own ideas they were true; and if ever a nobler body of men held state in any nation, I have yet to learn when or where. If we had had the shadow of Caleb Strong in the Governor's chair, not a volunteer for this war had gone out of Massachusetts.

I have not told quite all the reasons why Massachusetts did nothing. Men knew the war would cost money; that the dollars would in the end be raised, not by a direct tax, of which the poor man paid according to his little, and the rich man in proportion to his much; but by a tariff which presses light on property, and hard on the person—by a tax on the backs and mouths of the people. Some of the whigs were glad last spring, when the war came, for they hoped thereby to save the child of their old age, the tariff of '42. There are always some rich men, who say, "No matter what sort of a Government we have, so long as we get our dividends;" always some poor men, who say, "No matter how much the nation suffers, if we fill our hungry purses thereby." Well, they lost their virtue, lost their tariff, and gained just nothing; what they deserved to gain.

Now a third opportunity has come;—no, it has not come; we have brought it. The President wants a war tax on tea and coffee. Is that democratic, to tax every man's breakfast and supper, for the sake of getting more territory to whip negroes in? (Numerous cries of "Yes.") Then what do you think despotism would be? He asks a loan of $28,000,000 for this war. He wants $3,000,000 to spend privately for this war. In eight months past, he has asked, I am told, for $74,000,000. Seventy-four millions of dollars to conquer slave territory! Is that democratic too? He wants to increase the standing army, to have ten regiments more! A pretty business that. Ten regiments to gag the people in Faneuil Hall. Do you think that is democratic? Some men have just asked Massachusetts for $20,000 for the volunteers! It is time for the people to rebuke all this wickedness.

I think there is a good deal to excuse the volunteers. I blame them, for some of them know what they are about. Yet I pity them more, for most of them, I am told, are low, ignorant men; some of them drunken and brutal. From the uproar they make here to-night, arms in their hands, I think what was told me is true! I say, I pity them. They are my brothers; not the less brothers because low and misguided. If they are so needy that they are forced to enlist by poverty, surely I pity them. If they are of good families, and know better, I pity them still more! I blame most the men that have duped the rank and file! I blame the captains and colonels, who will have least of the hardships, most of the pay, and all of the " glory." I blame the men that made the war; the men that make money out of it. I blame the great party men of the land. Did not Mr. Clay say he hoped he could slay a Mexican? (Cries, "No, he didn't.") Yes, he did; said it on Forefather's day! Did not Mr. Webster, in the streets of Philadelphia, bid the volunteers, misguided young men, go and uphold the stars of their country? (Voices, "He did right!") No; he should have said the stripes of his country, for every volunteer to this wicked war is a stripe on the nation's back! Did not he declare this war unconstitutional, and threaten to impeach the President who made it, and then go and invest a son in it? Has it not been said here, "Our country, howsoever bounded," bounded by robbery or bounded by right lines! Has it not been said, all round; "Our country, right or wrong!"

I say, I blame not so much the volunteers as the famous men who deceive the nation! (Cries of "Throw him over; kill him, kill him!" and a flourish of bayonets.) Throw him over! you will not throw him over. Kill him! I shall walk home unarmed and unattended, and not a man of you will hurt one hair of my head.

I say again, it is time for the people to take up this matter. Your Congress will do nothing till you tell them

what and how. Your 29th Congress can do little good.
Its sands are nearly run, God be thanked! It is the most
infamous Congress we ever had. We began with the
Congress that declared Independence, and swore by the
Eternal Justice of God. We have come down to the 29th
Congress, which declared war existed by the act of
Mexico—declared a lie; the Congress that swore by the
Baltimore Convention! We began with George Wash-
ington, and have got down to James K. Polk.

It is time for the people of Massachusetts to instruct
their servants in Congress to oppose this war; to refuse all
supplies for it; to ask for the recall of the army into our
own land. It is time for us to tell them that not an inch
of slave territory shall ever be added to the realm. Let
us remonstrate; let us petition; let us command. If any
class of men have hitherto been remiss, let them come
forward now and give us their names—the merchants, the
manufacturers, the whigs and the democrats. If men love
their country better than their party or their purse, now
let them show it.

Let us ask the General Court of Massachusetts to cancel
every commission which the Governor has given to the
officers of the volunteers. Let us ask them to disband the
companies not yet mustered into actual service; and then,
if you like that, ask them to call a convention of the
people of Massachusetts, to see what we shall do in reference to the war; in reference to the annexation of more
territory; in reference to the violation of the Constitution.
(Loud groans from crowds of rude fellows in several parts
of the hall). That was a tory groan; they never dared
groan so in Faneuil Hall before; not even the British
tories, when they had no bayonets to back them up! I
say, let us ask for these things!

Your President tells us it is treason to talk so! Treason
is it! treason to discuss a war which the Government made,
and which the people are made to pay for? If it be
treason to speak against the war, what was it to make the
war, to ask for 50,000 men and $74,000,000 for the war?
Why, if the people cannot discuss the war they have got
to fight and to pay for, who under heaven can? Whose
business is it, if it is not yours and mine? If my country
is in the wrong, and I know it, and hold my peace, then

I am guilty of treason, moral treason. Why, a wrong—
it is only the threshold of ruin. I would not have my
country take the next step. Treason is it, to show that
this war is wrong and wicked! Why, what if George III.,
any time from '75 to '83, had gone down to Parliament
and told them it was treason to discuss the war then
waging against these colonies! What do you think the
Commons would have said? What would the Lords say?
Why, that king, foolish as he was, would have been
lucky, if he had not learned there was a joint in his
neck, and, stiff as he bore him, that the people knew how
to find it.

I do not believe in killing kings, or any other men; but
I do say, in a time when the nation was not in danger,
that no British king, for two hundred years past, would
have dared call it treason to discuss the war—its cause, its
progress, or its termination!

Now is the time to act! Twice we have let the occasion
slip; beware of the third time! Let it be infamous for
a New England man to enlist; for a New England
merchant to loan his dollars, or to let his ships in aid of
this wicked war; let it be infamous for a manufacturer to
make a cannon, a sword, or a kernel of powder, to kill
our brothers with, while we all know that they are in the
right, and we in the wrong.

I know my voice is a feeble one in Massachusetts. I
have no mountainous position from whence to look down
and overawe the multitude; I have no background of
political reputation to echo my words. I am but a
plain, humble man; but I have a background of
Truth to sustain me, and the Justice of Heaven arches
over my head! For your sakes, I wish I had that oceanic
eloquence whose tidal flow should bear on its bosom the
drift-weed which politicians have piled together, and
sap and sweep away the sand-hillocks of soldiery blown
together by the idle wind; that oceanic eloquence
which sweeps all before it, and leaves the shore hard,
smooth, and clean! But feeble as I am, let me beg of you,
fellow-citizens of Boston, men and brothers, to come
forward and protest against this wicked war, and the end
for which it is waged. I call on the whigs, who love their
country better than they love the tariff of '42; I call on

the democrats, who think Justice is greater than the Baltimore Convention—I call on the whigs and democrats to come forward and join with me in opposing this wicked war! I call on the men of Boston, on the men of the old Bay State, to act worthy of their fathers, worthy of their country, worthy of themselves! Men and brothers, I call on you all to protest against this most infamous war, in the name of the State, in the name of the country, in the name of man—yes, in the name of God; leave not your children saddled with a war debt, to cripple the nation's commerce for years to come. Leave not your land cursed with slavery, extended and extending, palsying the nation's arm and corrupting the nation's heart. Leave not your memory infamous among the nations, because you feared men, feared the Government; because you loved money got by crime, land plundered in war, loved land unjustly bounded; because you debased your country by defending the wrong she dared to do; because you loved slavery, loved war, but loved not the Eternal Justice of all-judging God. If my counsel is weak and poor, follow one stronger and more manly. I am speaking to men; think of these things, and then act like men!

III.

A SERMON OF THE MEXICAN WAR.—PREACHED AT THE MELODEON, ON SUNDAY, JUNE 25, 1848.

SOON after the commencement of the war against Mexico, I said something respecting it in this place. But while I was printing the sermon, I was advised to hasten the compositors in their work, or the war would be over before the sermon was out. The advice was like a good deal of the counsel that is given to a man who thinks for himself, and honestly speaks what he unavoidably thinks. It is now more than two years since the war began; I have hoped to live long enough to see it ended, and hoped to say a word about it when over. A month ago, this day, the 25th of May, the treaty of peace, so much talked of, was ratified by the Mexican Congress. A few days ago, it was officially announced by telegraph, to your collector in Boston, that the war with Mexico was at an end.

There are two things about this war quite remarkable. The first is, the manner of its commencement. It was begun illegally, without the action of the constitutional authorities; begun by the command of the President of the United States, who ordered the American army into a territory which the Mexicans claimed as their own. The President says, "It is ours;" but the Mexicans also claimed it, and were in possession thereof until forcibly expelled. This is a plain case; and, as I have elsewhere treated at length of this matter,* I will not dwell upon it again, except to mention a single fact but recently divulged. It is well known that Mr. Polk claimed the territory west of the Nueces and east of the Rio Grande, as forming a part of Texas, and therefore as forming part of the United States

---

* In the Massachusetts *Quarterly Review*, Vol. I., Art. I. See also the paper on the administration of Mr. Polk, in Vol. III., Art. VIII.

after the annexation of Texas. He contends that Mexico
began the war by attacking the American army while in
that territory and near the Rio Grande. But, from the
correspondence laid before the American Senate, in its secret
session for considering the treaty, it now appears that on
the 10th of November, 1845, Mr. Polk instructed Mr.
Slidell to offer a relinquishment of American claims against
Mexico, amounting to $5,000,000 or $6,000,000, for the
sake of having the Rio Grande as the western boundary of
Texas ; yes, for that very territory which he says was ours
without paying a cent. When it was conquered, a military
government was established there, as in other places in
Mexico.

The other remarkable thing about the war is, the
manner of its conclusion. The treaty of peace which has
just been ratified by the Mexican authorities, and which
puts an end to the war, was negotiated by a man who had
no more legal authority than any one of us has to do it.
Mr. Polk made the war, without consulting Congress, and
that body adopted the war by a vote almost unanimous.
Mr. Nicholas P. Trist made the treaty, without consulting
the President; yes, even after the President had ordered
him to return home. As the Congress adopted Mr.
Polk's war, so Mr. Polk adopted Mr. Trist's treaty; and
the war illegally begun is brought informally to a close.
Mr. Polk is now in the President's chair, seated on the
throne of the Union, although he made the war; and
Mr. Trist, it is said, is under arrest for making the treaty,
meddling with what was none of his business.

When the war began, there was a good deal of talk
about it here ; talk against it. But, as things often go in
Boston, it ended in talk. The newsboys made money out
of the war. Political parties were true to their wonted
principles, or their wonted prejudices. The friends of the
party in power could see no informality in the beginning
of hostilities; no injustice in the war itself; not even an
impolicy. They were offended if an obscure man preached
against it of a Sunday. The political opponents of the
party in power talked against the war, as a matter of
course; but, when the elections came, supported the men
that made it with unusual alacrity—their deeds serving as

commentary upon their words, and making further remark thereon, in this place, quite superfluous. Many men— who, whatever other parts of Scripture they may forget, never cease to remember that " Money answereth all things,"—diligently set themselves to make money out of the war and the new turn it gave to national affairs. Others thought that " glory" was a good thing, and so engaged in the war itself, hoping to return, in due time, all glittering with its honours.

So what with the one political party that really praised the war, and the other who affected to oppose it, and with the commercial party, who looked only for a market—this for merchandise, and that for "patriotism"—the friends of peace, who seriously and heartily opposed the war, were very few in number. True, the " sober second thought" of the people has somewhat increased their number; but they are still few, mostly obscure men.

Now peace has come, nobody talks much about it; the newsboys have scarce made a cent by the news. They fired cannons, a hundred guns on the Common, for joy at the victory of Monterey; at Philadelphia, Baltimore, Washington, New York, men illuminated their houses in honour of the battle of Buena Vista, I think it was; the custom-house was officially illuminated at Boston for that occasion. But we hear of no cannons to welcome the peace. Thus far, it does not seem that a single candle has been burnt in rejoicing for that. The newspapers are full of talk, as usual; flags are flying in the streets; the air is a little noisy with hurrahs; but it is all talk about the conventions at Baltimore and Philadelphia; hurrahs for Taylor and Cass. Nobody talks of the peace. Flags enough flap in the wind, with the names of rival candidates; but nowhere do the stripes and stars bear Peace as their motto. The peace now secured is purchased with such conditions imposed on Mexico, that while every one will be glad of it, no man that loves justice can be proud of it. Very little is said about the treaty. The distinguished senator from Massachusetts did himself honour, it seems to me, in voting against it on the ground that it enabled us to plunder Mexico of her land. But the treaty contains some things highly honourable to the character of the nation, of which we may well enough be proud, if ever of anything. I refer to the twenty-second and twenty-third articles, which provide for arbitration between the nations, if future difficulties should occur; and to the pains taken, in case of actual hostilities, for the security of all unarmed persons, for the protection of private property, and for the humane treatment of all prisoners taken in war. These ideas, and the language of these articles, are copied from the celebrated treaty between the United States and Prussia, the treaty of 1785. It is scarcely needful to add that they were then introduced by that great and good man, Benjamin Franklin, one of the negotiators of the treaty. They made a new epoch in diplomacy, and introduced a principle previously unknown in the law of nations. The insertion of these articles in the new treaty is, perhaps, the only thing connected with the war which an American can look upon with satisfaction. Yet this fact excites no attention.*

Still, while so little notice is taken of this matter, in public and private, it may be worth while for a minister, on Sunday, to say a word about the peace; and, now the war is over, to look back upon it, to see what it has cost, in money and in men, and what we have got by it; what its consequences have been, thus far, and are likely to be for the future; what new dangers and duties come from this cause interpolated into our nation. We have been long promised "indemnity for the past, and security for the future;" let us see what we are to be indemnified for, and what secured against. The natural justice of the war I will not look at now.

First, then, of the cost of the war. Money is the first thing with a good many men; the only thing with some; and an important thing with all. So, first of all, let me speak of the cost of the war in dollars. It is a little difficult to determine the actual cost of the war, thus far— even its direct cost—for the bills are not all in the hands of Government; and then, as a matter of political party-craft, the Government, of course, is unwilling to let the

---

* Mr. Trist introduced these articles into the treaty, without having instructions from the American Government to do so; the honour, therefore, is wholly due to him. There were some in the Senate who opposed these articles.

full cost become known before the next election is over. So it is to be expected that the Government will keep the facts from the people as long as possible. Most governments would do the same. But Truth has a right of way everywhere, and will recover it at last, spite of the adverse possession of a political party. The indirect cost of the war must be still more difficult to come at, and will long remain a matter of calculation, in which it is impossible to reach certainty. We do not know yet the entire cost of the Florida war, or the late war with England; the complete cost of the Revolutionary war must for ever be unknown.

It is natural for most men to exaggerate what favours their argument; but when I cannot obtain the exact figures, I will come a good deal within the probable amount. The military and naval appropriations for the year ending in June, 1847, were $40,865,155·96 ; for the next year, $31,377,679·92; the sum asked for the present year, till next June, $42,224,000; making a whole of $114,466,835·88. It is true that all this appropriation is not for the Mexican war, but it is also true that this sum does not include all the appropriations for the war. Estimating the sums already paid by the Government, the private claims presented, and to be presented, the $15,000,000 to be paid Mexico as purchase-money for the territory we take from her, the $5,000,000 or $6,000,000 to be paid our own citizens for their claims against her,—I think I am a good deal within the mark when I say the war will have cost $150,000,000 before the soldiers are at home, discharged, and out of the pay of the State. In this sum I do not include the bounty lands to be given to the soldiers and officers, nor the pensions to be paid them, their widows and orphans, for years to come. I will estimate that at $50,000,000 more, making a whole of $200,000,000 which has been paid or must be. This is the direct cost to the Federal Government, and of course does not include the sums paid by individual States, or bestowed by private generosity, to feed and clothe the volunteers before they were mustered into service. This may seem extravagant; but, fifty years hence, when party spirit no longer blinds men's eyes, and when the whole is a matter of history, I think it will be thought moderate, and be found a good

deal within the actual and direct cost. Some of this cost
will appear as a public debt. Statements recently made
respecting it can hardly be trusted, notwithstanding the
authority on which they rest. Part of this war debt is
funded already, part not yet funded. When the outstand-
ing demands are all settled, and the treasury notes redeemed,
there will probably be a war debt of not less than
$125,000,000. At least, such is the estimate of an im-
partial and thoroughly competent judge. But, not to
exaggerate, let us call it only $100,000,000.

It will, perhaps, be said, Part of this money, all that is
paid in pensions, is a charity, and therefore no loss. But
it is a charity paid to men who, except for the war, would
have needed no such aid; and, therefore, a waste. Of the
actual cost of the war, some three or four millions have
been spent in extravagant prices for hiring or purchasing
ships, in buying provisions and various things needed by
the army, and supplied by political favourites at exorbitant
rates. This is the only portion of the cost which is not a
sheer waste; here the money has only changed hands;
nothing has been destroyed, except the honesty of the parties concerned in such transactions. If a farmer hires
men to help him till the soil, the men earn their subsistence and their wages, and leave, besides, a profit to their
employer; when the season is over, he has his crops and
his improvements as the return for their pay and subsistence. But for all that the soldier has consumed, for his
wages, his clothes, his food and drink, the fighting tools
he has worn out, and the ammunition he has expended,
there is no available return to show; all that is a clear
waste. The beef is eaten up, the cloth worn away, the
powder is burnt, and what is there to show for it all?
Nothing but the "glory." You sent out sound men, and
they come back, many of them, sick and maimed; some of
them are slain.

The indirect pecuniary cost of the war is caused, first,
by diverting some 150,000 men, engaged in the war directly
or remotely, from the works of productive industry, to the
labours of war, which produce nothing; and, secondly, by
disturbing the regular business of the country, first by the
withdrawal of men from their natural work; then, by with-
drawing large quantities of money from the active capital

of the nation ; and, finally, by the general uncertainty
which it causes all over the land, thus hindering men from
undertaking or prosecuting successfully their various productive enterprises. If 150,000 men earn on the average
but $200 apiece, that alone amounts to $30,000,000. The
withdrawal of such an amount of labour from the common
industry of the country must be seriously felt. At any
rate, the nation has earned $30,000,000 less than it would
have done if these men had kept about their common
work.

But the diversion of capital from its natural and pacific
direction is a greater evil in this case. America is rich,
but her wealth consists mainly in land, in houses, cattle,
ships, and various things needed for human comfort and
industry. In money, we are poor. The amount of money
is small in proportion to the actual wealth of the nation,
and also in proportion to its activity, which is indicated
by the business of the nation. In actual wealth, the free
States of America are probably the richest people in the
world; but in money we are poorer than many other
nations. This is plain enough, though perhaps not very
well known, and is shown by the fact that interest, in
European States, is from two to four per cent. a year, and
in America from six to nine. The active capital of America is small. Now in this war a national debt has accumulated, which probably is or will soon be $100,000,000
or $125,000,000. All this great sum of money has, of
course, been taken from the active capital of the country,
and there has been so much less for the use of the farmer,
the manufacturer, and the merchant. But for this war,
these 150,000 men and these $100,000,000 would have
been devoted to productive industry; and the result would
have been shown by the increase of our annual earnings,
in increased wealth and comfort.

Then war produced uncertainty, and that distrust
amongst men. Therefore many were hindered from undertaking new works, and others found their old enterprises
ruined at once. In this way there has been a great loss,
which cannot be accurately estimated. I think no man,
familiar with American industry, would rate this indirect
loss lower than $100,000,000; some, perhaps, at twice as
much; but to avoid all possibility of exaggeration, let us

call it half the smallest of these sums, or $50,000,000, as the complete pecuniary cost of the Mexican war, direct and indirect.

What have we got to show for all this money? We have a large tract of territory, containing, in all, both east and west of the Rio Grande, I am told, between 700,000 and 800,000 square miles. Accounts differ as to its value. But it appears, from the recent correspondence of Mr. Slidell, that in 1845 the President offered Mexico, in money, $25,000,000 for that territory which we now acquire under this new treaty. Suppose it is worth more, suppose it is worth twice as much, or all the indirect cost of the war ($50,000,000), then the $200,000,000 are thrown away.

Now, for this last sum, we could have built a sufficient railroad across the Isthmus of Panama, and another across the continent, from the Mississippi to the Pacific. If such a road with its suitable equipment cost $100,000 a mile, and the distance should amount to 2000 miles, then the $200,000,000 would just pay the bills. That would have been the greatest national work of productive industry in the world. In comparison with it, the Lake Mœris and the Pyramids of Egypt, and the Wall of China, seem but the works of a child. It might be a work to be proud of till the world ends; one, too, which would advance the industry, the welfare, and general civilization of mankind to a great degree, diminishing, by half, the distance round the globe; saving millions of property and many lives each year; besides furnishing, it is thought, a handsome income from the original outlay. But, perhaps, that would not be the best use which might be made of the money; perhaps it would not have been wise to undertake that work. I do not pretend to judge of such matters, only to show what might be done with that sum of money, if we were disposed to construct works of such a character. At any rate, two Pacific railroads would be better than one Mexican war. We are seldom aware of the cost of war. If a single regiment of dragoons cost only $700,000 a year, which is a good deal less than the actual cost, that is considerably more than the cost of twelve colleges like Harvard University, with its schools for theology, law, and medicine; its scientific school, observatory, and all. We are, taken as a whole, a very ignorant people; and while we waste our school-money and school-time, must continue so.

A great man, who towers far above the common heads, full of creative thought, of the ideas which move the world, able to organize that thought into institutions, laws, practical works; a man of a million, a million-minded man, at the head of a nation, putting his thought into them; ruling not barely by virtue of his position, but by the intellectual and moral power to fill it; ruling not over men's heads, but in their minds and hearts, and leading them to new fields of toil, increasing their numbers, wealth, intelligence, comfort, morals, piety—such a man is a noble sight; a Charlemagne, or a Genghis Khan, a Moses leading his nation up from Egyptian bondage to freedom and the promised land. How have the eyes of the world been fixed on Washington! In darker days than ours, when all was violence, it is easy to excuse such men if they were warriors also, and made, for the time, their nation but a camp. There have been ages when the most lasting ink was human blood. In our day, when war is the exception, and that commonly needless, such a man, so getting the start of the majestic world, were a far grander sight. And with such a man at the head of this nation, a great man at the head of a free nation, able and energetic, and enterprising as we are, what were too much to hope? As it is, we have wasted our money, and got the honour of fighting such a war.

Let me next speak of the direct cost of the war in men. In April, 1846, the entire army of the United States consisted of 7244 men; the naval force of about 7500. We presented the gratifying spectacle of a nation 20,000,000 strong, with a sea-coast of 3000 or 4000 miles, and only 7000 or 8000 soldiers, and as many armed men on the sea, or less than 15,000 in all! Few things were more grateful to an American than this thought, that his country was so nearly free from the terrible curse of a standing army. At that time the standing army of France was about 480,000 men; that of Russia nearly 800,000 it is said. Most of the officers in the American army and navy, and most of the rank and file, had probably entered the service with no expectation of ever shedding the blood of men.

The navy and army were looked on as instruments of peace; as much so as the police of a city.

The first of last January there was, in Mexico, an American army of 23,695 regular soldiers, and a little more than 50,000 volunteers, the number cannot now be exactly determined, making an army of invasion of about 75,000 men. The naval forces, also, had been increased to 10,000. Estimating all the men engaged in the service of the army and navy; in making weapons of war and ammunition; in preparing food and clothing; in transporting those things and the soldiers from place to place, by land or sea, and in performing the various other works incident to military operations; it is within bounds to say that there were 80,000 or 90,000 men engaged indirectly in the works of war. But not to exaggerate, it is safe to say that 150,000 men were directly or indirectly engaged in the Mexican war. This estimate will seem moderate, when you remember that there were about 5000 teamsters connected with the army in Mexico.

Here, then, were 150,000 men whose attention and toil were diverted from the great business of productive industry to merely military operations, or preparations for them. Of course, all the labour of these men was of no direct value to the human race. The food and clothing and labour of a man who earns nothing by productive work of hand or head, is food, clothing, and labour thrown away —labour in vain. There is nothing to show for the things he has consumed. So all the work spent in preparing ammunition and weapons of war is labour thrown away, an absolute loss, as much as if it had been spent in making earthen pitchers and then in dashing them to pieces. A country is the richer for every serviceable plough and spade made in it, and the world the richer; they are to be used in productive work, and when worn out, there is the improved soil and the crops that have been gathered, to show for the wear and tear of the tools. So a country is the richer for every industrious shoemaker and blacksmith it contains; for his time and toil go to increase the sum of human comfort, creating actual wealth. The world also is better off, and becomes better through their influence. But a country is the poorer for every soldier it maintains, and the world poorer, as he adds nothing to the actual wealth of mankind; so is it the poorer for each sword and cannon made within its borders, and the world poorer, for these instruments cannot be used in any productive work, only for works of destruction.

So much for the labour of these 150,000 men; labour wasted in vain. Let us now look at the cost of life. It is not possible to ascertain the exact loss suffered up to this time, in killed, deceased by ordinary diseases, and in wounded; for some die before they are mustered into the service of the United States, and parts of the army are so far distant from the seat of Government that their recent losses are still unknown. I rely for information on the last report of the Secretary of War, read before the Senate, April 10, 1848, and recently printed. That gives the losses of parts of the army up to December last; other accounts are made up only till October, or till August. Recent losses will of course swell the amount of destruction. According to that report, on the American side there had been killed in battle, or died of wounds received therein, 1689 persons; there had died of diseases and accidents, 6173; 3743 have been wounded in battle, who were not known to be dead at the date of the report.

This does not include the deaths in the navy, nor the destruction of men connected with the army in various ways, as furnishing supplies and the like. Considering the sickness and accidents that have happened in the present year, and others which may be expected before the troops reach home, I may set down the total number of deaths on the American side, caused by the war, at 15,000, and the number of wounded men at 4000. Suppose the army on the average to have consisted of 50,000 men for two years, this gives a mortality of fifteen per cent. each year, which is an enormous loss even for times of war, and one seldom equalled in modern warfare.

Now, most of the men who have thus died or been maimed were in the prime of life, able-bodied and hearty men. Had they remained at home in the works of peace, it is not likely that more than 500 of the number would have died. So then 14,500 lives may be set down at once to the account of the war. The wounded men are of course to thank the war, and that alone, for their smart, and the life-long agony which they are called on to endure.

Such is the American loss. The loss of the Mexicans we cannot now determine. But they have been many times more numerous than the Americans; have been badly armed, badly commanded, badly trained, and besides, have been beaten in every battle; their number seemed often the cause of their ruin, making them confident before battle, and hindering their retreat after they were beaten. Still more, they have been ill provided with surgeons and nurses to care for the wounded, and were destitute of medicines. They must have lost in battle five or six times more than we have done, and have had a proportionate number of wounded. To "lie like a military bulletin" is a European proverb; and it is not necessary to trust reports which tell of 600 or 900 Mexicans left dead on the ground, while the Americans lost but five or six. But when we remember that only twelve Americans were killed during the bombardment of 'Vera Cruz, which lasted five days; that the citadel contained more than 5000 soldiers and over 400 pieces of cannon, we may easily believe the Mexican losses, on the whole, have been 10,000 men killed and perished of their wounds. Their loss by sickness would probably be smaller than our own, for the Mexicans were in their native climate, though often ill-furnished with clothes, with shelter, and provisions; so I will put down their loss by ordinary diseases at only 5000, making a total of 15,000 deaths. Suppose their number of wounded was four times as great as our own, or 20,000: I should not be surprised if this were only half the number.

Put all together, and we have in total, Americans and Mexicans, 24,000 men wounded, more or less, and the greater part maimed for life; and we have 30,000 men killed on the field of battle, or perished by the slow torture of their wounds, or deceased of diseases caused by extraordinary exposures; 24,000 men maimed; 30,000 dead!

You all remember the bill which so hastily passed Congress in May, 1846, and authorized the war previously begun. You perhaps have not forgot the preamble, "Whereas war exists by the act of Mexico." Well, that bill authorized the waste of $200,000,000 of American treasure, money enough to have built a railroad across the Isthmus of Panama, and another to connect the Mississippi and the Pacific Ocean; it demanded the disturbance of industry and commerce all over the land, caused by withdrawing $100,000,000 from peaceful investments, and diverting 150,000 Americans from their productive and peaceful works; it demanded a loss yet greater of the treasure of Mexicans; it commanded the maiming of 24,000 men for life, and the death of 30,000 men in the prime and vigour of manhood. Yet such was the state of feeling, I will not say of thought, in the Congress, that out of both houses only sixteen men voted against it. If a prophet had stood there he might have said to the representative of Boston, " You have just voted for the wasting of 200,000,000 of the very dollars you were sent there to represent; for the maiming of 24,000 men and the killing of 30,000 more—part by disease, part by the sword, part by the slow and awful lingerings of a wounded frame! Sir, that is the English of your vote." Suppose the prophet, before the votes were taken, could have gone round and told each member of Congress, " If there comes a war, you will perish in it;" perhaps the vote would have been a little different. It is easy to vote away blood, if it is not your own!

Such is the cost of the war in money and in men. Yet it has not been a very cruel war. It has been conducted with as much gentleness as a war of invasion can be. There is no agreeable way of butchering men. You cannot make it a pastime. The Americans have always been a brave people; they were never cruel. They always treated their prisoners kindly—in the Revolutionary war, in the late war with England. True, they have seized the Mexican ports, taken military possession of the custom-houses, and collected such duties as they saw fit; true, they sometimes made the army of invasion self-subsisting, and to that end have levied contributions on the towns they have taken; true, they have seized provisions which were private property, snatching them out of the hands of men who needed them; true, they have robbed the rich and the poor; true, they have burned and bombarded towns, have murdered men and violated women. All this must of course take place in any war. There will be the general murder and robbery committed on account of the nation, and the particular murder and robbery on account of the special individual. This also is to be expected. You cannot set a town on fire and burn down just half of it, making the flames stop exactly where you will. You cannot take the most idle, ignorant, drunken, and vicious men out of the low population in our cities and large towns, get them drunk enough or foolish enough to enlist, train them to violence, theft, robbery, murder, and then stop the man from exercising his rage or lust on his own private account. If it is hard to make a dog understand that he must kill a hare for his master, but never for himself; it is not much easier to teach a volunteer that it is a duty, a distinction, and a glory to rob and murder the Mexican people for the nation's sake, but a wrong, a shame, and a crime to rob or murder a single Mexican for his own sake. There have been instances of wanton cruelty, occasioned by private licentiousness and individual barbarity. Of these I shall take no further notice, but come to such as have been commanded by the American authorities, and which were the official acts of the nation.

One was the capture of Tabasco. Tabasco is a small town several hundred miles from the theatre of war, situated on a river about eighty miles from the sea, in the midst of a fertile province. The army did not need it, nor the navy. It did not lie in the way of the American operations; its possession would be wholly useless. But one Sunday afternoon, while the streets were full of men, women, and children, engaged in their Sunday business, a part of the naval force of America swept by; the streets running at right angles with the river, were enfiladed by the hostile cannon, and men, women, and children, unarmed and unresisting, were mowed down by the merciless shot. The city was taken, but soon abandoned, for its possession was of no use. The killing of those men, women, and children was as much a piece of murder, as it would be to come and shoot us to-day, and in this house. No valid excuse has been given for this cold-blooded massacre; none can be given. It was not battle, but wanton butchery. None but a Pequod Indian could excuse it. The theological newspapers in New England thought it a wicked thing in Dr. Palfrey to write a letter on Sunday, though he hoped thereby to help end the war. How many of them had any fault to find with this national butchery on the Lord's day? Fighting is bad enough any day; fighting for mere pay, or glory, or the love of fighting, is a wicked thing; but to fight on that day when the whole Christian world kneels to pray in the name of the Peacemaker; to butcher men and women and children, when they are coming home from church, with prayer-books in their hands, seems an aggravation even of murder; a cowardly murder, which a Hessian would have been ashamed of. "But, 'twas a famous victory."

One other instance, of at least apparent wantonness, took place at the bombardment of Vera Cruz. After the siege had gone on for a while, the foreign consuls in the town, "moved," as they say, "by the feeling of humanity excited in their hearts by the frightful results of the bombardment of the city," requested that the women and children might be allowed to leave the city, and not stay to be shot. The American General refused; they must stay and be shot.

Perhaps you have not an adequate conception of the effect produced by bombarding a town. Let me interest you a little in the details thereof. Vera Cruz is about as large as Boston was in 1810; it contains about 30,000 inhabitants. In addition, it is protected by a castle, the celebrated fortress of St. Juan d'Ulloa, furnished with more than 5000 soldiers and over 400 cannons. Imagine to yourself Boston as it was forty years ago, invested with a fleet on one side, and an army of 15,000 men on the land, both raining cannon-balls and bomb-shells upon your houses; shattering them to fragments, exploding in your streets, churches, houses, cellars, mingling men, women, and children in one promiscuous murder. Suppose this to continue five days and nights; imagine the condition of the city; the ruins, the flames; the dead, the wounded, the widows, the orphans; think of the fears of the men anticipating the city would be sacked by a merciless soldiery : think of the women! Thus you will have a faint notion of the picture of Vera Cruz at the end of March, 1847. Do you know the meaning of the name of the city? Vera Cruz is the True Cross. "See how these Christians love one another." The Americans are followers of the Prince of Peace; they have more missionaries amongst the "heathen" than any other nation, and the President, in his last Message, says, "No country has been so much favoured, or should acknowledge with deeper reverence the manifestations of the Divine protection." The Americans were fighting Mexico to dismember her territory, to plunder her soil, and plant thereon the institution of slavery, "the necessary background of freedom."

Few of us have ever seen a battle, and without that none can have a complete notion of the ferocious passions which it excites. Let me help your fancy a little by relating an anecdote which seems to be very well authenticated, and requires but little external testimony to render it credible. At any rate, it was abundantly believed a year ago; but times change, and what was then believed all round may now be "the most improbable thing in the world." At the battle of Buena Vista, a Kentucky regiment began to stagger under the heavy charge of the Mexicans. The American commander-in-chief turned to one who stood near him, and exclaimed, "By God, this will not do. This is not the way for Kentuckians to behave when called on to make good a battle. It will not answer, sir." So the General clenched his fist, knit his brows, and set his teeth hard together. However, the Kentuckians presently formed in good order and gave a deadly fire, which altered the battle. Then the old General broke out with a loud hurrah. "Hurrah for old Kentuck," he exclaimed, rising in his stirrups; "that's the way to do it. Give 'em hell, damn 'em," and tears of exultation rolled down his cheeks as he said it. You find the name of this General at the head of most of the whig newspapers in the United States. He is one of the most popular candidates for the Presidency. Cannons were fired for him, a hundred guns, on Boston Common, not long ago, in honour of his nomination for the highest office in the gift of a free and Christian people. Soon we shall probably have clerical certificates, setting forth, to the people of the North, that he is an exemplary Christian. You know how Faneuil Hall, the old "Cradle of Liberty," rang with "Hurrah for Taylor," but a few days ago. The seven wise men of Greece were famous in their day; but now nothing is known of them except a single pungent aphorism from each, "Know thyself," and the like. The time may come when our great men shall have suffered this same reduction, descending, all their robes of glory having vanished save a single thread. Then shall Franklin be known only as having said, "Don't give too much for the Whistle;" Patrick Henry for his "Give me Liberty or give me Death;" Washington for his "In Peace prepare for War;" Jefferson for his "All men are created equal;" and General Taylor shall be known only by his attributes rough and ready, and for his aphorism, "Give 'em hell, damn 'em." Yet he does not seem to be a ferocious man, but generous and kindly, it is said, and strongly opposed to this particular war, whose "natural justice" it seems he looked at, and which he thought was wicked at the beginning, though, on that account, he was none the less ready to fight it.

One thing more I must mention in speaking of the cost of men. According to the Report quoted just now, 4966 American soldiers had deserted in Mexico. Some of them had joined the Mexican army. When the American commissioners, who were sent to secure the ratification of the treaty, went to Queretaro, they found there a body of 200 American soldiers, and 800 more were at no great distance, mustered into the Mexican service. These men, it seems, had served out their time in the American camp, and notwithstanding they had, as the President says in his Message, "covered themselves with imperishable honours," by fighting men who never injured them, they were willing to go and seek a yet thicker mantle of this imperishable honour, by fighting against their own country! Why should they not? If it were right to kill Mexicans for a few dollars a month, why was it not also right to kill Americans, especially when it pays the most? Perhaps it is not an American habit to inquire into the justice of a war, only into the profit which it may bring. If the Mexicans pay best, in money, these 1000 soldiers made a good speculation. No doubt in Mexico military glory is at a premium, though it could hardly command a greater price just now than in America, where, however, the supply seems equal to the demand.

The numerous desertions and the readiness with which the soldiers joined the "foe," show plainly the moral

character of the men, and the degree of "patriotism" and
"humanity" which animated them in going to war. You
know the severity of military discipline; the terrible
beatings men are subjected to before they can become
perfect in the soldier's art; the horrible and revolting
punishments imposed on them for drunkenness, though
little pains were taken to keep the temptation from their
eyes, and for disobedience of general orders. You have
read enough of this in the newspapers. The officers of the
volunteers, I am told, have generally been men of little
education, men of strong passions and bad habits; many
of them abandoned men, who belonged to the refuse of
society. Such men run into an army as the wash of
the street runs into the sewers. When such a man gets
clothed with a little authority, in time of peace, you know
what use he makes of it; but when he covers himself with
the "imperishable honours" of his official coat, gets an
epaulet on his shoulder, a sword by his side, a commission in his pocket, and visions of "glory" in his head, you
may easily judge how he will use his authority, or may
read in the newspapers how he has used it. When there
are brutal soldiers, commanded by brutal captains, it is to
be supposed that much brutality is to be suffered.

Now desertion is a great offence in a soldier; in this
army it is one of the most common; for nearly ten per
cent. of the American army has deserted in Mexico, not
to mention the desertions before the army reached that
country. It is related that forty-eight men were hanged
at once for desertion; not hanged as you judicially murder
men in time of peace, privately, as if ashamed of the deed,
in the corner of a gaol, and by a contrivance which shortens
the agony, and makes death humane as possible. These
forty-eight men were hanged slowly; put to death with
painful procrastinations, their agony wilfully prolonged,
and death embittered by needless ferocity. But that is
not all: it is related, that these men were doomed to be
thus murdered on the day when the battle of Churubusco
took place. These men, awaiting their death, were told
they should not suffer till the American flag should wave
its stripes over the hostile walls. So they were kept in
suspense an hour, and then slowly hanged one by one.
You know the name of the officer on whom this barbarity

rests : it was Colonel Harney, a man whose reputation was black enough and base enough before. His previous deeds, however, require no mention here. But this man is now a General, and so on the high road to the Presidency, whenever it shall please our Southern masters to say the word. Some accounts say there were more than forty-eight who thus were hanged. I only give the number of those whose names lie printed before me as I write. Perhaps the number was less; it is impossible to obtain exact information in respect to the matter, for the Government has not yet published an account of the punishments inflicted in this war. The information can only be obtained by a "Resolution" of either house of Congress, and so is not likely to be had before the election. But at the same time with the execution, other deserters were scourged with fifty lashes each, branded with a letter D, a perpetual mark of infamy on their cheek, compelled to wear an iron yoke, weighing eight pounds, about their neck. Six men were made to dig the grave of their companions, and were then flogged with two hundred lashes each.

I wish this hanging of forty-eight men could have taken place in State Street, and the respectable citizens of Boston, who like this war, had been made to look on and see it all; that they had seen those poor culprits bid farewell to father, mother, wife, or child, looking wistfully for the hour which was to end their torment, and then, one by one, have seen them slowly hanged to death; that your representative, ye men of Boston, had put on all the halters! He did help put them on; that infamous vote — I speak not of the motive, it may have been as honourable as the vote itself was infamous—doomed these eight-and-forty men to be thus murdered.

Yes, I wish all this killing of the 2000 Americans on the field of battle, and the 10,000 Mexicans; all this slashing of the bodies of 24,000 wounded men; all the agony of the other 18,000, that have died of disease, could have taken place in some spot where the President of the United States and his Cabinet, where all the Congress who voted for the war, with the Baltimore conventions of '44 and '48, and the whig convention of Philadelphia, and the controlling men of both political parties, who care nothing for this bloodshed and misery they have idly caused, could have stood and seen it all; and then that the voice of the whole nation had come up to them and said, "This is your work, not ours. Certainly we will not shed our blood, nor our brothers' blood, to get never so much slave territory. It was bad enough to fight in the cause of freedom. In the cause of slavery—God forgive us for that! We have trusted you thus far, but please God we never will trust you again."

Let us now look at the effect of this war on the morals of the nation. The Revolutionary war was the contest for a great idea. If there were ever a just war it was that—a contest for national existence. Yet it brought out many of the worst qualities of human nature on both sides, as well as some of the best. It helped make a Washington, it is true, but a Benedict Arnold likewise. A war with a powerful nation, terrible as it must be, yet develops the energy of the people, promotes self-denial, and helps the growth of some qualities of a high order. It had this effect in England from 1798 to 1815. True, England for that time became a despotism, but the self-consciousness of the nation, its self-denial and energy, were amazingly stimulated; the moral effect of that series of wars was doubtless far better than of the infamous contest which she has kept up against Ireland for many years. Let us give even war its due: when a great boy fights with an equal, it may develop his animal courage and strength—for he gets as bad as he gives; but when he only beats a little boy that cannot pay back his blows, it is cowardly as well as cruel, and doubly debasing to the conqueror. Mexico was no match for America. We all knew that very well before the war began. When a nation numbering 8,000,000 or 9,000,000 of people can be successfully invaded by an army of 75,000 men, two-thirds of them volunteers, raw, and undisciplined; when the invaders with less than 15,000 can march two hundred miles into the very heart of the hostile country, and with less than 6000 can take and hold the capital of the nation, a city of 100,000 or 200,000 inhabitants, and dictate a peace, taking as much territory as they will—it is hardly fair to dignify such operations with the name of war. The little good which a long contest with an equal might produce in the

conqueror, is wholly lost. Had Mexico been a strong
nation, we should never have had this conflict. A few
years ago, when General Cass wanted a war with England,
"an old-fashioned war," and declared it "unavoidable,"
all the men of property trembled. The Northern men
thought of their mills and their ships; they thought how
Boston and New York would look after a war with our
sturdy old father over the sea; they thought we should
lose many millions of dollars and gain nothing. The men
of the South, who have no mills and no ships, and no large
cities to be destroyed, thought of their "peculiar institution;" they thought of a servile war; they thought what
might become of their slaves, if a nation which gave
$100,000,000 to emancipate her bondmen should send a
large army with a few black soldiers from Jamaica; should
offer money, arms, and freedom to all who would leave
their masters and claim their unalienable rights. They
knew the southern towns would be burnt to ashes, and the
whole South, from Virginia to the Gulf, would be swept
with fire; and they said, "Don't." The North said so,
and the South; they feared such a war with such a foe.
Everybody knows the effect which this fear had on southern politicians in the beginning of this century, and how
gladly they made peace with England soon as she was at
liberty to turn her fleet and her army against the most
vulnerable part of the nation. I am not blind to the
wickedness of England more than ignorant of the good
things she has done and is doing; a Paradise for the rich
and strong, she is still a Purgatory for the wise and the
good, and the Hell of the poor and the weak. I have no
fondness for war anywhere, and believe it needless and
wanton in this age of the world—surely needless and
wicked between Father England and Daughter America;
but I do solemnly believe that the moral effect of such an
old-fashioned war as Mr. Cass in 1845 thought unavoidable, would have been better than that of this Mexican
war. It would have ended slavery; ended it in blood, no
doubt, the worst thing to blot out an evil with; but ended
it, and for ever. God grant it may yet have a more peaceful termination. We should have lost millions of property
and thousands of men, and then, when peace came, we
should know what it was worth; and as the burnt child

dreads the fire, no future President, or Congress, or Convention, or Party, would talk much in favour of war for some years to come.

The moral effect of this war is thoroughly bad. It was unjust in the beginning. Mexico did not pay her debts; but though the United States, in 1783, acknowledged the British claims against ourselves, they were not paid till 1803; our claims against England, for her depredations in 1793, were not paid till 1804; our claims against France, for her depredations in 1806-13, were not paid us till 1834. The fact that Mexico refused to receive the resident Minister which the United States sent to settle the disputes, when a commissioner was expected—this was no ground of war. We have lately seen a British ambassador ordered to leave Spain within eight-and-forty hours, and yet the English Minister of Foreign Affairs, Lord Palmerston—no new hand at diplomacy—declares that this does not interrupt the concord of the two nations! We treated Mexico contemptuously before hostilities began; and when she sent troops into a territory which she had always possessed, though Texas had claimed it, we declared that that was an act of war, and ourselves sent an army to invade her soil, to capture her cities, and seize her territory. It has been a war of plunder, undertaken for the purpose of seizing Mexican territory, and extending over it that dismal curse which blackens, impoverishes, and barbarizes half the Union now, and swiftly corrupts the other half. It was not enough to have Louisiana a slave territory; not enough to make that institution perpetual in Florida; not enough to extend this blight over Texas—we must have yet more slave soil, one day to be carved into Slave States, to bind the Southern yoke yet more securely on the Northern neck; to corrupt yet more the politics, literature, and morals of the North. The war was unjust at its beginning; mean in its motives, a war without honourable cause; a war for plunder; a quarrel between a great boy and a little puny weakling who could not walk alone, and could hardly stand. We have treated Mexico as the three Northern powers treated Poland in the last century—stooped to conquer. Nay, our contest has been like the English seizure of Ireland. All the justice was on one side, the force, skill, and wealth, on the other.

I know men say the war has shown us that Americans could fight. Could fight—almost every male beast will fight, the more brutal the better. The long war of the Revolution, when Connecticut, for seven years, kept 5000 men in the field, showed that Americans could fight; Bunker Hill and Lexington showed that they could fight, even without previous discipline. If such valour be a merit, I am ready to believe that the Americans, in a great cause like that of Mexico, to resist wicked invasion, would fight as men never fought before. A republic like our own, where every free man feels an interest in the welfare of the nation, is full of the elements that make soldiers. Is that a praise? Most men think so, but it is the smallest honour of a nation. Of all glories, military glory, at its best estate, seems the poorest.

Men tell us it shows the strength of the nation, and some writers quote the opinions of European kings who, when hearing of the battles of Monterey, Buena Vista, and Vera Cruz, became convinced that we were a "great people." Remembering the character of these kings, one can easily believe that such was their judgment, and will not sigh many times at their fate, but will hope to see the day when the last king, who can estimate a nation's strength only by its battles, has passed on to impotence and oblivion. The power of America—do we need proof of that? I see it in the streets of Boston and New York; in Lowell and in Lawrence; I see it in our mills and our ships; I read it in those letters of iron written all over the North, where he may read that runs; I see it in the unconquered energy which tames the forest, the rivers, and the ocean; in the schoolhouses which lift their modest roof in every village of the North; in the churches that rise all over the freeman's land: would God that they rose higher, pointing down to man and to human duties, and up to God and immortal life! I see the strength of America in that tide of population which spreads over the prairies of the West, and, beating on the Rocky Mountains, dashes its peaceful spray to the very shores of the Pacific sea. Had we taken 150,000 men and $200,000,000, and built two railroads across the continent, that would have been a worthy sign of the nation's strength. Perhaps those kings could not see it; but sensible men could see it and be glad. This waste of treasure and this waste of blood is only a proof of weakness. War is a transient weakness of the nation, but slavery a permanent imbecility.

What falsehood has this war produced in the executive and legislative power; in both parties, whigs and democrats! I always thought that here in Massachusetts the whigs were the most to blame; they tried to put the disgrace of the war on the others, while the democratic party coolly faced the wickedness. Did far-sighted men know that there would be a war on Mexico, or else on the tariff or the currency, and prefer the first as the least evil?

See to what the war has driven two of the most famous men of the nation: one wished to "capture or slay a Mexican;"* the other could encourage the volunteers to fight a war which he had denounced as needless, "a war of pretexts," and place the men of Monterey before the men of Bunker Hill;† each could invest a son in that unholy cause. You know the rest: the fathers ate sour grapes, and the children's teeth were set on edge. When a man goes on board an emigrant ship, reeking with filth and fever, not for gain, not for "glory," but in brotherly love, catches the contagion, and dies a martyr to his heroic benevolence, men speak of it in corners, and it is soon forgot; there is no parade in the streets; society takes little pains to do honour to the man. How rarely is a pension given to his widow or his child; only once in the whole land, and then but a small sum.‡ But when a volunteer officer—for of the humbler and more excusable men that fall we take no heed, war may mow that crop of "vulgar deaths" with what scythe he will—falls or dies in the quarrel which he had no concern in, falls in a broil between the two nations, your newspapers extol the man, and with martial pomp, "sonorous metal blowing martial sounds," with all the honours of the most honoured dead, you lay away his body in the tomb. Thus is it that the nation teaches these little ones that it is better to kill than to make alive.

I know there are men in the army, honourable and

* See Mr. Clay's speech at the dinner in New Orleans on Forefathers' day.

† See Mr. Webster's speech to the volunteers at Philadelphia.

‡ A case of this sort had just occurred in Boston.

high-minded men, Christian men, who dislike war in general, and this war in special; but such is their view of official duty, that they obeyed the summons of battle, though with pain and reluctance. They knew not how to avoid obedience. I am willing to believe there are many such. But with volunteers, who, of their own accord, came forth to enlist, men not blinded by ignorance, not driven by poverty to the field, but only by hope of reward —what shall be said of them? Much may be said to excuse the rank and file, ignorant men, many of them in want—but for the leaders, what can be said? Had I a brother who, in the day of the nation's extremity, came forward with a good conscience, and perilled his life on the battle-field, and lost it "in the sacred cause of God and his country," I would honour the man, and when his dust came home, I would lay it away with his fathers'; with sorrow indeed, but with thankfulness of heart that, for conscience' sake, he was ready even to die. But had I a brother who, merely for his pay, or hope of fame, had voluntarily gone down to fight innocent men, to plunder their territory, and lost his life in that felonious essay—in sorrow and in silence, and in secrecy, would I lay down his body in the grave; I would not court display, nor mark it with a single stone.

See how this war has affected public opinion. How many of your newspapers have shown its true atrocity? how many of the pulpits? Yet, if any one is appointed to tell of public wrongs, it is the minister of religion. The Governor of Massachusetts* is an officer of a Christian church; a man distinguished for many excellencies, some of them by no means common: it is said he is opposed to the war in private, and thinks it wicked; but no man has lent himself as a readier tool to promote it. The Christian and the man seem lost in the office, in the Governor! What a lesson of falseness does all this teach to that large class of persons who look no higher than the example of eminent men for their instruction. You know what complaints have been made by the highest authority in the nation, because a few men dared to speak against the war. It was "affording aid and comfort to the enemy." If the war party had been stronger, and feared no public opinion,

* Mr. George N. Briggs.

we should have had men hanged for treason, because they spoke of this national iniquity! Nothing would have been easier. A "gag law" is not wholly unknown in America.

If you will take all the theft, all the assaults, all the cases of arson, ever committed in time of peace in the United States, since the settlement of Jamestown in 1608, and add to them all the cases of violence offered to woman, with all the murders, they will not amount to half the wrongs committed in this war for the plunder of Mexico. Yet the cry has been, and still is, "You must not say a word against it; if you do, you 'afford aid and comfort to the enemy.'" Not tell the nation that she is doing wrong? What a miserable saying is that; let it come from what high authority it may, it is a miserable saying. Make the case your own. Suppose the United States were invaded by a nation ten times abler for war than we are, with a cause no more just, intentions equally bad; invaded for the purpose of dismembering our territory and making our own New England the soil of slaves; would you be still? would you stand and look on tamely while the hostile hosts, strangers in language, manners, and religion, crossed your rivers, seized your ports, burnt your towns? No, surely not. Though the men of New England would not be able to resist with most celestial love, they would contend with most manly vigour; and I should rather see every house swept clean off the land, and the ground sheeted with our own dead; rather see every man, woman, and child in the land slain, than see them tamely submit to such a wrong. And so would you. No; sacred as life is, and dear as it is, better let it be trodden out by the hoof of war, rather than yield tamely to a wrong. But while you were doing your utmost to repel such formidable injustice, if in the midst of your invaders, men rose up and said, "America is in the right, and, brothers, you are wrong; you should not thus kill men to steal their land: shame on you!" how should you feel towards such? Nay, in the struggle with England, when our fathers perilled everything but honour, and fought for the unalienable rights of man, you all remember, how in England herself there stood up noble men, and with a voice that was heard above the roar of the populace, and an authority higher than the majesty of the throne, they said, "You do a wrong; you may ravage, but you cannot conquer. If I were an American, while a foreign troop remained in my land, I would never lay down my arms; no, never, never, never!"

But I wander a little from my theme, the effect of the war on the morals of the nation. Here are 50,000 or 75,000 men trained to kill. Hereafter they will be of little service in any good work. Many of them were the off-scouring of the people at first. Now, these men have tasted the idleness, the intemperance, the debauchery of a camp; tasted of its riot, tasted of its blood! They will come home before long, hirelings of murder. What will their influence be as fathers, husbands? The nation taught them to fight and plunder the Mexicans for the nation's sake; the Governor of Massachusetts called on them in the name of "patriotism" and "humanity" to enlist for that work: but if, with no justice on our side, it is humane and patriotic to fight and plunder the Mexicans on the nation's account, why not for the soldier to fight and plunder an American on his own account? Ay, why not?—that is a distinction too nice for common minds; by far too nice for mine.

See the effect on the nation. We have just plundered Mexico; taken a piece of her territory larger than the thirteen states which fought the Revolution, a hundred times as large as Massachusetts; we have burnt her cities, have butchered her men, have been victorious in every contest. The Mexicans were as unprotected women; we, armed men. See how the lust of conquest will increase. Soon it will be the ambition of the next President to extend the "area of freedom" a little further south; the lust of conquest will increase. Soon we must have Yucatan, Central America, all of Mexico, Cuba, Porto Rico, Hayti, Jamaica—all the islands of the Gulf. Many men would gladly, I doubt not, extend the "area of freedom" so as to include the free blacks of those islands. We have long looked with jealous eyes on West Indian emancipation—hoping the scheme would not succeed. How pleasant it would be to re-establish slavery in Hayti and Jamaica, in all the islands whence the gold of England or the ideas of France have driven it out. If the South wants this, would the North object? The possession of the West Indies would bring much money to New England, and what is the value of freedom compared to coffee and sugar and cotton?

I must say one word of the effect this war has had on political parties. By the parties I mean the leaders thereof, the men that control the parties. The effect on the democratic party, on the majority of Congress, on the most prominent men of the nation, has been mentioned before. It has shut their eyes to truth and justice; it has filled their mouths with injustice and falsehood. It has made one man "available" for the Presidency who was only known before as a sagacious general, that fought against the Indians in Florida, and acquired a certain reputation by the use of bloodhounds, a reputation which was rather unenviable, even in America. The battles in northern Mexico made him conspicuous, and now he is seized on as an engine to thrust one corrupt party out of power, and to lift in another party, I will not say less corrupt, I wish I could; it were difficult to think it more so. This latter party has been conspicuous for its opposition to a military man as ruler of a free people; recently it has been smitten with sudden admiration for military men, and military success, and tells the people, without a blush, that a military man fresh from a fight which he disapproved of, is most likely to restore peace, "because most familiar with the evils of war!" In Massachusetts the prevalent political party, as such, for some years, seems to have had no moral principle; however, it had a prejudice in favour of decency: now it has thrown that overboard, and has not even its respectability left. What are its "Resolutions?" Some men knew what they were worth long ago; now all men can see what they are worth.

The cost of the war in money and men I have tried to calculate, but the effect on the morals of the people, on the press, the pulpit, and the parties, and through them on the rising generation, it is impossible to tell. I have only faintly sketched the outline of that. The effect of the war on Mexico herself, we can dimly see in the distance. The Government of the United States has wilfully, wantonly broken the peace of the continent. The Revolutionary war was unavoidable; but for this invasion there is no excuse. That God, whose providence watches over the falling nation as the falling sparrow, and whose comprehensive plans are now advanced by the righteousness and now by the wrath of man; He who stilleth the waves of the sea and the tumult of the people, will turn all this wickedness to account in the history of man—of that I have no doubt. But that is no excuse for American crime. A greater good lay within our grasp, and we spurned it away.

Well, before long the soldiers will come back, such as shall ever come—the regulars and volunteers, the husbands of the women whom your charity fed last winter, housed and clad and warmed. They will come back. Come, New England, with your posterity of States, go forth to meet your sons returning all " covered with imperishable honours." Come, men, to meet your fathers, brothers. Come, women, to your husbands and your lovers; come. But what! is that the body of men who a year or two ago went forth so full of valour and of rum? Are these rags the imperishable honours that cover them? Here is not half the whole. Where is the wealth they hoped from the spoil of churches? But the men—"Where is my husband?" says one; "And my son?" says another. "They fell at Jalapa, one, and one at Cerro Gordo; but they fell covered with imperishable honour, for 'twas a famous victory." "Where is my lover?" screams a woman whom anguish makes respectable, spite of her filth and ignorance;—"And our father, where is he?" scream a troop of half-starved children, staring through their dirt and rags. "One died of the vomit at Vera Cruz. Your father, little ones, we scourged the naked man to death at Mixcoac."

But that troop which is left, who are in the arms of wife and child, they are the best sermon against war; this has lost an arm and that a leg; half are maimed in battle or sickened with the fever; all polluted with the drunkenness, idleness, debauchery, lust, and murder of a camp. Strip off this man's coat, and count the stripes welted into his flesh, stripes laid on by demagogues that love the people—"the dear people!" See how affectionately the war-makers branded the "dear soldiers" with a letter D, with a red-hot iron, in the cheek. The flesh will quiver as the irons burn; no matter: it is only for love of the people that all this is done, and we are all of us covered with imperishable honours! D stands for deserter—ay, and for demagogue—yes, and for demon too. Many a man shall come home with but half of himself, half his body, less than half his soul.

> "Alas! the mother that him bare,
> If she could stand in presence there,
> In that wan cheek and wasted air,
> She would not know her child."

"Better," you say, "for us better, and for themselves better by far, if they had left that remnant of a body in the common ditch where the soldier finds his 'bed of honour;' better have fed therewith the vultures of a foreign soil than thus come back." No; better come back, and live here, mutilated, scourged, branded, a cripple, a pauper, a drunkard, and a felon; better darken the windows of the gaol, and blot the gallows with unusual shame, to teach us all that such is war, and such the results of every "famous victory," such the imperishable honours that it brings, and how the war-makers love the men they rule!

O Christian America! O New England, child of the Puritans! Cradled in the wilderness, thy swaddling garments stained with martyrs' blood, hearing in thy youth the war-whoop of the savage and thy mother's sweet and soul-composing hymn:

> "Hush, my child, lie still and slumber,
> Holy angels guard thy bed;
> Heavenly blessings, without number,
> Rest upon thine infant head."

Come, New England, take the old banners of thy conquering host, the standards borne at Monterey, Palo Alto, Buena Vista, Vera Cruz, the "glorious stripes and stars" that waved over the walls of Churubusco, Contreras, Puebla, Mexico herself, flags blackened with battle and stiffened with blood, pierced by the lances and torn with the shot; bring them into thy churches, hang them up over altar and pulpit, and let little children, clad in white raiment and crowned with flowers, come and chant their lessons for the day.

"Blessed are the pure in heart, for they shall see God.

"Blessed are the peacemakers, for they shall be called the children of God."

Then let the priest say, "Righteousness exalteth a nation, but sin is a reproach unto any people. Blessed is the Lord my strength, which teacheth my hands to war, and my fingers to fight. Happy is that people that is in such a case. Yea, happy is that people whose God is the Lord, and Jesus Christ their Saviour."

Then let the soldiers who lost their limbs and the women who lost their husbands and their lovers in the strife, and the men—wiser than the children of light—who made money out of the war : let all the people, like people and like priest, say, " Amen."

But suppose these men were to come back to Boston on a day when, in civil style, as having never sinned yourself, and never left a man in ignorance and want to be goaded into crime, you were about to hang three men—one for murder, one for robbery with the armed hand, and one for burning down a house. Suppose, after the fashion of " the good old times," you were to hang those men in public, and lead them in long procession through your streets, and while you were welcoming these returned soldiers and taking their officers to feast in " the Cradle of Liberty," they should meet the sheriff's procession escorting those culprits to the gallows. Suppose the warriors should ask, " Why, what is that?" What would you say? Why, this : " These men, they broke the law of God, by violence, by fire and blood, and we shall hang them for the public good, and especially for the example, to teach the ignorant, the low, and the weak." Suppose those three felons, the halters round their neck, should ask also, " Why, what is that ?" You would say, " They are the soldiers just come back from war. For two long years they have been hard at work, burning cities, plundering a nation, and butchering whole armies of men. Sometimes they killed a thousand in a day. By their help, the nation has stolen seven hundred thousand square miles of land !" Suppose the culprits ask, " Where will you hang so many ?" " Hang them !" is the answer, " we shall only hang you. It is written in our Bible that one murder makes a villain, millions a hero. We shall feast these men full of bread and wine ; shall take their leader, a rough man and a ready, one who by perpetual robbery holds a hundred slaves and more, and make him a king over all the land. But as you only burnt, robbed, and murdered on so small a scale, and without the command of the President or the Congress, we shall hang you by the neck. Our Governor ordered these men to go and burn and rob and kill; now he orders you to be hanged, and you must not ask any more questions, for the hour is already come."

To make the whole more perfect—suppose a native of Loo-Choo, converted to Christianity by your missionaries in his native land, had come hither to have " the way of God " " expounded unto him more perfectly," that he might see how these Christians love one another. Suppose he should be witness to a scene like this!

To men who know the facts of war, the wickedness of this particular invasion and its wide-extending consequences, I fear that my words will seem poor and cold and tame. I have purposely mastered my emotion, telling only my thought. I have uttered no denunciation against the men who caused this destruction of treasure, this massacre of men, this awful degradation of the moral sense. The respectable men of Boston—" the men of property and standing " all over the State, the men that commonly control the politics of New England—tell you that they dislike the war. But they re-elect the men who made it. Has a single man in all New England lost his seat in any office because he favoured the war? Not a man. Have you ever known a northern merchant who would not let his ship for the war, because the war was wicked and he a Christian? Have you ever known a northern manufacturer who would not sell a kernel of powder, nor a cannon-ball, nor a coat, nor a shirt for the war? Have you ever known a capitalist, a man who lives by letting money, refuse to lend money for the war because the war was wicked? Not a merchant, not a manufacturer, not a capitalist. A little money—it can buy up whole hosts of men. Virginia sells her negroes; what does New England sell? There was once a man in Boston, a rich man too, not a very great man, only a good one who loved his country, and there was another poor man here, in the times that tried men's souls; but there was not money enough in all England, not enough promise of honours, to make Hancock and Adams false to their sense of right. Is our soil degenerate, and have we lost the breed of noble men?

No, I have not denounced the men who directly made the war, or indirectly edged the people on. Pardon me, thou prostrate Mexico, robbed of more than half thy soil, that America may have more slaves; thy cities burned, thy children slain, the streets of thy capital trodden by the alien foot, but still smoking with thy children's blood; pardon me if I seem to have forgotten thee! And you, ye butchered Americans, slain by the vomito, the gallows, and the sword; you, ye maimed and mutilated men, who shall never again join hands in prayer, never kneel to God once more upon the limbs He made you; you, ye widows, orphans of these butchered men, far off in that more sunny South, here in our own fair land; pardon me that I seem to forget your wrongs! And thou, my Country, my own, my loved, my native land, thou child of great ideas and mother of many a noble son, dishonoured now, thy treasure wasted, thy children killed or else made murderers, thy peaceful glory gone, thy Government made to pimp and pander for lust of crime; forgive me that I seem over-gentle to the men who did and do the damning deed which wastes thy treasure, spills thy blood, and stains thine honour's sacred fold! And you, ye sons of men everywhere, thou child of God, Mankind, whose latest, fairest hope is planted here in this new world,—forgive me if I seem gentle to thy enemies, and to forget the crime that so dishonours man, and makes this ground a slaughter-yard of men—slain, too, in furtherance of the basest wish! I have no words to tell the pity that I feel for them that did the deed. I only say, "Father, forgive them, for they know full well the sin they do!"

A sectarian church could censure a General for holding his candle in a Catholic cathedral; it was "a candle to the Pope;" yet never dared to blame the war. While we loaded a ship of war with corn, and sent off the Macedonian to Cork, freighted by private bounty to feed the starving Irishman, the State sent her ships to Vera Cruz, in a cause most unholy, to bombard, to smite, and to kill. Father! forgive the State; forgive the church. It was an ignorant State. It was a silent church—a poor, dumb dog, that dared not bark at the wolf who prowls about the fold, but only at the lamb.

Yet ye leaders of the land, know this,—that the blood of thirty thousand men cries out of the ground against you. Be it your folly or your crime, still cries the voice, "Where is thy brother?" That thirty thousand—in the name of humanity I ask, "Where are they?" In the name of justice I answer, "You slew them!"

It was not the people who made this war. They have often enough done a foolish thing. But it was not they who did this wrong. It was they who led the people; it was demagogues that did it. Whig demagogues and demagogues of the democrats; men that flatter the ignorance, the folly, or the sin of the people, that they might satisfy their own base purposes. In May, 1846, if the facts of the case could have been stated to the voters, and the question put to the whole mass of the people, "Shall we go down and fight Mexico, spending two hundred million of dollars, maiming four and twenty thousand men, and butchering thirty thousand; shall we rob her of half her territory?"—the lowest and most miserable part of the nation would have said as they did say, "Yes;" the demagogues of the nation would have said as they did say, "Yes;" perhaps a majority of the men of the South would have said so, for the humanity of the nation lies not there; but if it had been brought to the great mass of the people at the North,—whose industry and skill so increase the national wealth, whose intelligence and morals have given the nation its character abroad,—then they, the great majority of the land, would have said, "No. We will have no war! If we want more land, we will buy it in the open market, and pay for it honestly. But we are not thieves, nor murderers, thank God, and will not butcher a nation to make a slave-field out of her soil." The people would not have made this war.

Well, we have got a new territory, enough to make one hundred States of the size of Massachusetts. That is not all. We have beaten the armies of Mexico, destroyed the little strength she had left, the little self-respect, else she would not so have yielded and given up half her soil for a few miserable dollars. Soon we shall take the rest of her possessions. How can Mexico hold them now—weakened, humiliated, divided worse than ever within herself. Before many years, all of this northern continent will doubtless be in the hands of the Anglo-Saxon race. That of itself is not a thing to mourn at. Could we have extended our empire there by trade, by the Christian arts of peace, it would be a blessing to us and to Mexico; a blessing to the world. But we have done it in the worst way, by fraud and blood; for the worst purpose, to steal soil and convert the cities of men into the shambles for human flesh; have done it at the bidding of men whose counsels long have been a scourge and a curse—at the bidding of slaveholders. They it is that rule the land, fill the offices, buy up the North with the crumbs that fall from their political table, make the laws, declare hostilities, and leave the North to pay the bill. Shall we ever waken out of our sleep? shall we ever remember the duties we owe to the world and to God, who put us here on this new continent? Let us not despair.

Soon we shall have all the southern part of the continent, perhaps half the islands of the Gulf. One thing remains to do—that is, with the new soil we have taken, to extend order, peace, education, religion; to keep it from the blight, the crime, and the sin of slavery. That is for the nation to do; for the North to do. God knows the South will never do it. Is there manliness enough left in the North to do that? Has the soil forgot its wonted faith, and borne a different race of men from those who struggled eight long years for freedom? Do we forget our sires, forget our God? In the day when the monarchs of Europe are shaken from their thrones; when the Russian and the Turk abolish slavery; when cowardly Naples awakes from her centuries of sleep, and will have freedom; when France prays to become a Republic, and in her agony sweats great drops of blood; while the tories of the world look on and mock and wag their heads; and while the Angel of Hope descends with trusting words to comfort her,—shall America extend slavery? butcher a nation to get soil to make a field for slaves? I know how easily the South can buy office-hunters; whig or democrat, the price is still the same. The same golden eagle blinds the eyes of each. But can she buy the people of the North? Is honesty gone, and honour gone, your love of country gone, religion gone, and nothing manly left—not even shame? Then let us perish; let the Union perish! No; let that stand firm, and let the Northern men themselves be slaves; and let us go to our masters and say, "You are very few, we are very many; we have the wealth, the numbers, the intelligence, the religion of the land, but you have the power; do not be hard upon us; pray give us a little something, some humble offices; or if not these, at least a tariff, and we will be content."

Slavery has already been the blight of this nation, the curse of the North and the curse of the South. It has hindered commerce, manufactures, agriculture. It confounds your politics. It has silenced your ablest men. It has muzzled the pulpit, and stifled the better life out of the press. It has robbed three million men of what is dearer than life; it has kept back the welfare of seventeen millions more. You ask, O Americans, where is the harmony of the Union? It was broken by slavery. Where is the treasure we have wasted? It was squandered by slavery. Where are the men we sent to Mexico? They were murdered by slavery; and now the slave power comes forward to put her new minions, her thirteenth President, upon the nation's neck! Will the North say "Yes?"

But there is a Providence which rules the world—a plan in His affairs. Shall all this war, this aggression of the slave power, be for nothing? Surely not. Let it teach us two things: Everlasting hostility to slavery; everlasting love of Justice and of its Eternal Right. Then, dear as we may pay for it, it may be worth what it has cost—the money and the men. I call on you, ye men—fathers, brothers, husbands, sons—to learn this lesson, and, when duty calls, to show that you know it—know it by heart and at your fingers' ends! And you, ye women—mothers, sisters, daughters, wives—I call on you to teach this lesson to your children, and let them know that such a war is sin, and slavery sin, and, while you teach them to hate both, teach them to be men, and do the duties of noble, Christian, and manly men! Behind injustice there is ruin, and above man there is the everlasting God.

IV.

THE POLITICAL DESTINATION OF AMERICA AND THE SIGNS OF THE TIMES.—DELIVERED BEFORE SEVERAL LITERARY SOCIETIES, 1848.

EVERY nation has a peculiar character, in which it differs from all others that have been, that are, and possibly from all that are to come; for it does not yet appear that the Divine Father of the nations ever repeats himself and creates either two nations or two men exactly alike. However, as nations, like men, agree in more things than they differ, and in obvious things too, the special peculiarity of any one tribe does not always appear at first sight. But if we look through the history of some nation which has passed off from the stage of action, we find certain prevailing traits which continually reappear in the language and laws thereof; in its arts, literature, manners, modes of religion—in short, in the whole life of the people. The most prominent thing in the history of the Hebrews is their continual trust in God, and this marks them from their first appearance to the present day. They have accordingly done little for art, science, philosophy, little for commerce and the useful arts of life, but much for religion; and the psalms they sung two or three thousand years ago are at this day the hymns and prayers of the whole Christian world. Three great historical forms of religion, Judaism, Christianity, and Mahometanism, all have proceeded from them.

He that looks at the Ionian Greeks, finds in their story always the same prominent characteristic, a devotion to what is beautiful. This appears often to the neglect of what is true, right, and therefore holy. Hence, while they have done little for religion, their literature, architecture, sculpture, furnish us with models never surpassed, and perhaps not equalled. Yet they lack the ideal aspiration after religion that appears in the literature and art, and even language of some other people, quite inferior to the Greeks in elegance and refinement. Science, also, is most largely indebted to these beauty-loving Greeks, for truth is one form of loveliness.

If we take the Romans, from Romulus their first king, to Augustulus, the last of the Cæsars, the same traits of national character appear, only the complexion and dress thereof changed by circumstances. There is always the same hardness and materialism the same skill in organizing men, the same turn for affairs and genius for legislation. Rome borrowed her theology and liturgical forms; her art, science, literature, philosophy, and eloquence; even her art of war was an imitation. But law sprung up indigenous in her soil; her laws are the best gift she offers to the human race,—the "monument more lasting than brass," which she has left behind her.

We may take another nation, which has by no means completed its history, the Saxon race, from Hengist and Horsa to Sir Robert Peel; there also is a permanent peculiarity in the tribe. They are yet the same bold, handy, practical people as when their bark first touched the savage shores of Britain; not over religious; less pious than moral; not so much upright before God, as downright before men; servants of the understanding more than children of reason; not following the guidance of an intuition, and the light of an idea, but rather trusting to experiment, facts, precedents, and usages; not philosophical, but commercial; warlike through strength and courage, not from love of war or its glory; material, obstinate, and grasping, with the same admiration of horses, dogs, oxen, and strong drink; the same willingness to tread down any obstacle, material, human, or divine, which stands in their way; the same impatient lust of wealth and power; the same disposition to colonize and reannex other lands; the same love of liberty and love of law; the same readiness in forming political confederations.

In each of these four instances, the Hebrews, the Ionians, the Romans, and the Anglo-Saxon race, have had a nationality so strong, that while they have mingled with other nations in commerce and in war, as victors and vanquished, they have stoutly held their character through all; they have thus modified feebler nations joined with them. To take the last, neither the Britons nor the Danes affected very much the character of the Anglo-Saxons; they never turned it out of its course. The Normans gave the Saxon manners, refinement, letters, elegance. The Anglo-Saxon bishop of the eleventh century, dressed in untanned sheep-skins, " the woolly side out and the fleshy side in;" he ate cheese and flesh, drank milk and mead. The Norman taught him to wear cloth, to eat also bread and roots, to drink wine. But in other respects the Norman left him as he found him. England has received her kings and her nobles from Normandy, Anjou, the Provence, Scotland, Holland, Hanover, often seeing a foreigner ascend her throne; yet the sturdy Anglo-Saxon character held its own, spite of the new element infused into its blood: change the ministries, change the dynasties often as they will, John Bull is obstinate as ever, and himself changes not; no philosophy or religion makes him less material. No nation but the English could have produced a Hobbes, a Hume, a Paley, or a Bentham; they are all instantial and not exceptional men in that race.

Now this idiosyncrasy of a nation is a sacred gift; like the genius of a Burns, a Thorwaldsen, a Franklin, or a Bowditch, it is given for some divine purpose, to be sacredly cherished and patiently unfolded. The cause of the peculiarities of a nation or an individual man we cannot fully determine as yet, and so we refer it to the chain of causes which we call Providence. But the national persistency in a common type is easily explained. The qualities of father and mother are commonly transmitted to their children, but not always, for peculiarities may lie latent in a family for generations, and reappear in the genius or the folly of a child—often in the complexion and features: and, besides, father and mother are often no match. But such exceptions are rare, and the qualities of a race are always thus reproduced, the deficiency of one man getting counterbalanced by the redundancy of the next: the marriages of a whole tribe are not far from normal.

Some nations, it seems, perish through defect of this national character, as individuals fail of success through excess or deficiency in their character. Thus the Celts—that great flood of a nation which once swept over Germany, France, England, and, casting its spray far over the Alps, at one time threatened destruction to Rome itself—seem to have been so filled with love of individual independence, that they could never accept a minute organization of human rights and duties; and so their children would not group themselves into a city, as other races, and submit to a strong central power, which should curb individual will enough to insure national unity of action. Perhaps this was once the excellence of the Celts, and thereby they broke the trammels and escaped from the theocratic or despotic traditions of earlier and more savage times, developing the power of the individual for a time, and the energy of a nation loosely bound; but when they came in contact with the Romans, Franks, and Saxons, they melted away as snow in April—only, like that, remnants thereof yet lingering in the mountains and islands of Europe. No external pressure of famine or political oppression now holds the Celts in Ireland together, or gives them national unity of action enough to resist the Saxon foe. Doubtless in other days this very peculiarity of the Irish has done the world some service. Nations succeed each other as races of animals in the geological epochs, and, like them also, perish when their work is done.

The peculiar character of a nation does not appear nakedly, without relief and shadow. As the waters of the Rhone, in coming from the mountains, have caught a stain from the soils they have traversed which mars the cerulean tinge of the mountain snow that gave them birth, so the peculiarities of each nation become modified by the circumstances to which it is exposed, though the fundamental character of a nation, it seems, has never been changed. Only when the blood of the nation is changed by additions from another stock is the idiosyncrasy altered.

Now, while each nation has its peculiar genius or character which does not change, it has also and accordingly a particular work to perform in the economy of the world, a certain fundamental idea to unfold and develop. This is its national task, for in God's world, as in a shop, there is a regular division of labour. Sometimes it is a limited work, and when it is done the nation may be dismissed, and go to its repose. *Non omnia possumus omnes* is as true of nations as of men; one has a genius for one thing, another for something different, and the idea of each nation and its special work will depend on the genius of the nation. Men do not gather grapes of thorns.

In addition to this specific genius of the nation and its corresponding work, there are also various accidental or subordinate qualities, which change with circumstances, and so vary the nation's aspect that its peculiar genius and peculiar duty are often hid from its own consciousness, and even obscured to that of the philosophic looker-on. These subordinate peculiarities will depend first on the peculiar genius, idea and work of the nation, and next on the transient circumstances, geographical, climatic, historical and secular, to which the nation has been exposed. The past helped form the circumstances of the present age, and they the character of the men now living. Thus new modifications of the national type continually take place; new variations are played, but on the same old strings and of the same old tune. Once circumstances made the Hebrews entirely pastoral, now as completely commercial; but the same trust in God, the same national exclusiveness, appear as of old. As one looks at the history of the Ionians, Romans, Saxons, he sees unity of national character, a continuity of idea and of work; but it appears in the midst of variety, for while these remained ever the same to complete the economy of the world, subordinate qualities—sentiments, ideas, actions—changed to suit the passing hour. The nation's *course* was laid towards a certain point, but they stood to the right hand or the left, they sailed with much canvas or little, and swift or slow, as the winds and waves compelled: nay, sometimes the national ship "heaves to," and lies with her "head to the wind," regardless of her destination; but when the storm is overblown resumes her course. Men will carelessly think the ship has no certain aim, but only drifts.

The most marked characteristic of the American nation is Love of Freedom; of man's natural rights. This is so plain to a student of American history, or of American politics, that the point requires no arguing. We have a genius for liberty: the American idea is freedom, natural rights. Accordingly, the work providentially laid out for us to do seems this,—to organize the rights of man. This is a problem hitherto unattempted on a national scale, in human history. Often enough attempts have been made to organize the powers of priests, kings, nobles, in a theocracy, monarchy, oligarchy, powers which had no foundation in human duties or human rights, but solely in the selfishness of strong men. Often enough have the mights of men been organized, but not the rights of man. Surely there has never been an attempt made on a national scale to organize the rights of man as man; rights resting on the nature of things; rights derived from no conventional compact of men with men; not inherited from past generations, nor received from parliaments and kings, nor secured by their parchments; but rights that are derived straightway from God, the Author of Duty and the Source of Right, and which are secured in the great charter of our being.

At first view it will be said, the peculiar genius of America is not such, nor such her fundamental idea, nor that her destined work. It is true that much of the national conduct seems exceptional when measured by that standard, and the nation's course as crooked as the Rio Grande; it is true that America sometimes seems to spurn liberty, and sells the freedom of three million men for less than three million annual bales of cotton; true, she often tramples, knowingly, consciously, tramples on the most unquestionable and sacred rights. Yet, when one looks through the whole character and history of America, spite of the exceptions, nothing comes out with such relief as this love of freedom, this idea of liberty, this attempt to organize right. There are numerous subordinate qualities which conflict with the nation's idea and work, coming from our circumstances, not our soul, as well as many others which help the nation perform her providential work. They are signs of the times, and it is important to look carefully among the most prominent of them, where, indeed, one finds striking contradictions.

The first is an impatience of authority. Every thing

must render its reason, and show cause for its being. We
will not be commanded, at least only by such as we choose
to obey. Does some one say, "Thou shalt," or "Thou
shalt not," we ask, "Who are you?" Hence comes a
seeming irreverence. The shovel hat, the symbol of
authority, which awed our fathers, is not respected unless
it covers a man, and then it is the man we honour, and
no longer the shovel hat. "I will complain of you to the
government!" said a Prussian nobleman to a Yankee
stage-driver, who uncivilly threw the nobleman's trunk
to the top of the coach. "Tell the government to go to
the devil!" was the symbolical reply.

Old precedents will not suffice us, for we want something anterior to all precedents; we go beyond what is
written, asking the cause of the precedent and the reason
of the writing. "Our fathers did so," says some one.
"What of that?" say we. "Our fathers—they were
giants, were they? Not at all, only great boys, and we
are not only taller than they, but mounted on their
shoulders to boot, and see twice as far. My dear wise
man, or wiseacre, it is we that are the ancients, and have
forgotten more than all our fathers knew. We will take
their wisdom joyfully, and thank God for it, but not their
authority, we know better; and of their nonsense not a
word. It was very well that they lived, and it is very
well that they are dead. Let them keep decently buried,
for respectable dead men never walk."

Tradition does not satisfy us. The American scholar
has no folios in his library. The antiquary unrolls his
codex, hid for eighteen hundred years in the ashes of
Herculaneum, deciphers its fossil wisdom, telling us what
great men thought in the bay of Naples, and two thousand years ago. "What do you tell of that for?" is the
answer to his learning. "What has Pythagoras to do
with the price of cotton? You may be a very learned
man; you can read the hieroglyphics of Egypt, I dare
say, and know so much about the Pharaohs, it is a pity
you had not lived in their time; when you might have
been good for something; but you are too old-fashioned
for our business, and may return to your dust." An eminent American, a student of Egyptian history, with a
scholarly indignation declared, "There is not a man who

G 2

cares to know whether Shoophoo lived one thousand years before Christ, or three."

The example of other and ancient States does not terrify or instruct us. If slavery were a curse to Athens, the corruption of Corinth, the undoing of Rome, and all history shows it was so, we will learn no lesson from that experience, for we say, "We are not Athenians, men of Corinth, nor pagan Romans, thank God, but free republicans, Christians of America. We live in the nineteenth century, and though slavery worked all that mischief then and there, we know how to make money out of it, twelve hundred millions of dollars, as Mr. Clay counts the cash."

The example of contemporary nations furnishes us little warning or guidance. We will set our own precedents, and do not like to be told that the Prussians or the Dutch have learned some things in the education of the people before us, which we shall do well to learn after them. So when a good man tells us of their schools and their colleges, "patriotic" schoolmasters exclaim, "It is not true; our schools are the best in the world! But if it were true, it is unpatriotic to say so; it aids and comforts the enemy." Jonathan knows little of war; he has heard his grandfather talk of Lexington and Saratoga; he thinks he should like to have a little touch of battle on his own account: so when there is difficulty in setting up the fence betwixt his estate and his neighbours, he blusters for awhile, talks big, and threatens to strike his father; but, not having quite the stomach for that experiment, falls to beating his other neighbour, who happens to be poor, weak, and of a sickly constitution; and when he beats her at every step,—

> "For 'tis no war, as each one knows,
> When only one side deals the blows,
> And t'other bears 'em,"—

Jonathan thinks he has covered himself with "imperishable honours," and sets up his general for a great king. Poor Jonathan—he does not know the misery, the tears, the blood, the shame, the wickedness, and the sin he has set a-going, and which one day he is to account for with God, who forgets nothing!

Yet while we are so unwilling to accept the good principles, to be warned by the fate, or guided by the success,

of other nations, we gladly and servilely copy their faults,
their follies, their vice and sin. Like all upstarts, we
pique ourselves on our imitation of aristocratic ways.
How many a blusterer in Congress,—for there are two
denominations of blusterers, differing only in degree, your
great blusterer in Congress and your little blusterer in a
bar-room,—has roared away hours long against aristocratic
influence, in favour of the " pure democracy," while he
played the oligarch in his native village, the tyrant over
his hired help, and though no man knows who his grandfather was, spite of the herald's office, conjures up some
trumpery coat of arms ! Like a clown, who, by pinching
his appetite, has bought a gaudy cloak for Sabbath wear-
ing, we chuckle inwardly at our brave apery of foreign
absurdities, hoping that strangers will be astonished at us
—which, sure enough, comes to pass. Jonathan is as
vain as he is conceited, and expects that the Fiddlers, and
the Trollopes, and others, who visit us periodically as the
swallows, and likewise for what they can catch, shall only
extol, or at least stand aghast at the brave spectacle we
offer, of " the freest and most enlightened nation in the
world;" and if they tell us that we are an ill-mannered
set, raw and clownish, that we pick our teeth with a fork,
loll back in our chairs, and make our countenance hateful
with tobacco, and that with all our excellences we are a
nation of "rowdies,"—why, we are offended, and our feelings are hurt. There was an African chief, long ago, who
ruled over a few miserable cabins, and one day received a
French traveller from Paris, under a tree. With the
exception of a pair of shoes, our chief was as naked as a
pestle, but with great complacency he asked the traveller,
" What do they say of me at Paris ?"

Such is our dread of authority, that we like not old
things; hence we are always a-changing. Our house
must be new, and our book, and even our church. So we
choose a material that soon wears out, though it often out-
lasts our patience. The wooden house is an apt emblem
of this sign of the times. But this love of change appears
not less in important matters. We think " Of old things
all are over old, of new things none are new enough."
So the age asks of all institutions their right to be: What
right has the government to existence? Who gave the

majority a right to control the minority, to restrict trade,
levy taxes, make laws, and all that? If the nation goes
into a committee of the whole and makes laws, some little
man goes into a committee of one and passes his counter
resolves. The State of South Carolina is a nice example
of this self-reliance, and this questioning of all authority.
That little brazen State, which contains only about half so
many free white inhabitants as the single city of New
York, but which none the less claims to have monopolized
most of the chivalry of the nation, and its patriotism, as
well as political wisdom—that chivalrous little State says,
"If the nation does not make laws to suit us; if it does
not allow us to imprison all black seamen from the North;
if it prevents the extension of Slavery wherever we wish
to carry it—then the State of South Carolina will nullify,
and leave the other nine-and-twenty States to go to ruin!"

Men ask what right have the churches to the shadow of
authority which clings to them—to make creeds, and to
bind and to loose! So it is a thing which has happened,
that when a church excommunicates a young stripling for
heresy, he turns round, fulminates his edict, and excommunicates the church. Said a sly Jesuit to an American
Protestant at Rome, "But the rites and customs and
doctrines of the Catholic church go back to the second
century, the age after the apostles!" "No doubt of it,"
said the American, who had also read the Fathers, "they
go back to the times of the apostles themselves; but that
proves nothing, for there were as great fools in the first
century as the last. A fool or a folly is no better because
it is an old folly or an old fool. There are fools enough
now, in all conscience. Pray don't go back to prove their
apostolical succession."

There are always some men who are born out of due
season, men of past ages, stragglers of former generations,
who ought to have born before Dr. Faustus invented
printing, but who are unfortunately born now, or, if born
long ago, have been fraudulently and illegally concealed
by their mothers, and are now, for the first time, brought
to light. The age lifts such aged juveniles from the
ground, and bids them live, but they are sadly to seek in
this day; they are old-fashioned boys; their authority is
called in question; their traditions and old-wives' fables

are laughed at, at any rate disbelieved; they get pro-
fanely elbowed in the crowd—men not knowing their
great age and consequent venerableness; the shovel hat,
though apparently born on their head, is treated with
disrespect. The very boys laugh pertly in their face when
they speak, and even old men can scarce forbear a smile,
though it may be a smile of pity. The age affords such
men a place, for it is a catholic age, large-minded, and
tolerant,—such a place as it gives to ancient armour,
Indian Bibles, and fossil bones of the mastodon; it puts
them by in some room seldom used, with other old furniture, and allows them to mumble their anilities by themselves; now and then takes off its hat; looks in, cha-
ritably, to keep the mediæval relics in good heart, and
pretends to listen, as they discourse of what comes of
nothing and goes to it; but in matters which the age
cares about, commerce, manufactures, politics, which it
cares much for, even in education, which it cares far too
little about, it trusts no such counsellors, nor tolerates nor
ever affects to listen.

Then there is a philosophical tendency, distinctly
visible; a groping after ultimate facts, first principles,
and universal ideas. We wish to know first the fact, next
the law of that fact, and then the reason of the law. A
sign of this tendency is noticeable in the titles of books;
we have no longer "treatises" on the eye, the ear, sleep,
and so forth, but in their place we find works professing to
treat of the "philosophy" of vision, of sound, of sleep.
Even in the pulpits, men speak about the "philosophy" of
religion; we have philosophical lectures, delivered to men
of little culture, which would have amazed our grand-
fathers, who thought a shoemaker should never go beyond
his last, even to seek for the philosophy of shoes. "What
a pity," said a grave Scotchman, in the beginning of this
century, "to teach the beautiful science of geometry to
weavers and cobblers." Here nothing is too good or high
for any one tall and good enough to get hold of it. What
audiences attend the Lowell lectures in Boston—two or
three thousand men, listening to twelve lectures on the
philosophy of fish! It would not bring a dollar or a vote,
only thought to their minds! Young ladies are well versed
in the philosophy of the affections, and understand the

theory of attraction, while their grandmothers, good easy souls, were satisfied with the possession of the fact. The circumstance, that philosophical lectures get delivered by men like Walker, Agassiz, Emerson, and their coadjutors, men who do not spare abstruseness, get listened to, and even understood, in town and village, by large crowds of men, of only the most common culture; this indicates a philosophical tendency, unknown in any other land or age. Our circle of professed scholars, men of culture and learning, is a very small one, while our circle of thinking men is disproportionately large.   The best thought of France and Germany finds a readier welcome here than in our parent land: nay, the newest and the best thought of England finds its earliest and warmest welcome in America. It was a little remarkable, that Bacon and Newton should be reprinted here, and La Place should have found his translator and expositor coming out of an insurance office in Salem! Men of no great pretensions object to an accomplished and eloquent politician: "That is all very well; he made us cry and laugh, but the discourse was not philosophical; he never tells us the reason of the thing; he seems not only not to know it, but not to know that there *is* a reason for the thing, and if not, what is the use of this bobbing on the surface?"   Young maidens complain of the minister, that he has no philosophy in his sermons, nothing but precepts, which they could read in the Bible as well as he; perhaps in heathen Seneca.   He does not feed their souls.

One finds this tendency where it is least expected: there is a philosophical party in politics, a very small party it may be, but an actual one. They aim to get at everlasting ideas and universal laws, not made by man, but by God, and for man, who only finds them; and from them they aim to deduce all particular enactments, so that each statute in the code shall represent a fact in the universe; a point of thought in God; so, indeed, that legislation shall be divine in the same sense that a true system of astronomy is divine—or the Christian religion—the law corresponding to a fact.   Men of this party, in New England, have more ideas than precedents, are spontaneous more than logical; have intuitions, rather than intellectual convictions, arrived at by the process of reasoning.   They think it is not philosophical to take a young scoundrel and shut him up with a party of old ones, for his amendment; not philosophical to leave children with no culture, intellectual, moral, or religious, exposed to the temptations of a high and corrupt civilization, and then, when they go astray—as such barbarians needs must, in such temptations—to hang them by the neck for the example's sake. They doubt if war is a more philosophical mode of getting justice between two nations, than blows to settle a quarrel between two men. In either case they do not see how it follows that he who can strike the hardest blow is always in the right. In short, they think that judicial murder, which is hanging, and national murder, which is war, are not more philosophical than homicide, which one man commits on his own private account.

Theological sects are always the last to feel any popular movement. Yet all of them, from the Episcopalians to the Quakers, have each a philosophical party, which bids fair to outgrow the party which rests on precedent and usage, to overshadow and destroy it. The Catholic church itself, though far astern of all the sects, in regard to the great movements of the age, shares this spirit, and abroad, if not here, is well nigh rent asunder by the potent medicine which this new Daniel of philosophy has put into its mouth. Everywhere in the American churches there are signs of a tendency to drop all that rests merely on tradition and hearsay, to cling only to such facts as bide the test of critical search, and such doctrines as can be verified in human consciousness here and to-day. Doctors of divinity destroy the faith they once preached.

True, there are antagonistic tendencies; for, soon as one pole is developed, the other appears; objections are made to philosophy, the old cry is raised—" Infidelity," " Denial," " Free-thinking." It is said that philosophy will corrupt the young men, will spoil the old ones, and deceive the very elect. "Authority and tradition," say some, " are all we need consult; reason must be put down, or she will soon ask terrible questions." There is good cause for these men warring against reason and philosophy; it is purely in self-defence. But this counsel and that cry come from those quarters before mentioned, where the men of past ages have their place, where the forgotten is re-collected, the obsolete preserved, and the useless held in esteem. The counsel is not dangerous; the bird of night, who overstays his hour, is only troublesome to himself, and was never known to hurt a dovelet or a mouseling after sunrise. In the night only is the owl destructive. Some of those who thus cry out against this tendency, are excellent men in their way, and highly useful, valuable as conveyancers of opinions. So long as there are men who take opinions as real estate, "to have and to hold for themselves and their heirs for ever," why should there not be such conveyancers of opinions, as well as of land? And as it is not the duty of the latter functionary to ascertain the quality or the value of the land, but only its metes and bounds, its appurtenances, and the title thereto; to see if the grantor is regularly seized and possessed thereof, and has good right to convey and devise the same, and to make sure that the whole conveyance is regularly made out—so is it with these conveyancers of opinion; so should it be, and they are valuable men. It is a good thing to know that we hold, under Scotus, and Ramus, and Albertus Magnus, who were regularly seized of this or that opinion. It gives an absurdity the dignity of a relic. Sometimes these worthies, who thus oppose reason and her kin, seem to have a good deal in them, and, when one examines, he finds more than he looked for. They are like a nest of boxes from Hingham and Nuremburg, you open one, and behold another; that, and lo! a third. So you go on, opening and opening, and finding and finding, till at last you come to the heart of the matter, and then you find a box that is very little, and entirely empty.

Yet, with all this tendency—and it is now so strong that it cannot be put down, nor even howled down, much as it may be howled over—there is a lamentable want of first principles, well known and established; we have rejected the authority of tradition, but not yet accepted the authority of truth and justice. We will not be treated as striplings, and are not old enough to go alone as men. Accordingly, nothing seems fixed. There is a perpetual see-sawing of opposite principles. Somebody said ministers ought to be ordained on horseback, because they are to remain so short a time in one place. It would be as emblematic to inaugurate American politicians, by swearing them on a weathercock. The great men of the land have as many turns in their course as the Euripus or the Missouri. Even the facts given in the spiritual nature of man are called in question. An eminent Unitarian divine regards the existence of God as a matter of opinion, thinks it cannot be demonstrated, and publicly declares that it is "not a certainty." Some American Protestants no longer take the Bible as the standard of ultimate appeal, yet venture not to set up in that place reason, conscience, the soul getting help of God; others, who affect to accept the Scripture as the last authority, yet, when questioned as to their belief in the miraculous and divine birth of Jesus of Nazareth, are found unable to say yes or no, not having made up their minds.

In politics, it is not yet decided whether it is best to leave men to buy where they can buy cheapest, and sell where they can sell dearest, or to restrict that matter.

It was a clear case to our fathers, in '76, that all men were "created equal," each with "Unalienable Rights." That seemed so clear, that reasoning would not make it appear more reasonable; it was taken for granted, as a self-evident proposition. The whole nation said so. Now, it is no strange thing to find it said that negroes are not "created equal" in unalienable rights with white men. Nay, in the Senate of the United States, a famous man declares all this talk a dangerous mistake. The practical decision of the nation looks the same way. So, to make our theory accord with our practice, we ought to recommit the Declaration to the hands which drafted that great State paper, and instruct Mr. Jefferson to amend the document, and declare that "All men are created equal, and endowed by their Creator with certain unalienable rights, if born of white mothers; but if not, not."

In this lack of first principles, it is not settled in the popular consciousness, that there is such a thing as an absolute right, a great law of God, which we are to keep, come what will come. So the nation is not upright, but goes stooping. Hence, in private affairs, law takes the place of conscience, and, in public, might of right. So the bankrupt pays his shilling in the pound, and gets his discharge, but afterwards, becoming rich, does not think

of paying the other nineteen shillings. He will tell you
the law is his conscience; if that be satisfied, so is he.
But you will yet find him letting money at one or two
per cent. a month, contrary to law; and then he will tell
you that paying a debt is a matter of law, while letting
money is only a matter of conscience. So he rides either
indifferently—now the public hack, and now his own private nag, according as it serves his turn.

So a rich State borrows money and "repudiates" the
debt, satisfying its political conscience, as the bankrupt
his commercial conscience, with the notion that there is
no absolute right; that expediency is the only justice, and
that King People can do no wrong. No calm voice of
indignation cries out from the pulpit and the press, and
the heart of the people, to shame the repudiators into
decent morals; because it is not settled in the popular
mind that there is any absolute right. Then, because we
are strong and the Mexicans weak, because we want their
land for a slave-pasture, and they cannot keep us out of it,
we think that is reason enough for waging an infamous
war of plunder. Grave men do not ask about "the
natural justice" of such an undertaking, only about its
cost. Have we not seen an American Congress vote a
plain lie, with only sixteen dissenting voices in the whole
body; has not the head of the nation continually repeated
that lie; and do not both parties, even at this day, sustain the vote?

Now and then there rises up an honest man, with a
great Christian heart in his bosom, and sets free a score or
two of slaves inherited from his father; watches over and
tends them in their new-found freedom: or another, who,
when legally released from payment of his debts, restores
the uttermost farthing. We talk of this and praise it, as
an extraordinary thing. Indeed it is so; justice is an
unusual thing, and such men deserve the honour they thus
win. But such praise shows that such honesty is a rare
honesty. The northern man, born on the battle-ground of
freedom, goes to the South and becomes the most tyrannical of slave-drivers. The son of the Puritan, bred up
in austere ways, is sent to Congress to stand up for truth
and right, but he turns out a "dough-face," and betrays
the duty he went to serve. Yet he does not lose his place,

for every dough-faced representative has a dough-faced constituency to back him.

It is a great mischief that comes from lacking first principles, and the worst part of it comes from lacking first principles in morals. Thereby our eyes are holden so that we see not the great social evils all about us. We attempt to justify slavery, even to do it in the name of Jesus Christ. The whig party of the North loves slavery; the democratic party does not even seek to conceal its affection therefor. A great politician declares the Mexican war wicked, and then urges men to go and fight it; he thinks a famous general not fit to be nominated for President, but then invites men to elect him. Politics are national morals, the morals of Thomas and Jeremiah, multiplied by millions. But it is not decided yet that honesty is the best policy for a politician; it is thought that the best policy is honesty, at least as near it as the times will allow. Many politicians seem undecided how to turn, and so sit on the fence between honesty and dishonesty. Mr. Facing-bothways is a popular politician in America just now, sitting on the fence between honesty and dishonesty, and, like the blank leaf between the Old and New Testaments, belonging to neither dispensations. It is a little amusing to a trifler to hear a man's fitness for the Presidency defended on the ground that he has no definite convictions or ideas!

There was once a man who said he always told a lie when it would serve his special turn. It is a pity he went to his own place long ago. He seemed born for a party politician in America. He would have had a large party, for he made a great many converts before he died, and left a numerous kindred busy in the editing of newspapers, writing addresses for the people, and passing " resolutions."

It must strike a stranger as a little odd that a republic should have a slaveholder for President five-sixths of the time, and most of the important offices be monopolized by other slaveholders; a little surprising that all the pulpits and most of the presses should be in favour of slavery, at least not against it. But such is the fact. Everybody knows the character of the American government for some years past, and of the American parties in politics. " Like

master, like man," used to be a true proverb in old England,
and "Like people, like ruler," is a true proverb in America;
true now.   Did a decided people ever choose dough-faces?
—a people that loved God and man, choose representatives
that cared for neither truth nor justice?   Now and then,
for dust gets into the brightest eyes; but did they ever
choose such men continually?   The people are always
fairly represented; our representatives do actually represent us, and in more senses than they are paid for.
Congress and the Cabinet are only two thermometers hung
up in the capital, to show the temperature of the national
morals.

But amid this general uncertainty there are two capital
maxims which prevail amongst our hucksters of politics:
to love your party better than your country, and yourself
better than your party.   There are, it is true, real statesmen amongst us, men who love justice and do the right;
but they seem lost in the mob of vulgar politicians and
the dust of party editors.

Since the nation loves freedom above all things, the
name democracy is a favourite name.   No party could
live a twelvemonth that should declare itself anti-demo-
cratic.   Saint and sinner, statesman and politician, alike
love the name.   So it comes to pass that there are two
things which bear that name; each has its type and its
motto.   The motto of one is, "You are as good as I, and
let us help one another."   That represents the democracy
of the Declaration of Independence, and of the New Testament; its type is a free school, where children of all ranks
meet under the guidance of intelligent and Christian men,
to be educated in mind, and heart, and soul.   The other
has for its motto, "I am as good as you, so get out of
my way."   Its type is the bar-room of a tavern—dirty,
offensive, stained with tobacco, and full of drunken, noisy,
quarrelsome "rowdies," just returned from the Mexican
war, and ready for a "buffalo hunt," for privateering, or
to go and plunder any one who is better off than themselves, especially if also better.   That is not exactly the
democracy of the Declaration, or of the New Testament;
but of—no matter whom.

Then, again, there is a great intensity of life and purpose. This displays itself in our actions and speeches; in our speculations; in the "revivals" of the more serious sects; in the excitements of trade; in the general character of the people. All that we do we overdo. It appears in our hopefulness; we are the most aspiring of nations. Not content with half the continent, we wish the other half. We have this characteristic of genius: we are dissatisfied with all that we have done. Somebody once said we were too vain to be proud. It is not wholly so; the national idea is so far above us that any achievement seems little and low. The American soul passes away from its work soon as it is finished. So the soul of each great artist refuses to dwell in his finished work, for that seems little to his dream. Our fathers deemed the Revolution a great work; it was once thought a surprising thing to found that little colony on the shores of New England; but young America looks to other revolutions, and thinks she has many a Plymouth colony in her bosom. If other nations wonder at our achievements, we are a disappointment to ourselves, and wonder we have not done more. Our national idea out-travels our experience, and all experience. We began our national career by setting all history at defiance—for that said, "A republic on a large scale cannot exist." Our progress since has shown that we were right in refusing to be limited by the past. The political ideas of the nation are transcendant, not empirical. Human history could not justify the Declaration of Independence and its large statements of the new idea: the nation went behind human history and appealed to human nature.

We are more spontaneous than logical; we have ideas, rather than facts or precedents. We dream more than we remember, and so have many orators and poets, or poetasters, with but few antiquaries and general scholars. We are not so reflective as forecasting. We are the most intuitive of modern nations. The very party in politics which has the least culture, is richest in ideas which will one day become facts. Great truths—political, philosophical, religious—lie a-burning in many a young heart which cannot legitimate nor prove them true, but none the less feels, and feels them true. A man full of new truths finds a ready audience with us. Many things which come dis-

guised as truths under such circumstances pass current
for a time, but by and by their bray discovers them. The
hope which comes from this intensity of life and intuition
of truths is a national characteristic. It gives courage,
enterprise, and strength. They can who think they can.
We are confident in our star; other nations may see it or
not, we know it is there above the clouds. We do not
hesitate at rash experiments—sending fifty thousand soldiers
to conquer a nation with eight or nine millions of people.
We are up to everything, and think ourselves a match
for anything. The young man is rash, for he only hopes,
having little to remember; he is excitable, and loves excitement; change of work is his repose; he is hot and
noisy, sanguine and fearless, with the courage that comes
from warm blood and ignorance of dangers; he does not
know what a hard, tough, sour old world he is born into.
We are a nation of young men. We talked of annexing
Texas and northern Mexico, and did both; now we grasp
at Cuba, Central America,—all the continent,—and speak
of a railroad to the Pacific as a trifle for us to accomplish.
Our national deeds are certainly great, but our hope and
promise far outbrags them all.
    If this intensity of life and hope has its good side, it
has also its evil; with much of the excellence of youth we
have its faults—rashness, haste, and superficiality. Our
work is seldom well done. In English manufactures there
is a certain solid honesty of performance; in the French a
certain air of elegance and refinement: one misses both
these in American works. It is said America invents the
most machines, but England builds them best. We lack
the phlegmatic patience of older nations. We are always
in a hurry, morning, noon, and night. We are impatient
of the process, but greedy of the result ; so that we make
short experiments but long reports, and talk much though
we say little. We forget that a sober method is a short
way of coming to the end, and that he who, before he
sets out, ascertains where he is going and the way thither,
ends his journey more prosperously than one who settles
these matters by the way. Quickness is a great deside-
ratum with us. It is said an American ship is known far
off at sea by the quantity of canvas she carries. Rough
and ready is a popular attribute. Quick and off would be

a symbolic motto for the nation at this day, representing one phase of our character. We are sudden in deliberation; the "one-hour rule" works well in Congress. A committee of the British Parliament spends twice or thrice our time in collecting facts, understanding and making them intelligible, but less than our time in speech-making after the report; speeches there commonly being for the purpose of facilitating the business, while here one sometimes is half ready to think, notwithstanding our earnestness, that the business is to facilitate the speaking. A State revises her statutes with a rapidity that astonishes a European. Yet each revision brings some amendment, and what is found good in the constitution or laws of one State gets speedily imitated by the rest; each new State of the North becoming more democratic than its predecessor.

We are so intent on our purpose that we have no time for amusement. We have but one or two festivals in the year, and even then we are serious and reformatory. Jonathan thinks it a very solemn thing to be merry. A Frenchman said we have but two amusements in America—theology for the women and politics for the men; preaching and voting. If this be true, it may help to explain the fact that most men take their theology from their wives, and women politics from their husbands. No nation ever tried the experiment of such abstinence from amusement. We have no time for sport, and so lose much of the poetry of life. All work and no play does not always make a dull boy, but it commonly makes a hard man.

We rush from school into business early; we hurry while in business; we aim to be rich quickly, making a fortune at a stroke, making or losing it twice or thrice in a lifetime. "Soft and fair, goes safe and far," is no proverb to our taste. We are the most restless of people. How we crowd into cars and steamboats; a locomotive would well typify our fuming, fizzing spirit. In our large towns life seems to be only a scamper. Not satisfied with bustling about all day, when night comes we cannot sit still, but alone of all nations have added rockers to our chairs.

All is haste, from the tanning of leather to the educa-

tion of a boy, and the old saw holds its edge good as ever
—"the more haste the worse speed." The young stripling, innocent of all manner of lore, whom a judicious
father has barrelled down in a college, or law-school, or
theological seminary, till his beard be grown, mourns over
the few years he must spend there awaiting that operation.
His rule is, "to make a spoon or spoil a horn ;" he longs
to be out in the world "making a fortune," or "doing
good," as he calls what his father better names "making
noisy work for repentance, and doing mischief." So he
rushes into life not fitted, and would fly towards heaven,
this young Icarus, his wings not half fledged. There
seems little taste for thoroughness. In our schools as our
farms, we pass over much ground, but pass over it poorly.

In education the aim is not to get the most we can, but
the least we can get along with. A ship with over-much
canvas and over-little ballast were no bad emblem of many
amongst us. In no country is it so easy to get a reputation for learning—accumulated thought, because so few
devote themselves to that accumulation. In this respect
our standard is low. So a man of one attainment is sure
to be honoured, but a man of many and varied abilities is
in danger of being undervalued. A Spurzheim would be
warmly welcomed, while a Humboldt would be suspected
of superficiality, as we have not the standard to judge him
by. Yet in no country in the world is it so difficult to
get a reputation for eloquence, as many speak, and that
well. It is surprising with what natural strength and
beauty the young American addresses himself to speak.
Some hatter's apprentice, or shoemaker's journeyman, at a
temperance or anti-slavery meeting, will speak words like
the blows of an axe, that cut clean and deep. The country
swarms with orators, more abundantly where education is
least esteemed—in the West or South.

We have secured national unity of action for the white
citizens, without much curtailing individual variety of
action, so we have at the North pretty well solved that
problem which other nations have so often boggled over;
we have balanced the centripetal power, the government
and laws, with the centrifugal power, the mass of individuals, into harmonious proportions. If one were to leave
out of sight the three million slaves, one-sixth part of the

population, the problem might be regarded as very happily solved. As the consequences of this, in no country is there more talent, or so much awake and active. In the South this unity is attained by sacrificing all the rights of three million slaves, and almost all the rights of the other coloured population. In despotic countries this unity is brought about by the sacrifice of freedom, individual variety of action, in all except the despot and his favourites; so, much of the nation's energy is stifled in the chains of the State, while here it is friendly to institutions which are friendly to it, goes to its work, and approves itself in the vast increase of wealth and comfort throughout the North, where there is no class of men which is so oppressed that it cannot rise. One is amazed at the amount of ready skill and general ability which he finds in all the North, where each man has a little culture, takes his newspaper, manages his own business, and talks with some intelligence of many things—especially of politics and theology. In respect to this general intellectual ability and power of self-help, the mass of people seem far in advance of any other nation. But at the same time our scholars, who always represent the nation's higher modes of consciousness, will not bear comparison with the scholars of England, France, and Germany, men thoroughly furnished for their work. This is a great reproach and mischief to us, for we need most accomplished leaders, who by their thought can direct this national intensity of life. Our literature does not furnish them; we have no great men there; Irving, Channing, Cooper, are not names to conjure with in literature. One reads thick volumes devoted to the poets of America, or her prose writers, and finds many names which he wonders he never heard of before; but when he turns over their works, he finds consolation and recovers his composure.

American literature may be divided into two departments: the permanent literature, which gets printed in books, that sometimes reach more than one edition; and the evanescent literature, which appears only in the form of speeches, pamphlets, reviews, newspaper articles, and the like extempore productions. Now our permanent literature, as a general thing, is superficial, tame, and weak; it is not American; it has not our ideas, our contempt of

authority, our philosophical turn, nor even our uncertainty
as to first principles, still less our national intensity, our
hope, and fresh intuitive perceptions of truth. It is a
miserable imitation. Love of freedom is not there. The
real national literature is found almost wholly in speeches,
pamphlets, and newspapers. The latter . are pretty
thoroughly American: mirrors in which we see no very
flattering likeness of our morals or our manners. Yet the
picture is true : that vulgarity, that rant, that bragging
violence, that recklessness of truth and justice, that dis-
regard of right and duty, are a part of the nation's every-
day life. Our newspapers are low and "wicked to a
fault ;" only in this weakness are they un-American. Yet
they exhibit, and abundantly, the four qualities we have
mentioned as belonging to the signs of our times. As a
general rule, our orators are also American, with our good
and ill. Now and then one rises who has studied Demos-
thenes in Leland or Francis, and got a second-hand acquaintance with old models: a man who uses literary
common-places, and thinks himself original and classic
because he can quote a line or so of Horace, in a Western
House of Representatives, without getting so many words
wrong as his reporter ; but such men are rare, and after
making due abatement for them, our orators all over the
land are pretty thoroughly American, a little turgid, hot,
sometimes brilliant, hopeful, intuitive, abounding in half
truths, full of great ideas ; often inconsequent ; sometimes
coarse; patriotic, vain, self-confident, rash, strong, and
young-mannish. Of course the most of our speeches are
vulgar, ranting, and worthless ; but we have produced some
magnificent specimens of oratory, which are fresh, original,
American, and brand new.

The more studied, polished, and elegant literature is not
so ; that is mainly an imitation. It seems not a thing of
native growth. Sometimes, as in Channing, the thought
and the hope are American, but the form and the colour-
ing old and foreign. We dare not be original; our
American pine must be cut to the trim pattern of the
English yew, though the pine bleed at every clip. This
poet tunes his lyre at the harp of Goethe, Milton, Pope, or
Tennyson. His songs might be better sung on the Rhine
than the Kennebec. They are not American in form or

feeling; they have not the breath of our air; the smell of our ground is not in them. Hence our poet seems cold and poor. He loves the old mythology; talks about Pluto —the Greek devil, the fates and furies—witches of old time in Greece, but would blush to use our mythology, or breathe the name in verse of our devil, or our own witches, lest he should be thought to believe what he wrote. The mother and sisters, who with many a pinch and pain sent the hopeful boy to college, must turn over the classical dictionary before they can find out what the youth would be at in his rhymes. Our poet is not deep enough to see that Aphrodite came from the ordinary waters, that Homer only hitched into rhythm and furnished the accomplish-ment of verse to street-talk, nursery tales, and old men's gossip in the Ionian towns; he thinks what is common is unclean. So he sings of Corinth and Athens, which he never saw, but has not a word to say of Boston, and Fall River, and Baltimore, and New York, which are just as meet for song. He raves of Thermopylæ and Marathon, with never a word for Lexington and Bunker Hill, for Cowpens, and Lundy's Lane, and Bemis's Heights. He loves to tell of the Ilyssus, of "smooth-sliding Mincius, crowned with vocal reeds," yet sings not of the Petapsco, the Susquehanna, the Aroostook, and the Willimantick. He prates of the narcissus and the daisy, never of American dandelions and blue-eyed grass; he dwells on the lark and the nightingale, but has not a thought for the brown thrasher and the bobolink, who every morning in June rain down such showers of melody on his affected head. What a lesson Burns teaches us, addressing his "rough bur-thistle," his daisy, "wee crimson tippit thing," and finding marvellous poetry in the mouse whose nest his plough turned over! Nay, how beautifully has even our sweet poet sung of our own Green river, our waterfowl, of the blue and fringed gentian, the glory of autumnal days.

Hitherto, spite of the great reading public, we have no permanent literature which corresponds to the American idea. Perhaps it is not time for that; it must be organ-ized in deeds before it becomes classic in words; but as yet we have no such literature which reflects even the surface of American life, certainly nothing which portrays our intensity of life, our hope, or even our daily doings and drivings, as the Odyssey paints old Greek life, or Don Quixote and Gil Blas portray Spanish life. Literary men are commonly timid; ours know they are but poorly fledged as yet, so dare not fly away from the parent tree, but hop timidly from branch to branch. Our writers love to creep about in the shadow of some old renown, not venturing to soar away into the unwinged air, to sing of things here and now, making our life classic. So, without the grace of high culture, and the energy of American thought, they become weak, cold, and poor; are "curious, not knowing, not exact, but nice." Too fastidious to be wise, too unlettered to be elegant, too critical to create, they prefer a dull saying that is old to a novel form of speech, or a natural expression of a new truth. In a single American work,—and a famous one too,—there are over sixty similes, not one original, and all poor. A few men, conscious of this defect, this sin against the Holy Spirit of Literature, go to the opposite extreme, and are American-mad; they wilfully talk rude, write innumerous verse, and play their harps all jangling, out of tune. A yet fewer few are American without madness. One such must not here be passed by, alike philosopher and bard, in whose writings "ancient wisdom shines with new-born beauty," and who has enriched a genius thoroughly American in the best sense, with a cosmopolitan culture and literary skill, which were wonderful in any land. But of American literature in general, and of him in special, more shall be said at another time.

Another remarkable feature is our excessive love of material things. This is more than a Utilitarianism, a preference of the useful over the beautiful. The Puritan at Plymouth had a corn-field, a cabbage-garden, and a patch for potatoes, a school-house, and a church, before he sat down to play the fiddle. He would have been a fool to reverse this process. It were poor economy and worse taste to have painters, sculptors, and musicians, while the rude wants of the body are uncared for. But our fault in this respect is, that we place too much the charm of life in mere material things,—houses, lands, well-spread tables, and elegant furniture,—not enough in man, in virtue, wisdom, genius, religion, greatness of soul, and nobleness of life. We mistake a perfection of the means of manliness for the end—manhood itself. Yet the housekeeping of a Shakspeare, Milton, Franklin, had only one thing worth boasting of. Strange to say, that was the master of the house. A rich and vulgar man once sported a coach and four, and at its first turn out rode into the great commercial street of a large town in New England. "How fine you must feel with your new coach and four," said one of his old friends, though not quite so rich. "Yes," was the reply, "as fine as a beetle in a gold snuff-box." All of his kindred are not so nice and discriminating in their self-consciousness.

This practical materialism is a great affliction to us. We think a man cannot be poor and great also. So we see a great man sell himself for a little money, and it is thought "a good operation." A conspicuous man, in praise of a certain painter, summed up his judgment with this: "Why, sir, he has made twenty thousand dollars by his pictures." "A good deal more than Michael Angelo, Leonardo, and Raphael together," might have been the reply. But it is easier to weigh purses than artistic skill. It was a characteristic praise bestowed in Boston on a distinguished American writer, that his book brought him more money than any man had ever realized for an original work in this country. "Commerce," said Mr. Pitt, "having got into both houses of Parliament, privilege must be done away," —the privilege of wit and genius, not less than rank. Clergymen estimate their own and their brothers' importance, not by their apostolical gifts, or even apostolic succession, but by the value of the living.

All other nations have this same fault, it may be said. But there is this difference: in other nations the things of a man are put before the man himself; so a materialism which exalts the accidents of the man—rank, wealth, birth, and the like—above the man, is not inconsistent with the general idea of England or Austria. In America it is a contradiction. Besides, in most civilized countries, there is a class of men living on inherited wealth, who devote their lives to politics, art, science, letters, and so are above the mere material elegance which surrounds them. That class has often inflicted a deep wound on society, which festers long and leads to serious trouble in the system, but

at the same time it redeems a nation from the reproach of
mere material vulgarity; it has been the source of refinement, and has warmed into life much of the wisdom and
beauty which have thence spread over all the world.   In
America there is no such class.   Young men inheriting
wealth very rarely turn to anything noble; they either
convert their talents into gold, or their gold into furniture,
wines, and confectionary.   A young man of wealth does
not know what to do with himself or it; a rich young
woman seems to have no resource but marriage!   Yet it
must be confessed, that at least in one part of the United
States wealth flows freely for the support of public institutions of education.

Here it is difficult for a man of science to live by his
thought.   Was Bowditch one of the first mathematicians
of his age?   He must be at the head of an annuity office.
If Socrates should set up as a dealer in money, and outwit
the brokers as formerly the Sophists, and shave notes as
skilfully as of old, we should think him a great man.
But if he adopted his old plan, what should we say of
him?

Manliness is postponed and wealth preferred.   "What
a fine house is this," one often says: "what furniture;
what feasting.   But the master of the house!—why, every
stone out of the wall laughs at him.   He spent all of himself in getting this pretty show together, and now it is
empty, and mocks its owner.   He is the emblematic coffin
at the Egyptian feast."   "Oh, man!" says the looker-on,
"why not furnish thyself with a mind, and conscience, a
heart and a soul, before getting all this brass and mahogany together; this beef and these wines?"   The poor
wight would answer,—"Why, sir, there were none such
in the market!"   The young man does not say, "I will
first of all things be a man, and so being, will have this
thing and the other," putting the agreeable after the
essential.   But he says, "First of all, by hook or by crook,
I will have money, the manhood may take care of itself."
He has it,—for tough and hard as the old world is, it is
somewhat fluid before a strong man who resolutely grapples
with difficulty and will swim through; it can be made to
serve his turn.   He has money, but the man has evaporated
in the process; when you look he is not there.   True, other

nations have done the same thing, and we only repeat their experiment. The old devil of conformity says to our American Adam and Eve, "Do this and you shall be as gods," a promise as likely to hold good as the devil's did in the beginning. A man was meant for something more than a tassel to a large estate, and a woman to be more than a rich housekeeper.

With this offensive materialism we copy the vices of feudal aristocracy abroad, making our vulgarity still more ridiculous. We are ambitious or proud of wealth, which is but labour stored up, and at the same time are ashamed of labour, which is wealth in process. With all our talk about democracy, labour is thought less honourable in Boston than in Berlin and Leipsic. Thriving men are afraid their children will be shoemakers, or ply some such honourable and useful craft. Yet little pains are taken to elevate the condition or improve the manners and morals of those who do all the manual work of society. The strong man takes care that his children and himself escape that condition. We do not believe that all stations are alike honourable if honourably filled; we have little desire to equalize the burdens of life, so that there shall be no degraded class; none cursed with work, none with idleness. It is popular to endow a college; vulgar to take an interest in common schools. Liberty is a fact, equality a word, and fraternity, we do not think of yet.

In this struggle for material wealth and the social rank which is based thereon, it is amusing to see the shifting of the scenes; the social aspirations of one, and the contempt with which another rebuts the aspirant. An old man can remember when the most exclusive of men, and the most golden, had scarce a penny in their purse, and grumbled at not finding a place where they would. Now the successful man is ashamed of the steps he rose by. The gentleman who came to Boston half a century ago, with all his worldly goods tied up in a cotton handkerchief, and that not of so large a pattern as are made now-a-days, is ashamed to recollect that his father was a currier, or a blacksmith, or a skipper at Barnstable or Beverly; ashamed, also, of his forty or fifty country cousins, remarkable for nothing but their large hands and their excellent memory. Nay, he is ashamed of his own humble beginnings, and

sneers at men starting as he once started. The generation
of English "Snobs" came in with the Conqueror, and
migrated to America at an early day, where they continue
to thrive marvellously—the chief "conservative party" in
the land.

Through this contempt for labour, a certain affectation
runs through a good deal of American society, and makes
our aristocracy vulgar and contemptible. What if Burns
had been ashamed of his plough, and Franklin had lost his
recollection of the candle-moulds and the composing stick?
Mr. Chubbs, who got rich to-day, imitates Mr. Swipes, who
got rich yesterday, buys the same furniture, gives similar
entertainments, and counts himself "as good a man as
Swipes, any day." Nay, he goes a little beyond him, puts
his servants in livery, with the "Chubbs arms" on the
button; but the new-found family arms are not descriptive
of the character of the Chubbses, or of their origin and
history—only of their vanity. Then Mr. Swipes looks
down on poor Chubbs, and curls his lip with scorn; calls
him a "parvenu," "an upstart," "a plebeian;" speaks of
him as one of "that sort of people," "one of your ordinary
men;" "thrifty and well off in the world, but a little
vulgar." At the same time Mr. Swipes looks up to Mr.
Bung, who got rich the day before yesterday, as a gentleman of old family and quite distinguished, and receives
from that quarter the same treatment he bestows on his
left-hand neighbour. The real gentleman is the same all
the world over. Such are by no means lacking here,
while the pretended gentlemen swarm in America.
Chaucer said a good word long ago:

> "—This is not mine intendément
> To clepen no wight in no age
> Only gentle for his lineáge;
> But whoso that is virtuous,
> And in his port not outragéous:
> When such one thou see'st thee beforn,
> Though he be not gentle born,
> Thou mayest well see this in soth,
> That he is gentle, because he doth
> As 'longeth to a gentleman;
> Of them none other deem I can;
> For certainly withouten drede,
> A churl is deeméd by his deed,
> Of high or low, as ye may see,
> Or of what kindred that he be."

It is no wonder vulgar men, who travel here and eat our dinners, laugh at this form of vulgarity. Wiser men see its cause, and prophesy its speedy decay. Every nation has its aristocracy, or controlling class: in some lands it is permanent, an aristocracy of blood; men that are descended from distinguished warriors, from the pirates and freebooters of a rude age. The nobility of England are proud of their fathers' deeds, and emblazon the symbols thereof in their family arms, emblems of barbarism. Ours is an aristocracy of wealth, not got by plunder, but by toil, thrift, enterprise; of course it is a moveable aristocracy: the first families of the last century are now forgot, and their successors will give place to new names. Now earning is nobler than robbing, and work is before war; but we are ashamed of both, and seek to conceal the noble source of our wealth. An aristocracy of gold is far preferable to the old and immoveable nobility of blood, but it has also its peculiar vices: it has the effrontery of an upstart, despises its own ladder, is heartless and lacks noble principle, vulgar and cursing. This lust of wealth, however, does us a service, and gives the whole nation a stimulus which it needs, and, low as the motive is, drives us to continual advancement. It is a great merit for a nation to secure the largest amount of useful and comfortable and beautiful things which can be honestly earned, and used with profit to the body and soul of man. Only when wealth becomes an idol, and material abundance is made the end, not the means, does the love of it become an evil. No nation was ever too rich, or over-thrifty, though many a nation has lost its soul by living wholly for the senses.

Now and then we see noble men living apart from this vulgarity and scramble; some rich, some poor, but both content to live for noble aims, to pinch and spare for virtue, religion, for truth and right. Such men never fail from any age or land, but everywhere they are the exceptional men. Still they serve to keep alive the sacred fire in the hearts of young men, rising amid the common mob as oaks surpass the brambles or the fern.

In these secondary qualities of the people which mark the special signs of the times, there are many contradictions, quality contending with quality; all by no means balanced into harmonious relations. Here are great faults not less than great virtues. Can the national faults be corrected? Most certainly; they are but accidental, coming from our circumstances, our history, our position as a people—heterogeneous, new, and placed on a new and untamed continent. They come not from the nation's soul; they do not belong to our fundamental idea, but are hostile to it. One day our impatience of authority, our philosophical tendency, will lead us to a right method, that to fixed principles, and then we shall have a continuity of national action. Considering the pains taken by the fathers of the better portion of America to promote religion here, remembering how dear is Christianity to the heart of all, conservative and radical—though men often name as Christian what is not—and seeing how truth and right are sure to win at last,—it becomes pretty plain that we shall arrive at true principles, laws of the universe, ideas of God; then we shall be in unison also with it and Him. When that great defect—lack of first principles—is corrected, our intensity of life, with the hope and confidence it inspires, will do a great work for us. We have already secured an abundance of material comforts hitherto unknown; no land was ever so full of corn and cattle, clothing, comfortable houses, and all things needed for the flesh. The desire of those things, even the excessive desire thereof, performs an important part in the divine economy of the human race; nowhere is its good effect more conspicuous than in America, where in two generations the wild Irishman becomes a decent citizen, orderly, temperate, and intelligent. This done or even a-doing, as it is now, we shall go forth to realize our great national idea, and accomplish the great work of organizing into institutions the unalienable rights of man. The great obstacle in the way of that is African slavery—the great exception in the nation's history; the national sin. When that is removed, as soon it must be, lesser but kindred evils will easily be done away; the truth which the land-reformers, which the associationists, the free-traders, and others, have seen, dimly or clearly, can readily be carried out. But while this monster vice continues, there is little hope of any great and permanent national reform. The positive things which we chiefly need for this work, are first, education, next, education, and then education, a vigorous development of the mind, conscience, affections, religious power of the whole nation. The method and the means for that I shall not now discuss.

The organization of human rights, the performance of human duties, is an unlimited work. If there shall ever be a time when it is all done, then the race will have finished its course. Shall the American nation go on in this work, or pause, turn off, fall, and perish? To me it seems almost treason to doubt that a glorious future awaits us. Young as we are, and wicked, we have yet done something which the world will not let perish. One day we shall attend more emphatically to the rights of the hand, and organize labour and skill; then to the rights of the head, looking after education, science, literature, and art; and again to the rights of the heart, building up the State with its laws, society with its families, the church with its goodness and piety. One day we shall see that it is a shame, and a loss, and a wrong, to have a criminal, or an ignorant man, or a pauper, or an idler, in the land; that the gaol, and the gallows, and the almshouse are a reproach which need not be. Out of new sentiments and ideas, not seen as yet, new forms of society will come, free from the antagonism of races, classes, men—representing the American idea in its length, breadth, depth, and height, its beauty, and its truth, and then the old civilization of our time shall seem barbarous and even savage. There will be an American art commensurate with our idea and akin to this great continent; not an imitation, but a fresh, new growth. An American literature also must come with democratic freedom, democratic thought, democratic power—for we are not always to be pensioners of other lands, doing nothing but import and quote; a literature with all of German philosophic depth, with English solid sense, with French vivacity and wit, Italian fire of sentiment and soul, with all of Grecian elegance of form, and more than Hebrew piety and faith in God. We must not look for the maiden's ringlets on the baby's brow; we are yet but a girl; the nameless grace of maturity, and womanhood's majestic charm, are still to come. At length we must have a system of education, which shall uplift the humblest, rudest, worst born child in all the land; which shall bring forth and bring up noble men.

An American State is a thing that must also be; a State of free men who give over brawling, resting on industry, justice, love, not on war, cunning, and violence—a State where liberty, equality, and fraternity are deeds as well as words. In its time the American Church must also appear, with liberty, holiness, and love for its watchwords, cultivating reason, conscience, affection, faith, and leading the world's way in justice, peace, and love. The Roman Church has been all men know what and how; the American Church, with freedom for the mind, freedom for the heart, freedom for the soul, is yet to be, sundering no chord of the human harp, but tuning all to harmony. This also must come; but hitherto no one has risen with genius fit to plan its holy walls, conceive its columns, project its towers, or lay its corner-stone. Is it too much to hope all this? Look at the arena before us—look at our past history. Hark! there is the sound of many million men, the trampling of their freeborn feet, the murmuring of their voice; a nation born of this land that God reserved so long a virgin earth, in a high day married to the human race,—rising, and swelling, and rolling on, strong and certain as the Atlantic tide; they come numerous as ocean waves when east winds blow, their destination commensurate with the continent, with ideas vast as the Mississippi, strong as the Alleghanies, and awful as Niagara; they come murmuring little of the past, but, moving in the brightness of their great idea, and casting its light far on to other lands and distant days—come to the world's great work, to organize the rights of man.

V.

SOME THOUGHTS ON THE FREE SOIL PARTY AND
THE ELECTION OF GENERAL TAYLOR, DECEM-
BER, 1848.

THE people of the United States have just chosen an
officer, who, for the next four years, will have more power
than any monarch of Europe ; yet three years ago he was
scarcely known out of the army in Florida, and even now
has appeared only in the character of a successful general.
His supporters at the North intend, by means of his
election, to change the entire commercial policy of the
country, and perhaps, also, its financial policy ; they contemplate, or profess to contemplate, a great change.   Yet
the election has been effected without tumult or noise;
not a soldier has drawn his bayonet; scarcely has a
constable needed his official rod to keep order withal. In
Europe, at the same time, the beginning of a change in
the national dynasty or the national policy is only at-
tempted by violence, by soldiers with arms ready for fight,
by battle and murder. One day or another, men will be
wise enough to see the cause of this difference, and insular
statesmen in England, who now sneer at the new government in America, may learn that democracy has at least
one quality—that of respecting law and order, and may
live to see ours the oldest government in the whole Caucasian race.

Since the election is now over, it is worth while to look
a moment at the politics and political parties of the
country, that we may gain wisdom for the future, and
perhaps hope ; at any rate, may see the actual condition of
things. Each political party is based on an Idea, which
corresponds to a Truth, or an Interest. It commonly

happens that the idea is represented as an interest, and the interest as an idea, before either becomes the foundation of a large party. Now when a new idea is introduced to any party, or applied to any institution, if it be only auxiliary to the old doctrines incarnated therein, a regular growth and new development take place; but when the new idea is hostile to the old, the development takes place under the form of a revolution, and that will be greater or less in proportion to the difference between the new idea and the old doctrine; in proportion to their relative strength and value. As Aristotle said of seditions, a revolution comes on slight occasions, but not of slight causes;* the occasion may be obvious and obviously trivial, but the cause obscure and great. The occasion of the French Revolution of 1848 was afforded by the attempt of the king to prevent a certain public dinner : he had a legal right to prevent it. The cause of the Revolution was a little different; but some men in America and England, at first, scarcely looked beyond the occasion, and, taking that for the cause, thought the Frenchmen fools to make so much ado about a trifle, and that they had better eat their *soupe maigre* at home, and let their victuals stop their mouths. The occasion of the American Revolution may be found in the Stamp-Act, or the Sugar-Act, the Writs of Assistance, or the Boston Port-Bill; some men, even now, see no further, and logically conclude the colonists made a mistake, because for a dozen years they were far worse off than before the "Rebellion," and have never been so lightly taxed since. Such men do not see the cause of the Revolution, which was not an unwillingness to pay taxes, but a determination to govern themselves.

At the present day it is plain that a revolution, neither slow nor silent, is taking place in the political parties of America. The occasion thereof is the nomination of a man for the presidency, who has no political or civil experience, but who has three qualities that are important in the eyes of the leading men who have supported and pushed him forward: one is, that he is an eminent slaveholder, whose interests and accordingly whose ideas are identical with those of the slaveholders; the next, that he

---

* Γίγνονται μὲν οὖν αἱ στάσεις οὐ περὶ μικρῶν ἀλλ' ἐκ μικρῶν, στασιάζουσι δὲ περὶ μεγάλων.—Aristotle's *Polit.*, Lib. V., Chap. 4, § 1.

is not hostile to the doctrines of northern manufacturers respecting a protective tariff; and the third, that he is an eminent and very successful military commander. The last is an accidental quality, and it is not to be supposed that the intelligent and influential men at the North and South who have promoted his election, value him any more on that account, or think that mere military success fits him for his high office, and enables him to settle the complicated difficulties of a modern State. They must know better; but they must have known that many men of little intelligence are so taken with military glory that they will ask for no more in their hero; it was foreseen, also, that honest and intelligent men of all parties would give him their vote because he had never been mixed up with the intrigues of political life. Thus "far-sighted" politicians of the North and South, saw that he might be fairly elected, and then might serve the purposes of the slaveholder, or the manufacturer of the North. The military success of General Taylor, an accidental merit, was only the occasion of his nomination by the whigs; his substantial merit was found in the fact, that he was supposed, or known, to be favourable to the "peculiar institution" of the South, and the protective policy of the manufacturers at the North: this was the cause of his formal nomination by the Whig Convention of Philadelphia, and his real nomination by members of the whig party at Washington. The men of property at the South wanted an extension of slavery; the men of property at the North, a high protective tariff; and it was thought General Taylor could serve both purposes, and promote the interests of the North and South.

Such is the occasion of the revolution in political parties: the cause is the introduction of a new idea into these parties entirely hostile to some of their former doctrines. In the electioneering contest, the new idea was represented by the words "Free Soil." For present practice it takes a negative form: "No more Slave States, no more Slave Territory," is the motto. But these words and this motto do not adequately represent the idea, only so much thereof as has been needful in the present crisis.

Before now there has been much in the political history of America to provoke the resentment of the North.

England has been ruled by various dynasties; the American chair has been chiefly occupied by the Southern House, the Dynasty of Slaveholders: now and then a member of the Northern House has sat on that seat, but commonly it has been a "Northern man with Southern principles," never a man with mind to see the great idea of America, and will to carry it out in action. Still the spirit of liberty has not died out of the North; the attempt to put an eighth slaveholder in the chair of "the model republic," gave occasion for that spirit to act again.

The new idea is not hostile to the distinctive doctrine of either political party; neither to free-trade, nor to protection; so it makes no revolution in respect to them: it is neutral, and leaves both as it found them. It is not hostile to the general theory of the American State, so it makes no revolution there; this idea is assumed as self-evident, in the Declaration of Independence. It is not inimical to the theory of the Constitution of the United States, as set forth in the preamble thereto, where the design of the Constitution is declared to be "To form a more perfect union, establish justice, insure domestic tranquillity, provide for the common defence, promote the general welfare, and secure the blessings of liberty to ourselves and our posterity."

There are clauses in the Constitution, which are exceptions to this theory, and hostile to the design mentioned above; to such, this idea will one day prove itself utterly at variance, as it is now plainly hostile to one part of the practice of the American Government, and that of both the parties.

We have had several political parties since the Revolution: the federalists, and anti-federalists, — the latter shading off into republicans, democrats, and loco focos; the former tapering into modern whigs, in which guise some of their fathers would scarcely recognise the family type. We have had a protective party and an anti-protective party; once there was a free-trade party, which no longer appears in politics. There has been a National Bank party, which seems to have gone to the realm of things lost on earth. In the rise and fall of these parties, several dramas, tragic and comic, have been performed on the American boards, where "One man in his time plays many parts," and stout representatives of the Hartford Convention find themselves on the same side with worshippers of the Gerrymander, and shouting the same cry. It is kindly ordered that memory should be so short, and brass so common. None of the old parties is likely to return; the living have buried the dead. "We are all federalists," said Mr. Jefferson, "we are all democrats," and truly, so far as old questions are concerned. It is well known that the present representatives of the old federal party have abjured the commercial theory of their predecessors; and the men who were "Jacobins" at the beginning of the century, curse the new French Revolution by their gods. At the presidential election of 1840, there were but two parties in the field—democrats and whigs. As they both survive, it is well to see what interests or what ideas they represent.

They differ accidentally in the possession and the desire of power; in the fact that the former took the initiative, in annexing Texas, and in making the Mexican war, while the latter only pretended to oppose either, but zealously and continually co-operated in both. Then, again, the democratic party sustains the sub-treasury system, insisting that the government shall not interfere with banking, shall keep its own deposits, and give and take only specie in its business with the people. The whig party, if we understand it, has not of late developed any distinctive doctrine, on the subject of money and financial operations, but only complained of the action of the sub-treasury; yet, as it sustained the late Bank of the United States, and appropriately followed as chief mourner at the funeral thereof, uttering dreadful lamentations and prophecies which time has not seen fit to accomplish, it still keeps up a show of differing from the democrats on this matter. These are only accidental or historical differences, which do not practically affect the politics of the nation to any great degree.

The substantial difference between the two is this: the whigs desire a tariff of duties which shall directly and intentionally protect American industry, or, as we understand it, shall directly and intentionally protect manufacturing industry, while the commercial and agricultural interests are to be protected indirectly, not as if they were valuable in themselves, but were a collateral security to the manufacturing interest: a special protection is desired for the great manufactures, which are usually conducted by large capitalists—such as the manufacture of wool, iron, and cotton. On the other hand, the democrats disclaim all direct protection of any special interest, but, by raising the national revenue from the imports of the nation, actually afford a protection to the articles of domestic origin to the extent of the national revenue, and much more. That is the substantial difference between the two parties—one which has been much insisted on at the late election, especially at the North.

Is this difference of any practical importance at the present moment? There are two methods of raising the revenue of a country: first, by direct taxation,—a direct tax on the person, a direct tax on the property; second, by indirect taxation. To a simple-minded man direct taxation seems the only just and equal mode of collecting the public revenue: thereby, the rich man pays in proportion to his much, the poor to his little. This is so just and obvious, that it is the only method resorted to, in towns of the North, for raising their revenue. But while it requires very little common sense and virtue to appreciate this plan in a town, it seems to require a good deal to endure it in a nation. The four direct taxes levied by the American government since 1787 have been imperfectly collected, and only with great difficulty and long delay. To avoid this difficulty, the government resorts to various indirect modes of taxation, and collects the greater part of its revenue from the imports which reach our shores. In this way a man's national tax is not directly in proportion to his wealth, but directly in proportion to his consumption of imported goods, or directly to that of domestic goods, whose price is enhanced by the duties laid on the foreign article. So it may happen that an Irish labourer, with a dozen children, pays a larger national tax than a millionaire who sees fit to live in a miserly style. Besides, no one knows when he pays or what. At first it seems as if the indirect mode of taxation made the burden light, but in the end it does not always prove so. The remote effect thereof is sometimes remarkable. The tax of one per cent. levied in Massachusetts on articles sold

by auction, has produced some results not at all antici-
pated.

Now since neither party ventures to suggest direct taxation, the actual question between the two is not between
free trade and protection, but only between a protective
and a revenue tariff. So the real and practical question
between them is this : Shall there be a high tariff or a low
one ? At first sight a man not in favour of free trade
might think the present tariff gave sufficient protection to
those great manufactures of wool, cotton, and iron, and as
much as was reasonable. But the present duty is perhaps
scarcely adequate to meet the expenses of the nation, for
with new territory new expenses must come ; there is a
large debt to be discharged, its interest to be paid ; large
sums will be demanded as pensions for the soldiers. Since
these things are so, it is but reasonable to conclude that,
under the administration of the whigs or democrats, a
pretty high tariff of duties will continue for some years to
come. So the great and substantial difference between the
two parties ceases to be of any great and substantial importance.

In the mean time another party rises up, representing
neither of these interests ; without developing any peculiar
views relative to trade or finance, it proclaims the doctrine
that there must be no more slave territory, and no more
slave States. This doctrine is of great practical importance, and one in which the free soil party differs substantially from both the other parties. The idea on which
the party rests is not new; it does not appear that the
men who framed the Constitution, or the people who
accepted it, ever contemplated the extension of slavery
beyond the limits of the United States at that time; had
such a proposition been then made, it would have been
indignantly rejected by both. The principle of the Wilmot Proviso boasts the same origin as the Declaration of
Independence. The state of feeling at the North occasioned by the Missouri Compromise is well known, but
after that there was no political party opposed to slavery.
No President has been hostile to it; no Cabinet; no Congress. In 1805, Mr. Pickering, a Senator from Massachusetts, brought forward his bill for amending the Constitution, so that slaves should not form part of the basis

of representation ; but it fell to the ground, not to be lifted up by his successors for years to come. The refusal of John Quincy Adams, while President, to recognise the independence of Hayti, and his efforts to favour the slave power, excited no remark. In 1844, for the first time the anti-slavery votes began seriously to affect the presidential election. At that time the whigs had nominated Mr. Clay as their candidate, a man of great powers, of popular manners, the friend of northern industry, but still more the friend of southern slavery, and more directly identified with that than any man in so high a latitude. The result of the anti-slavery votes is well known. The bitterest reproaches have been heaped on the men who voted against him as the incarnation of the slave power; the annexation of Texas, though accomplished by a whig senate, and the Mexican war, though only sixteen members of Congress voted against it, have both been laid to their charge ; and some have even affected to wonder that men conscientiously opposed to slavery could not forget their principle for the sake of their party, and put a most decided slaveholder, who had treated not only them but their cause with scorn and contempt, in the highest place of power.

The whig party renewed its attempt to place a slaveholder in the President's chair, at a time when all Europe was rising to end for ever the tyranny of man. General Taylor was particularly obnoxious to the anti-slavery men. He is a slaveholder, holding one or two hundred men in bondage, and enlarging that number by recent purchases; he employs them in the worst kind of slave labour, the manufacture of sugar ; he leaves them to the mercy of overseers, the dregs and refuse of mankind; he has just returned from a war undertaken for the extension of slavery ; he is a southern man with southern interests, and opinions favourable to slavery, and is uniformly represented by his supporters at the South, as decidedly opposed to the Wilmot Proviso, and in favour of the extension of slavery. We know this has been denied at the North; but the testimony of the South settles the question. The convention of democrats in South Carolina, when they also nominated him, said well, "His interests are our interests: . . . . we know that on this great, paramount, and leading question of the rights of the South [to extend slavery over the new territory], he is for us and he is with us." Said a newspaper in his own State, " General Taylor is from birth, association, and conviction, identified with the South and her institutions, being one of the most extensive slaveholders in Louisiana, and supported by the slaveholding interest; is opposed to the Wilmot Proviso, and in favour of procuring the privilege to the owners of slaves to remove with them to newly acquired territory."

The southerners evidently thought the crisis an important one. The following is from the distinguished whig senator, Mr. Berrien:—

" I consider it the most important Presidential election, especially to southern men, which has occurred since the foundation of the government.

" We have great and important interests at stake. If we fail to sustain them now, we may be forced too soon to decide whether we will remain in the Union, at the mercy of a band of fanatics or political jugglers, or reluctantly retire from it for the preservation of our domestic institutions, and all our rights as freemen. If we are united, we can sustain them ; if we divide on the old party issues, we must be victims.

" With a heart devoted to their interests on this great question, and without respect to party, I implore my fellow-citizens of Georgia, whig and democratic, to forget for the time their party divisions : to know each other only as southern men: to act upon the truism uttered by Mr. Calhoun, that on this vital question—the preservation of our domestic institutions—the southern man who is furthest from us is nearer to us than any northern man can be ; that General Taylor is identified with us, in feeling and interest, was born in a slaveholding State, educated in a slaveholding State, is himself a slaveholder ; that his slave property constitutes the means of support to himself and family ; that he cannot desert us without sacrificing his interest, his principle, the habits and feelings of his life ; and that with him, therefore, our institutions are safe. I beseech them, therefore, from the love which they bear to our noble State, to rally under the banner of Zachary Taylor, and, with one united voice, to send him by acclamation to the executive chair."

All this has been carefully kept from the sight of the people at the North.

There have always been men in America who were opposed to the extension and the very existence of slavery. In 1787, the best and the most celebrated statesmen were publicly active on the side of freedom. Some thought slavery a sin, others a mistake, but nearly all in the Convention thought it an error. South Carolina and Georgia were the only States thoroughly devoted to slavery at that time. They threatened to withdraw from the Union, if it were not sufficiently respected in the new Constitution. If the other States had said, "You may go, soon as you like, for hitherto you have been only a curse to us, and done little but brag," it would have been better for us all. However, partly for the sake of keeping the peace, and still more for the purpose of making money by certain concessions of the South, the North granted the southern demands. After the adoption of the Constitution, the anti-slavery spirit cooled down; other matters occupied the public mind. The long disasters of Europe; the alarm of the English party, who feared their sons should be "conscripts in the armies of Napoleon," and the violence of the French party, who were ready to compromise the dignity of the nation, and add new elements to the confusion in Europe; the subsequent conflict with England, and then the efforts to restore the national character, and improve our material condition,—these occupied the thought of the nation, till the Missouri Compromise again disturbed the public mind. But that was soon forgotten; little was said about slavery. In the eighteenth century, it was discussed in the colleges and newspapers, even in the pulpits of the North; but, in the first quarter of the nineteenth, little was heard of it. Manufactures got established at the North, and protected by duties; at the South, cotton was cultivated with profit, and a heavy duty protected the slave-grown sugar of Louisiana. The pecuniary interests of North and South became closely connected, and both seemed dependent on the peaceable continuance of slavery. Little was said against it, little thought, and nothing done. Southern masters voluntarily brought their slaves to New England, and took them back, no one offering the African the conventional shelter of the law, not to speak of the natural shelter of justice. We well remember the complaint made somewhat later, when a Judge decided that a slave, brought here by his master's consent, became, from that moment, free !

But where sin abounded, grace doth much more abound. There rose up one man who would not compromise, nor be silent,—who would be heard.* He spoke of the evil,

* William Lloyd Garrison.

spoke of the sin—for all true reforms are bottomed on religion, and while they seem adverse to many interests, yet represent the idea of the Eternal. He found a few others, a very few, and began the anti-slavery movement. The "platform" of the new party was not an interest, but an idea—that "All men are created equal, and endowed by their Creator with certain unalienable rights." Every truth is also a fact; this was a fact of human consciousness, and a truth of necessity.

The time has not come to write the history of the abolitionists,—other deeds must come before words; but we cannot forbear quoting the testimony of one witness, as to the state of anti-slavery feeling in New England in 1831. It is the late Hon. Harrison Gray Otis, a former mayor of Boston, who speaks in his recent letter.

"The first information received by me, of a disposition to agitate this subject in our State, was from the Governors of Virginia and Georgia, severally remonstrating against an incendiary newspaper, published in Boston, and, as they alleged, thrown broadcast among their plantations, inciting to insurrection and its horrid results. It appeared, on inquiry, that no member of the city government [of Boston] had ever heard of the publication. Some time afterwards it was reported to me by the city officers, that they had ferreted out the paper and its editor; that his office was an obscure hole, his only visible auxiliary a negro boy, and his supporters a very few insignificant persons of all colours. This information . . . I communicated to the above-named governors, with an assurance of my belief that the new fanaticism had not made, nor was likely to make, proselytes among the respectable classes of our people."

Such was the state of things in 1831. Anti-slavery had " an obscure hole " for its head-quarters; the one agitator, who had filled the two doughty Governors of Virginia and Georgia with uncomfortable forebodings, had a "negro boy" "for his only visible auxiliary," and none of the respectable men of Boston had heard of the hole, of the agitator, of the negro boy, or even of the agitation. One thing must be true: either the man and the boy were pretty vigorous, or else there was a great truth in that obscure hole; for, in spite of the governors and the mayors, spite of the many able men in the South and the North, spite, also, of the wealth and respectability of the whole land, it is a plain case that the abolitionists have shaken the nation, and their idea is the idea of the time; and the party which shall warmly welcome that is destined before long to override all the other parties.

One thing must be said of the leaders of the anti-slavery movement. They asked for nothing but justice; not justice for themselves—they were not Socratic enough to ask that,—but only justice for the slave; and to obtain that, they forsook all that human hearts most love. It is rather a cheap courage that fought at Monterey and Palo Alto, a bravery that can be bought for eight dollars a month; the patriotism which hurras for "our side," which makes speeches at Faneuil Hall, nay, which carries torchlights in a procession, is not the very loftiest kind of patriotism; even the man who stands up at the stake, and in one brief hour of agony anticipates the long torment of disease, does not endure the hardest, but only the most obvious kind of martyrdom. But when a man, for conscience' sake, leaves a calling that would insure him bread and respectability; when he abjures the opinions which give him the esteem of honourable men; when, for the sake of truth and justice, he devotes himself to liberating the most abused and despised class of men, solely because they are men and brothers; when he thus steps forth in front of the world, and encounters poverty and neglect, the scorn, the loathing, and the contempt of mankind—why, there is something not very common in that. There was once a Man who had not where to lay his head, who was born in "an obscure hole," and had not even a negro boy for his "auxiliary;" who all his life lived with most obscure persons—eating and drinking with publicans and sinners; who found no favour with mayors or governors, and yet has had some influence on the history of the world. When intelligent men mock at small beginnings, it is surprising they cannot remember that the greatest institutions have had their times which tried men's souls, and that they who have done all the noblest and best work of mankind, sometimes forgot self-interest in looking at a great truth; and though they had not always even a negro boy to help them, or an obscure hole to lay their heads in, yet found the might of the universe was on the side of right, and themselves workers with God!

The abolitionists did not aim to found a political party; they set forth an idea. If they had set up the interest of the whigs or the democrats, the manufacturers or the merchants, they might have formed a party and had a high place in it, with money, ease, social rank and a great name in the party—newspapers. Some of them had political talents, ideas more than enough, the power of organizing men, the skill to manage them, and a genius for eloquence. With such talents, it demands not a little manliness to keep out of politics and in the truth.

To found a political party there is no need of a great moral idea : the whig party has had none such this long time ; the democratic party pretends to none and acts on none ; each represents an interest which can be estimated in dollars ; neither seems to see that behind questions of political economy there is a question of political morality, and the welfare of the nation depends on the answer we shall give ! So long as the abolitionists had nothing but an idea, and but few men had that, there was no inducement for the common run of politicians to join them ; they could make nothing by it, so nothing of it. The guardians of education, the trustees of the popular religion, did not like to invest in such funds. But still the idea went on, spite of the most entire, the most bitter, the most heartless and unrelenting opposition ever known in America. No men were ever hated as the abolitionists ; political parties have joined to despise, and sectarian churches to curse them. Yet the idea has gone on, till now all that is most pious in the sects, most patriotic in the parties, all that is most Christian in modern philanthropy, is on its side. It has some representative in almost every family, save here and there one whose God is mammon alone, where the parents are antediluvian and the children born old and conservative, with no faculty but memory to bind them to mankind. It has its spokesmen in the House and the Senate. The tide rises and swells, and the compact wall of the whig party, the tall ramparts of the democrats, are beginning to " cave in."

As the idea has gained ground, men have begun to see that an interest is connected with it, and begun to look after that. One thing the North knows well—the art of calculation, and of ciphering. So it begins to ask questions as to the positive and comparative influence of the slave power on the country. Who fought the Revolution ? Why the North, furnishing the money and the men, Massachusetts alone sending fourteen thousand soldiers more than all the present slave States. Who pays the national taxes? The North, for the slaves pay but a trifle. Who owns the greater part of the property, the mills, the shops, the ships? The North. Who writes the books—the histories, poems, philosophies, works of science, even the sermons and commentaries on the Bible? Still the North. Who sends their children to school and college? The North. Who builds the churches, who founds the Bible societies, Education societies, Missionary societies, the thousand-and-one institutions for making men better and better off? Why the North. In a word, who is it that in seventy years has made the nation great, rich, and famous for her ideas and their success all over the world? The answer is, still the North, the North.

Well, says the calculator, but who has the offices of the nation? The South. Who has filled the Presidential chair forty-eight years out of sixty? Nobody but slave-holders. Who has held the chief posts of honour? The South. Who occupy the chief offices in the army and navy? The South. Who increases the cost of the post-office and pays so little of its expense?* The South. Who is most blustering and disposed to quarrel? The South. Who made the Mexican war? The South. Who sets at nought the Constitution? The South. Who would bring the greatest peril in case of war with a strong enemy? Why the South, the South. But what is the South most noted for abroad? For her three million slaves; and the North? for her wealth, freedom, education, religion!

. Then the calculator begins to remember past times— opens the account-books and turns back to old charges: five slaves count the same as three freemen, and the three million slaves, which at home are nothing but property, entitle their owners to as many representatives in Congress as are now sent by all the one million eight hundred thousand freemen who make the entire population of Maine,

---

* The following table shows the facts of the case :

| Cost of post-office in slave States for the year ending July 1st, 1847, $1,318,541 Receipts from post-office, 624,380 | Cost of post-office in free States for the year ending July 1st, 1847, $1,038,219 Receipts from post-office, 1,459,631 |

So the Southern post-office cost the nation $694,161, and the Northern post-office paid the nation $421,412, making a difference of $1,115,573 against the South.

New Hampshire, Vermont, Rhode Island, and Massachusetts, and have created a vast amount of property, worth more than all the slave States put together! Then the North must deliver up the fugitive slaves, and Ohio must play the traitor, the kidnapper, the bloodhound, for Kentucky! The South wanted to make two slave States out of Florida, and will out of Texas; she makes slavery perpetual in both; she is always bragging as if she made the Revolution, while she only laid the Embargo, and began the late war with England,—but that is going further back than is needful. The South imprisons our coloured sailors in her ports, contrary to justice, and even contrary to the Constitution. She drove our commissioners out of South Carolina and Louisiana, when they were sent to look into the matter and legally seek for redress. She affronts the world with a most odious despotism, and tried to make the English return her runaway slaves, making the nation a reproach before the world; she insists on kidnapping men even in Boston; she declares that we shall not abolish slavery in the capital of the Union; that she will extend it in spite of us from sea to sea. She annexed Texas for a slave-pasture, and then made the Mexican war to enlarge that pasture, but the North must pay for it; she treads the Constitution under her feet, the North under her feet, justice and the unalienable rights of man under her feet.

The North has charged all these items and many more; now they are brought up for settlement, and, if not cancelled, will not be forgot till the Muse of History gives up the ghost; some Northern men have the American sentiment, and the American idea, put the man before the dollar, counting man the substance, property the accident. The sentiment and idea of liberty are bottomed on Christianity, as that on human nature; they are quite sure to prevail; the spirit of the nation is on their side—the spirit of the age and the everlasting right.

It is instructive to see how the political parties have hitherto kept clear of anti-slavery. It is "no part of the whig doctrine;" the democrats abhor it. Mr. Webster, it is true, once claimed the Wilmot Proviso as his thunder, but he cannot wield it, and so it slips out of his hands, and runs round to the chair of his brother senator from New

Hampshire.* No leading politician in America has ever
been a leader against slavery. Even Mr. Adams only went
as he was pushed. True, among the whigs there are Giddings, Palfrey, Tuck, Mann, Root, and Julian; among the
democrats there is Hale—and a few others; but what are
they among so many? The members of the family of
Truth are unpopular, they make excellent servants but
hard masters, while the members of the family of Interest
are all respectable, and are the best company in the world;
their livery is attractive; their motto, "The almighty
dollar," is a passport everywhere. Now it happens that
some of the more advanced members of the family of Truth
fight their way into "good society," and make matrimonial
alliances with some of the poor relations of the family of
Interest. Straightway they become respectable: the church
publishes the banns; the marriage is solemnized in the
most Christian form; the attorney declares it legal. So
the gospel and law are satisfied, Truth and Interest made
one, and many persons after this alliance may be seen
in the company of Truth who before knew not of her
existence.

The free soil party has grown out of the anti-slavery
movement. It will have no more slave territory, but does
not touch slavery in the States, or between them, and says
nothing against the compromises of the Constitution; the
time has not come for that. The party has been organized in haste, and is composed, as are all parties, of
most discordant materials, some of its members seeming
hardly familiar with the idea; some are not yet emanci-
pated from old prejudices, old methods of action, and old
interests; but the greater part seem hostile to slavery in
all its forms. The immediate triumph of this new party
is not to be looked for; not desirable. In Massachusetts
they have gained large numbers in a very short period,
and under every disadvantage. What their future history
is to be, we will not now attempt to conjecture; but this is
plain, that they cannot remain long in their present position; either they will go back, and, after due penance,
receive political absolution from the church of the whigs,
or the democrats,—and this seems impossible,—or else they

* Mr. John P. Hale.

must go forward where the idea of justice impels them. One day the motto, "No more slave territory" will give place to this, " No slavery in America." The revolution in ideas is not over till that is done, nor the corresponding revolution in deeds while a single slave remains in America. A man who studies the great movements of mankind feels sure that that day is not far off; that no combination of northern and southern interest, no declamation, no violence, no love of money, no party zeal, no fraud and no lies, no compromise, can long put off the time. Bad passions will ere long league with the holiest love of right, and that wickedness may be put down with the strong hand which might easily be ended at little cost and without any violence, even of speech. One day the democratic party of the North will remember the grievances which they have suffered from the South, and, if they embrace the idea of freedom, no constitutional scruple will long hold them from destroying the "peculiar institution." What slavery is in the middle of the nineteenth century is quite plain; what it will be at the beginning of the twentieth it is not difficult to foresee. The slave power has gained a great victory: one more such will cost its life. South Carolina did not forget her usual craft in voting for a northern man that was devoted to slavery.

Let us now speak briefly of the conduct of the election. It has been attended, at least in New England, with more intellectual action than any election that I remember, and with less violence, denunciation, and vulgar appeals to low passions and sordid interest. Massachusetts has shown herself worthy of her best days; the free soil vote may be looked on with pride, by men who conscientiously cast their ballot the other way. Men of ability and integrity have been active on both sides, and able speeches have been made, while the vulgarity that marked the "Harrison campaign" has not been repeated.

In this contest the democratic party made a good confession, and "owned up" to the full extent of their conduct. They stated the question at issue, fairly, clearly, and entirely; the point could not be mistaken. The Baltimore Convention dealt honestly in declaring the political opinions of the party; the opinions of their candidate on the great party questions, and the subject of slavery, were made known with exemplary clearness and fidelity. The party did not fight in the dark; they had no dislike to holding slaves, and they pretended none. In all parts of the land they went before the people with the same doctrines and the same arguments; everywhere they "repudiated" the Wilmot Proviso. This gave them an advantage over a party with a different policy. They had a platform of doctrines; they knew what it was; the party stood on the platform; the candidate stood on it.

The whig party have conducted differently; they did not publish their confession of faith. We know what was the whig platform in 1840 and in 1844. But what is it in 1848? Particular men may publish their opinions, but the doctrines of the party are "not communicated to the public." For once in the history of America there was a whig convention which passed no "Resolutions;" it was the Convention at Philadelphia. But on one point, of the greatest importance too, it expressed the opinions of the whigs: it rejected the Wilmot Proviso, and Mr. Webster's thunder, which had fallen harmless and without lightning from his hands, was "kicked out of the meeting!" As the party had no platform, so their candidate had no political opinions. "What!" says one, "choose a President who does not declare his opinions,—then it must be because they are perfectly well known!" Not at all: General Taylor is raw in politics, and has not taken his first "drill!" "Then he must be a man of such great political and moral ability, that his will may take the place of reason!" Not at all: he is known only as a successful soldier, and his reputation is scarcely three years old. Mr. Webster declared his nomination "not fit to be made," and nobody has any authentic statement of his political opinions; perhaps not even General Taylor himself.

In the electioneering campaign there has been a certain duplicity in the supporters of General Taylor: at the North it was maintained that he was not opposed to the Wilmot Proviso, while at the South quite uniformly the opposite was maintained. This duplicity had the appearance of dishonesty. In New England the whigs did not meet the facts and arguments of the free soil party; in the beginning of the campaign the attempt was made, but was afterwards comparatively abandoned; the matter of slavery was left out of the case, and the old question of the sub-treasury and the tariff was brought up again, and a stranger would have thought, from some whig newspapers, that that was the only question of any importance. Few men were prepared to see a man of the ability and experience of Mr. Webster in his electioneering speeches pass wholly over the subject of slavery. The nation is presently to decide whether slavery is to extend over the new territory or not; even in a commercial and financial point of view, this is far more important than the question of banks and tariffs; but when its importance is estimated by its relation to freedom, right, human welfare in general,—we beg the pardon of American politicians for speaking of such things, —one is amazed to find the whig party of the opinion that it is more important to restore the tariff of 1842 than to prohibit slavery in a country as large as the thirteen States which fought the Revolution! It might have been ex-pected of little, ephemeral men,—minute politicians, who are the pest of the State,—but when at such a crisis a great man rises,* amid a sea of upturned faces, to instruct the lesser men, and forgets right, forgets freedom, forgets man, and forgets God, talking only of the tariff and of banks, why a stranger is amazed, till he remembers the peculiar relation of the great man to the moneyed men,—that he is their attorney, retained, paid, and pensioned to do the work of men whose interest it is to keep the ques-tion of slavery out of sight. If General Cavaignac had received a pension from the manufacturers of Lyons and of Lisle, to the amount of half a million of francs, should we be surprised if he forgot the needy millions of the land? Nay, only if he did not forget them!

It was a little hardy to ask the anti-slavery men to vote for General Taylor; it was like asking the members of a temperance society to choose an eminent distiller for presi-dent of their association. Still, we know that honest anti-slavery men did honestly vote for him. We know nothing to impeach the political integrity of General Taylor; the simple fact that he is a slaveholder, seems reason enough why he should not be President of a nation who believe that "All men are created equal, and endowed by their

* Hon. Daniel Webster.

Creator with certain unalienable rights." Men will be astonished in the next century to learn that the "model republic," had such an affection for slaveholders. Here is a remarkable document, which we think should be preserved:

DEED OF SALE.

"JOHN HAGARD, SR., TO ZACHARIAH TAYLOR.

"*Received for Record*, 18th *Feb.*, 1843.

" *This Indenture*, made this twenty-first day of April, eighteen hundred and forty-two, between John Hagard, Sr., of the City of New Orleans, State of Louisiana, of one part, and Zachariah Taylor, of the other part, *Witnesseth*, that the said John Hagard, Sr., for and in consideration of the sum of *Ninety-Five Thousand Dollars* to him in hand paid, and secured to be paid, as hereafter stated by the said Zachariah Taylor, at and before the sealing and delivering of these Presents, has this day bargained, sold, and delivered, conveyed, and confirmed, and by these Presents does bargain, sell, deliver, and confirm unto the said Zachariah Taylor, his heirs and assigns, for ever, all that plantation and tract of land : . . . .

" ALSO, all the following Slaves—Nelson, Milley, Peldea, Mason, Willis, Rachel, Caroline, Lucinda, Ramdall, Wirman, Carson, Little Ann, Winna, Jane, Tom, Sally, Gracia, Big Jane, Louisa, Maria, Charles, Barnard, Mira, Sally, Carson, Paul, Sansford, Mansfield, Harry Oden, Harry Horley, Carter, Henrietta, Ben, Charlotte, Wood, Dick, Harrietta, Clarissa, Ben, Anthony, Jacob, Hamby, Jim, Gabriel, Emeline, Armstead, George, Wilson, Cherry, Peggy, Walker, Jane, Wallace, Bartlett, Martha, Letitia, Barbara, Matilda, Lucy, John, Sarah, Bigg Ann, Allen, Tom, George, John, Dick, Fielding, Nelson, or Isom, Winna, Shellod, Lidney, Little Cherry, Puck, Sam, Hannah, or Anna, Mary, Ellen, Henrietta, and two small children :—Also, all the Horses, Mules, Cattle, Hogs, Farming Utensils, and Tools, now on said Plantation—together with all and singular the hereditaments, appurtenances, privileges, and advantages unto the said Land and Slaves belonging or appertaining. *To have and to hold* the said Plantation and tract of Land and Slaves, and other property above described, unto the said Zachariah Taylor, his heirs and assigns, for ever, and to his and to their only proper use, benefits, and behoof, for ever. And the said John Hagard, Sr., for himself, his heirs, executors, and administrators, does covenant, promise, and agree to and with said Zachariah Taylor, his heirs and assigns, that the aforesaid Plantation and tract of Land and Slaves, and other property, with the appurtenances, unto the said Zachariah Taylor, his heirs and assigns, against the claim or claims of all persons whomsoever claiming or to claim the same, or any part or parcel thereof, shall and will warrant, and by these Presents ·for ever defend.

· " *In Testimony Whereof*, the said John Hagard, Sr., has hereunto set his hand and seal, the day and year first above written."

If this document had been discovered among some Egyptian papyri, with the date 1848 before Christ, it would have been remarkable as a sign of the times. In a republic, nearly four thousand years later, it has a meaning which some future historian will appreciate.

The free soil party have been plain and explicit as the democrats; they published their creed in the celebrated Buffalo platform. The questions of sub-treasury and tariff are set aside; "No more slave territory" is the watchword. In part they represent an interest, for slavery is an injury to the North in many ways, and to a certain extent puts the North into the hands of the South; but chiefly an idea. Nobody thought they would elect their candidate, whosoever he might be; they could only arrest public attention and call men to the great questions at issue, and so, perhaps, prevent the evil which the South was bent on accomplishing. This they have done, and done well. The result has been highly gratifying. It was pleasant and encouraging to see men ready to sacrifice their old party attachments and their private interests, oftentimes, for the sake of a moral principle. I do not mean to say that there was no moral principle in the other parties—I know better. But it seems to me that the free soilers committed a great error in selecting Mr. Van Buren as their candidate. True, he is a man of ability, who has held the highest offices and acquitted himself honourably in all; but he had been the "Northern man, with Southern principles;" had shown a degree of subserviency to the South, which was remarkable, if not singular or strange: his promise, made and repeated in the most solemn manner, to veto any act of Congress, abolishing slavery in the capital, was an insult to the country, and a disgrace to himself. He had a general reputation for instability, and want of political firmness. It is true, he had opposed the annexation of Texas, and lost his nomination in 1844 by that act; but it is also true that he advised his party to vote for Mr. Polk, who was notoriously in favour of annexation. His nomination, I must confess, was unfortunate; the Buffalo Convention seems to have looked at his availability more than his fitness, and in their contest for a principle, began by making a compromise of that very principle itself. It was thought he could "carry" the State of New York; and so a man who was not a fair representative of the idea, was set up. It was a bad beginning. It is better to be defeated a thousand times, rather than seem to succeed by a compromise of the principle contended for. Still, enough has been done, to show the nation that the dollar is not almighty; that the South is not always to insult the North, and rule the land, annexing, plundering, and making slaves when she will; that the North has men who will not abandon the great sentiment of freedom, which is the boast of the nation and the age.

General Taylor is elected by a large popular vote; some voted for him on account of his splendid military success; some because he is a slaveholder, and true to the interests of the slave-power; some because he is a "good whig," and wants a high tariff of duties. But we think there are men who gave him their support, because he has never been concerned in the intrigues of a party, is indebted to none for past favours, is pledged to none, bribed by none, and intimidated by none; because he seems to be an honest man, with a certain rustic intelligence; a plain blunt man, that loves his country and mankind. We hope this was a large class. If he is such a man, he will enter upon his office under favourable auspices, and with the best wishes of all good men.

But what shall the free soil party do next? they cannot go back,—conscience waves behind them her glittering wings and bids them on; they cannot stand still, for as yet their measures and their watchword do not fully represent their idea. They must go forward, as the early aboli-tionists went, with this for their motto: "No slavery in America." "He that would lead men, must walk but one step before them," says somebody. Well, but he must think many steps before them, or they will presently tread him under their feet. The present success of the idea is doubtful; the interests of the South will demand the ex-tension of slavery;* the interests of the party now coming

* The following extract, from the *Charleston Mercury*, shows the feel-ing of the South. "Pursuant to a call, a meeting of the citizens of Orangeburg District was held to-day, 6th November, in the court-house, which was well filled on the occasion. . . . . Gen. D. F. Jamison then rose, and moved the appointment of a committee of twenty-five, to take into consideration the continued agitation by Congress of the ques-tion of slavery; . . . the committee, through their chairman, Gen. Jamison, made the following report :—

"The time has arrived when the slaveholding States of the confederacy must take decided action upon the continued attacks of the North against their domestic institutions, or submit in silence to that humiliating posi-tion in the opinions of mankind, that longer acquiescence must inevitably reduce them to. . . . . The agitation of the subject of slavery commenced in the fanatical murmurings of a few scattered abolitionists, into power, will demand their peculiar boon. So another compromise is to be feared, and the extension of slavery

to whom it was a long time confined; but now it has swelled into a torrent of popular opinion at the North; it has invaded the fireside and the church, the press and the halls of legislation; it has seized upon the deliberations of Congress, and at this moment is sapping the foundations, and about to overthrow the fairest political structure that the ingenuity of man has ever devised.

"The overt efforts of abolitionism were confined for a long period to annoying applications to Congress, under colour of the pretended right of petition; it has since directed the whole weight of its malign influence against the annexation of Texas, and had well-nigh cost to the country the loss of that important province; but emboldened by success and the inaction of the South, in an unjust and selfish spirit of national agrarianism it would now appropriate the whole public domain. It might well have been supposed that the undisturbed possession of the whole of Oregon Territory would have satisfied the non-slaveholding States. This they now hold, by the incorporation of the ordinance of 1787 into the bill of the last session for establishing a territorial government for Oregon. That provision, however, was not sustained by them from any apprehension that the territory could ever be settled from the States of the South, but it was intended as a gratuitous insult to the southern people, and a malignant and unjustifiable attack upon the institution of slavery.

"We are called upon to give up the whole public domain to the fanatical cravings of abolitionism, and the unholy lust of political power. A territory, acquired by the whole country for the use of all, where treasure has been squandered like chaff, and southern blood poured out like water, is sought to be appropriated by one section, because the other chooses to adhere to an institution held not only under the guaranties that brought this confederacy into existence, but under the highest sanction of Heaven. Should we quietly fold our hands under this assumption on the part of the non-slaveholding States, the fate of the South is sealed, the institution of slavery is gone, and its existence is but a question of time. . . . . Your committee are unwilling to anticipate what will be the result of the combined wisdom and joint action of the southern portion of the confederacy on this question; but as an initiatory step to a concert of action on the part of the people of South Carolina, they respectfully recommend, for the adoption of this meeting, the following resolutions :—

"*Resolved*, That the continued agitation of the question of slavery, by the people of the non-slaveholding States, by their legislatures, and by their representatives in Congress, exhibits not only a want of national courtesy, which should always exist between kindred States, but is a palpable violation of good faith towards the slaveholding States, who adopted the present Constitution 'in order to form a more perfect union.'

"*Resolved*, That while we acquiesce in adopting the boundary between the slaveholding and non-slaveholding States, known as the Missouri. Compromise line, we will not submit to any further restriction upon the rights of any southern man to carry his property and his institutions. into territory acquired by southern treasure and by southern blood.

"*Resolved*, That should the Wilmot Proviso, or any other restriction, be applied by Congress to the territories of the United States. south of 36 deg. 30 min. north latitude, we recommend to our representative in

yet further West.   But the ultimate triumph of the
genius of freedom is certain.   In Europe, it shakes the
earth. with mighty tread ; thrones fall before its conquering feet.   While in the eastern continent, kings, armies,
emperors, are impotent before that power, shall a hundred
thousand slaveholders stay it here with a bit of parch-
ment ?

Congress, as the decided opinion of this portion of his district, to leave
his seat in that body, and return home.

"*Resolved,* That we respectfully suggest to both houses of the legislature of South Carolina, to adopt a similar recommendation as to our
senators in Congress from this State.

"*Resolved,* That upon the return home of our senators and representatives in Congress, the legislature of South Carolina should be forthwith
assembled to adopt such measures as the exigency may demand.

"The resolutions were then submitted, *seriatim,* and, together with
the report, were unanimously adopted."

VI.

A DISCOURSE OCCASIONED BY THE DEATH OF JOHN
QUINCY ADAMS. DELIVERED AT THE MELODEON,
IN BOSTON, MARCH 5, 1848.

WITHIN a few days one of the most distinguished statesmen of the age has passed away; a man who has long
been before the public, familiarly known in the new world
and the old. He was one of the prominent monuments of
the age. It becomes us to look at his life, works, and
public character, with an impartial eye; to try him by
the Christian standard. Let me extenuate nothing, add
nothing, and set down nought from any partial love or
partial hate. His individuality has been so marked in a
long life, his good and evil so sharply defined, that one
can scarcely fail to delineate its most important features.

God has made some men great and others little. The
use of great men is to serve the little men; to take care of
the human race, and act as practical interpreters of justice
and truth. This is not the Hebrew rule, nor the heathen,
nor the common rule, only the Christian. The great man
is to be the servant of mankind, not they of him. Perhaps
greatness is always the same thing in kind, differing only
in mode and in form, as well as degree. The great man
has more of human nature than other men, organized in
him. So far as that goes, therefore, he is more me than I
am myself. We feel that superiority in all our intercourse
with great men, whether kings, philosophers, poets, or
saints. In kind we are the same; different in degree.

In nature we find individuals, not orders and genera;
but for our own convenience in understanding and recol-
lecting, we do a little violence to nature, and put the
individuals into classes. In this way we understand better
both the whole and each of its parts. Human nature

furnishes us with individual great men; for convenience
we put them into several classes, corresponding to their
several modes or forms of greatness. It is well to look at
these classes before we examine any one great man; this
will render it easier to see where he belongs and what he
is worth. Actual service is the test of actual greatness;
he who renders, of himself, the greatest actual service to
mankind, is actually the greatest man. There may be
other tests for determining the potential greatness of men,
or the essential; this is the Christian rule for determining
the actual greatness. Let us arrange these men in the
natural order of their work.

First of all, there are great men who discover general
truths, great ideas, universal laws, or invent methods of
thought and action. In this class the vastness of a man's
genius may be measured, and his relative rank ascertained
by the transcendency of his ideas, by the newness of his
truth, by its practical value, and the difficulty of attaining
it in his time, and under his peculiar circumstances. In
literature it is such men who originate thoughts, and put
them into original forms; they are the great men of letters.
In philosophy we meet with such; and they are the great
men of science. Thus Socrates discovered the philosophical method of minute analysis that distinguished his
school, and led to the rapid advance of knowledge in the
various and even conflicting academies, which held this
method in common, but applied it in various ways, well or
ill, and to various departments of human inquiry; thus
Newton discovered the law of gravitation, universal in
nature, and by the discovery did immense service to mankind. In politics we find similar, or analogous men, who
discover yet other laws of God, which bear the same relation to men in society that gravitation bears to the orbs in
heaven, or to the dust and stones in the street; men that
discover the first truths of politics, and teach the true
method of human society. Such are the great men in
politics.

We find corresponding men in religion; men who discover an idea so central that all sectarianism of parties or
of nations seems little in its light; who discover and teach
the universal law which unifies the race, binding man to
man, and men to God; who discover the true method of

religion conducting to natural worship without limitation, to free piety, free goodness, free thought. To my mind such are the greatest of great men, when measured by the transcendency of their doctrine and the service they render to all. By the influence of their idea, letters, philosophy, and politics become nobler and more beautiful, both in their forms and their substance.

Such is the class of discoverers; men who get truth at first hand, truth pertaining either especially to literature, philosophy, politics, religion, or at the same time to each and all of them.

The next class consists of such as organize these ideas, methods, truths, and laws; they concretize the abstract, particularize the general; they apply philosophy to practical purposes, organizing the discoveries of science into a railroad, a mill, a steam-ship, and by their work an idea becomes fact. They organize love into families, justice into a state, piety into a church. Wealth is power, knowledge is power, religion power; they organize all these powers, wealth, knowledge, religion, into common life, making divinity humanity, and that society.

This organizing genius is a very great one, and appears in various forms. One man spreads his thought out on the soil, whitening the land with bread-corn; another applies his mind to the rivers of New England, making them spin and weave for the human race; this man will organize his thought into a machine with one idea, joining together fire and water, iron and wood, animating them into a new creature, ready to do man's bidding; while that with audacious hand steals the lightning of heaven, organizes his plastic thought within that pliant fire, and sends it of his errands to fetch and carry tidings between the ends of the earth.

Another form of this mode of greatness is seen in politics, in organizing men. The man spreads his thought out on mankind, puts men into true relations with one another and with God; he organizes strength, wisdom, justice, love, piety; balances the conflicting forces of a nation, so that each man has his natural liberty as complete as if the only man, yet, living in society, gathers advantages from all the rest. The highest degree of this organizing

power is the genius for legislation, which can enact justice
and eternal right into treaties and statutes, codifying the
divine thought into human laws, making absolute religion
common life and daily custom, and balancing the centripetal power of the mass, with the centrifugal power of the
individual, into a well-proportioned state, as God has
balanced these two conflicting forces into the rhythmic
ellipses above our heads.   It need not be disguised, that
politics are the highest business for men of this class, nor
that a great statesman or legislator is the greatest example
of constructive skill.   It requires some ability to manage
the brute forces of Nature, or to combine profitably nine-
and-thirty clerks in a shop; how much more to arrange
twenty millions of intelligent, free men, not for a special
purpose, but for all the ends of universal life !

Such is the second class of great men; the organizers,
men of constructive heads, who form the institutions of the
world, the little and the great.

The next class consists of men who administer the institutions after they are founded.   To do this effectually and
even eminently, it requires no genius for original organization of truths freshly discovered, none for the discovery
of truths, outright.   It requires only a perception of those
truths, and an acquaintance with the institutions wherein
they have become incarnate; a knowledge of details, of
formulas, and practical methods, united with a strong will
and a practised understanding—what is called a turn for
affairs, tact, or address; a knowledge of routine and an
acquaintance with men.   The successs of such men will
depend on these qualities; they " know the ropes " and
the soundings, the signs of the times; can take advantage
of the winds and the tides.

In a shop, farm, ship, factory, or army, in a Church
or a State, such men are valuable; they cannot be dis-
pensed with; they are wheels to the carriage; without
them cannot a city be inhabited.   They are always
more numerous than both the other classes; more such are
needed, and therefore born.   The American mind, just
now, runs eminently in this direction.   These are not
men of theories, or of new modes of thought or action, but
what are called practical men, men of a few good rules,

men of facts and figures, not so full of ideas as of precedents. They are called common-sense men; not having
too much common-sense to be understood. They are not
likely to be fallen in with far off at sea; quite as seldom
out of their reckoning in ordinary weather. Such men
are excellent statesmen in common times, but in times of
trouble, when old precedents will not suit the new case,
and men must be guided by the nature of man, not his
history, they are not strong enough for the place, and get
pushed off by more constructive heads.

These men are the administrators, or managers. If
they have a little less of practical sense, such men fall a
little below, and turn out only critics, of whom I will not
now stop to discourse.

To have a railroad, there must have been first the discoverers, who found out the properties of wood and iron,
fire and water, and their latent power to carry men over
the earth; next the organizers, who put these elements
together, surveyed the route, planned the structure, set
men to grade the hill, to fill the valley, and pave the road
with iron bars; and then the administrators, who after all
that is done, procure the engines, engineers, conductors,
ticket-distributors, and the rest of the "hands;" they buy
the coal and see it is not wasted, fix the rates of fare,
calculate the savings, and distribute the dividends. The
discoverers and organizers often fare hard in the world,
lean men, ill-clad and suspected, often laughed at, while
the administrator is thought the greater man, because he
rides over their graves and pays the dividends, where the
organizer only called for the assessments, and the discoverer told what men called a dream. What happens in
a railroad happens also in a Church, or a State.

Let us for a moment compare these three classes of great
men. Measured by the test referred to, the discoverers
are the greatest of all. They anticipate the human race,
with long steps, striding before their kind. They learn
not only from the history of man, but man's nature; not
by empirical experience alone, but by a transcendent intuition of truth, now seen as a law, now as an idea. They
are wiser than experience, and by divination through their
nobler nature, know at once what the human race has not
learned in its thousands of years, kindling their lamp at

the central fire now streaming from the sky, now rushing broad-sheeted and terrible as ground-lightning from the earth. Of such men there are but few, especially in the highest mode of this greatness. A single One makes a new world, and men date ages after him.

Next in order of greatness, comes the organizer. He, also, must have great intellect, and character. It is no light work to make thoughts things. It requires mind to make a mill out of a river, bricks, iron, and stone, and set all the Connecticut to spinning cotton. But to construct a State, to harness fittingly twenty million men, animated by such divergent motives, possessing interests so unlike— this is the greatest work of constructive skill. To translate the ideas of the discoverer into institutions, to yoke men together by mere " abstractions," universal laws, and by such yoking save the liberty of all and secure the welfare of each—that is the most creative of poetry, the most constructive of sciences. In modern times, it is said, Napoleon is the greatest example of this faculty; not a discoverer, but an organizer of the highest power and on the largest scale. In human history he seems to have had no superior, perhaps no equal.

Some callings in life afford little opportunity to develop the great qualities above alluded to. How much genius lies latent no man can know; but he that walks familiarly with humble men often stumbles over masses of unsunned gold, where men proud in emptiness looked only for common dust. How many a Milton sits mute and inglorious in his shop; how many a Cromwell rears only corn and oxen for the world's use, no man can know. Some callings help to light, some hide and hinder. But there is none which demands more ability than politics; they develop greatness, if the man have the germ thereof within him. True, in politics, a man may get along with a very little ability, without being a discoverer or an organizer; were it otherwise, we should not be blessed with a very large House, or a crowded Senate. Nay, experience shows that in ordinary times one not even a great administrator may creep up to a high place and hang on there awhile. Few able administrators sit on the thrones of Europe at this day. But if power be in the man, the hand of politics will draw out the spark.

In America, politics more than elsewhere demand greatness, for ours is, in theory, the government of all, for all, and by all. It requires greater range of thought to discover the law for all than for a few; after the discovery thereof it is more difficult to construct a democracy than a monarchy, or an aristocracy, and after that is organized, it is more difficult to administer. It requires more manhood to wield at will " the fierce democratie" of America than to rule England or France; yet the American institutions are germane to human nature, and by that fact are rendered more easy, complicated as they are.

In politics, when the institutions are established, men often think there is no room for discoverers and organizers; that administrators alone are needed, and choose accordingly. But there are ideas well known, not yet organized into institutions: that of free-trade, of peace, of universal freedom, universal education, universal comfort, in a word, the idea of human brotherhood. These wait to be constructed into a State without injustice, without war, without slavery, ignorance, or want. It is hardly true that Infinity is dry of truths, unseen as yet; there are truths enough waiting to be discovered; all the space betwixt us and God is full of ideas, waiting for some Columbus to disclose new worlds. Men are always saying there is no new thing under the sun, but when the discoverer comes, they see their mistake. We want the new eye.

Now, it is quite plain where we are to place the distinguished person of whom I speak. Mr. Adams was not a discoverer; not an organizer. He added no truth to mankind, not known before, and even well known; he made no known truth a fact. He was an administrator of political institutions. Taking the whole land into consideration, comparing him with his competitors, measuring him by his apparent works, at first sight he does not seem very highly eminent in this class of political administrators. Nay, some would set him down, not an administrator so much as a political critic.

Here there is danger of doing him injustice, by neglecting a fact so obvious, that it is seldom seen. Mr. Adams was a northern man, with northern habits, methods, and opinions. By the North, I mean the free States.

The chief business of the North is to get empire over nature; all tends to that. Young men of talents become merchants, merchant-manufacturers, merchant-traders. The object directly aimed at, is wealth; not wealth by plunder, but by productive work. Now, to get dominion over nature, there must be education, universal education, otherwise there is not enough intelligent industry, which alone insures that dominion. With wide-spread intelligence, property will be widely distributed, and, of course, suffrage and civil power will get distributed. All is incomplete without religion. I deny not that these peculiarities of the North, come, also, from other sources, but they all are necessary to attain the chief object thereof— dominion over the material world. The North subdues nature by thought, and holds her powers in thrall. As results of this, see the increase in wealth which is signified by northern railroads, ships, mills, and shops; in the colleges, schools, churches, which arise; see the skill developed in this struggle with nature, the great enterprises which come of that, the movements of commerce, manufactures, the efforts—and successful, too—for the promotion of education, of religion. All is democratic, and becomes more so continually, each descendant founding institutions more liberal than those of the parent State. Men designedly, and, as their business, become merchants, mechanics, and the like; they are politicians by exception, by accident, from the necessity of the case. Few northern men are politicians by profession; they commonly think it better to be a collector or a postmaster, than a Senator, estimating place by money, not power. Northern politicians are bred as lawyers, clergymen, mechanics, farmers, merchants. Political life is an accident, not an end.

In the South the aim is to get dominion over men; so, the whole working population must be in subjection, in slavery. While the North makes brute nature half intelligent, the South makes human nature half brutal, the man becoming a thing. Talent tends to politics, not trade. Young men of ability go to the army or navy, to the public offices, to diplomatic posts, in a word, to politics. They learn to manage men. To do this, they not only learn what men think, but why they think it. The young man of the North seeks a fortune; of the South, a reputation and political power. The politician of the South makes politics the study and work of his whole life; all else is accidental and subordinate. He begins low, but ends high; he mingles with men; has bland and agreeable manners; is frank, honourable, manly, and knows how to persuade.

See the different results of causes so unlike. The North manages the commercial affairs of the land, the ships, mills, farms, and shops; the spiritual affairs, literature, science, morals, education, religion;—writes, calculates, instructs, and preaches. But the South manages the political affairs, and has free-trade or tariff, war or peace, just as she will. Of the eight Presidents who were elected in fifty years, only three were northern men. Each of them has retired from office, at the end of a single term, in possession of a fortune, but with little political influence. Each of the five southern Presidents has been twice elected; only one of them was rich. There is no accident in all this. The State of Rhode Island has men that can administer the Connecticut or the Mississippi; that can organize Niagara into a cotton factory; yes, that can get dominion over the ocean and the land: but the State of South Carolina has men that can manage the Congress, can rule the North and South, and make the nation do their bidding.

So the South succeeds in politics, but grows poor, and the North fails in politics, but thrives in commerce and the arts. There great men turn to politics, here to trade. It is so in time of peace, but, in the day of trouble, of storms, of revolution like the old one, men of tall heads will come up from the ships and the shops, the farms and the colleges of the North, born discoverers and organizers, the aristocracy of God, and sit down in the nation's councils to control the State. The North made the revolution, furnished the men, the money, the ideas, and the occasion for putting them into form. At the making of the Constitution, the South out-talked the North; put in such claims as it saw fitting, making the best bargain it could, violating the ideas of the Revolution, and getting the North, not only to consent to slavery, but to allow it to be represented in Congress itself. Now, the South breaks the Constitution just when it will, puts northern sailors in its gaols, and the North dares not complain, but bears it "with a patient

shrug." An eastern merchant is great on a southern exchange, makes cotton rise or fall, but no northern politician has much weight at the South, none has ever been
twice elected President. The North thinks it is a great
thing to get an inoffensive northern man as Speaker, in
the House of Representatives. The South is an aristocracy, which the democracy of the North would not
tolerate a year, were it at the North itself. Now it rules
the land, has the northern masses, democrats and whigs,
completely under its thumb. Does the South say, " Go,"
they hasten; "Come," they say, "Here we are;" "Do
this," they obey in a moment; "Whist," there is not a
mouse stirring in all the North. Does the South say
"Annex," it is done; "Fight," men of the North put on
the collar, lie lies, issue their proclamations, enrol their
soldiers, and declare it is moral treason for the most insignificant clergyman to preach against the war.

All this needs to be remembered in judging of Mr.
Adams. True he was regularly bred to politics, and "to
the manor born;" but he was a New England man, with
northern notions, northern habits, and though more than
fifty years in public life, yet he seems to have sought the
object of New England far more than the-object of the
South. Measure his greatness by his service; but that is
not to be measured by immediate and apparent success.

In a notice so brief as this I can say but little of the
details of Mr. Adams's life, and purposely pass over many
things, dwelling mainly on such as are significant of his
character. He was born at Quincy, the 11th of July,
1767; in 1777 he went to Europe with his father, then
Minister to France. He remained in Europe most of the
time, his powers developing with rapidity and promise of
future greatness, till 1785, when he returned and entered
the junior class in Harvard College. In 1787, he gradu-
ated with distinguished honours. He studied law at Newburyport, with Judge Parsons, till 1790, and was a lawyer
in Boston, till 1794.

That may be called the period of his education. He
enjoyed the advantages of a residence abroad, which
enabled him to acquire a knowledge of foreign languages,
modes of life, and habits of thought. His father's position

brought the son in contact with the ablest men of the age. He was Secretary of the American minister to Russia at the age of fourteen. He early became acquainted with Franklin and Jefferson, men who had a powerful influence on his youthful mind. For three years he was a student with Judge Parsons, a very remarkable man. These years, from 1767 to 1794, form a period marked by intense mental activity in America and in Europe. The greatest subjects which claim human attention, the laws that lie at the foundation of society, the State, the church, and the family, were discussed as never before. Mr. Adams drew in liberty and religion from his mother's breast. His cradle rocked with the Revolution. When eight years old, from a hill-top hard by his house he saw the smoke of Charlestown, burning at the command of the oppressor. The lullaby of his childhood was the roar of cannon at Lexington and Bunker Hill. He was born in the gathering of the storm, of a family that felt the blast, but never bent thereto; he grew up in its tumult. Circumstances like these make their mark on the character.

His attention was early turned to the most important matters. In 1793, he wrote several papers in the "Centinel," at Boston, on neutral rights, advising the American government to remain neutral in the quarrel between France, our ally, and others; the papers attracted the attention of Washington, who appointed the author Minister to Holland. He remained abroad in various diplomatic services in that country, in Russia and England, till 1801, when he was recalled by his father, and returned home. It was an important circumstance, that he was abroad during that time when the nation divided into two great parties. He was not called on to take sides with either; he had a vantage ground whence he could overlook both, approve their good and shun their evil. The effect of this is abundantly evident in all his life. He was not dyed in the wool by either political party,—the moral sense of the man drowned in the process of becoming a federalist or a democrat.

In 1802, he was elected to the Senate of Massachusetts, yet not wholly by the votes of one party. In 1803, he was chosen to the Senate of the United States. In the Massachusetts Legislature he was not a strict party man;

he was not elected to the Senate by a strictly party vote. In 1806, he was inaugurated as Professor of Rhetoric and Oratory at Harvard University, and continued in that office about three years. In 1808, he resigned his place in the Senate. In 1809, he was sent by Mr. Madison as Minister to Russia, and remained abroad in various ministries and commissions, till 1817, when he returned, and became Secretary of State under Mr. Monroe. This office he filled till he became President, in 1825. In 1829, failing of re-election, he retired to private life. In 1831, he was elected as one of the Representatives to Congress from Massachusetts, and continued there till his death, the first President that ever sat in an American Congress.

It will be fifty-four years the thirtieth of next May, since he began his public career. What did he aim at in that long period? At first sight, it is easy to see the aim of some of the conspicuous men of America. It has obviously been the aim of Mr. Clay to build up the "American System," by the establishment of protective duties; that of Mr. Calhoun to establish free trade, leaving a man to buy where he can buy cheapest, and sell where he can sell dearest. In respect to these matters the two are exactly opposite to one another—antithetic as the poles. But each has also, and obviously, another aim,—to build up the institution of slavery in the South. In this they agree, and if I understand them aright, this is the most important political design of each; for which Mr. Calhoun would forego even free trade, and Mr. Clay would "compromise" even a tariff. Looked at in reference to their aims, there is a certain continuity of action in both these gentlemen. I speak not now of another object which both have equally and obviously aimed at; not of the personal, but the political object.

At first sight, it does not appear that Mr. Adams had any definite scheme of measures which he aimed to establish; there is no obvious unity of idea, or continuity of action, that forces itself upon the spectator. He does not seem to have studied the two great subjects of our political economy, finance and trade, very deeply, or even with any considerable width of observation or inquiry; he had no financial or commercial hobby. He has worked with every party, and against every party; all have claimed, none

held him. Now he sides with the federalists, then with
the democrats; now he opposes France, showing that her
policy is that of pirates; now he contends against England;
now he works in favour of General Jackson, who put down
the nullification of South Carolina with a rough hand;
then he opposes the general in his action against the
Bank; now he contends for the Indians, then for the
Negroes; now attacks Masonry, and then Free Trade. He
speaks in favour of claiming and holding "the whole of
Oregon;" then against annexing Texas.

But there is one sentiment which runs through all his
life: an intense love of freedom for all men; one idea, the
idea that each man has unalienable rights. These are
what may be called the American sentiment, and the
American idea; for they lie at the basis of American
institutions, except the "patriarchal," and shine out in all
our history—I should say, our early history. These two
form the golden thread on which Mr. Adams's jewels are
strung. Love of human freedom in its widest sense is the
most marked and prominent thing in his character. This
explains most of his actions. Studied with this in mind,
his life is pretty consistent. This explains his love of the
Constitution. He early saw the peculiarity of the American
government; that it rested in theory on the natural rights
of man, not on a compact, not on tradition, but on somewhat anterior to both, on the unalienable rights universal
in man, and equal in each. He looked on the American
Constitution as an attempt to organize these rights; resting, therefore, not on force, but natural law; not on power,
but right. But with him the Constitution was not an
idol; it was a means, not an end. He did more than expound it; he went back of the Constitution, to the Declaration of Independence, for the ideas of the Constitution;
yes, back of the Declaration to Human Nature and the
Laws of God, to legitimate these ideas. The Constitution
is a compromise between those ideas and institutions and
prejudices existing when it was made; not an idol, but a
servant. He saw that the Constitution is "not the work
of eternal justice, ruling through the people," but the work
" of man; frail, fallen, imperfect man, following the dictates
of his nature, and aspiring to be perfect."* Though a

* See *Social Compact*, etc. Providence, 1848, p. 31, *et al.*

"constitutionalist," he did not worship the Constitution. He was much more than a "defender of the Constitution,"—a defender of Human Rights.

Mr. Adams had this American sentiment and idea in an heroic degree. Perhaps no political man now living has expressed them so fully. With a man like him, not very genial or creative, having no great constructive skill, and not without a certain pugnacity in his character, this sentiment and idea would naturally develop themselves in a negative form, that of opposition to Wrong, more often than in the positive form of direct organization of the Right; would lead to criticism oftener than to creation. Especially would this be the case if other men were building up institutions in opposition to this idea. In him they actually take the form of what he called "The unalienable right of resistance to oppression." His life furnishes abundant instances of this. He thought the Indians were unjustly treated, cried out against the wrong; when President, endeavoured to secure justice to the Creeks in Georgia, and got into collision with Governor Troup. He saw, or thought he saw, that England opposed the American idea, both in the new world and the old. In his zeal for freedom he sometimes forgot the great services of England in that same cause, and hated England, hated her with great intensity of hatred, hated her political policy, her monarchy, and her aristocracy, mocked at the madness of her king, for he thought England stood in the way of freedom.* Yet he loved the English name and the English blood, was "proud of being himself descended from that stock," thinking it worth noting, "that Chatham's language was his mother tongue, and Wolfe's great name compatriot with his own." He confessed no nation had done more for the cause of human improvement. He loved the Common Law of England, putting it far above the Roman Law, perhaps not without doing a little injustice to the latter.† The common law was a rude and

* See *Address at Washington*, 4th of July, 1821. Second Edition, Cambridge, *passim*.

† Reference is made to his *speech in the House of Representatives*, May 8th and 9th, 1840. (Boston, 1840.) It is a little remarkable that the false principle of the common law, on which Mr. Adams was commenting, as laid down by Blackstone, is corrected by a writer, M. Pothier, who rests on the civil law for his authority. See pp. 6–8, and 20, 21.

barbarous code. But human liberty was there; a trial by
jury was there; the habeas corpus was there. It was the
law of men "regardful of human rights."

This sentiment led him to defend the right of petition
in the House of Representatives, as no other man had
dared to do. He cared not whether it was the petition of
a majority, or a minority; of men or women, free men or
slaves. It might be a petition to remove him from a committee, to expel him from the House, a petition to dissolve
the Union—he presented it none the less. To him there
was but one nature in all, man or woman, bond or free, and
that was human nature, the most sacred thing on earth.
Each human child had unalienable rights, and though that
child was a beggar or slave, had rights, which all the
power in the world, bent into a single arm, could not
destroy nor abate, though it might ravish away. This
induced him to attempt to procure the right of suffrage
for the coloured citizens of the District of Columbia.

This sentiment led him to oppose tyranny in the House
of Representatives, the tyranny of the majority. In one
of his juvenile essays, published in 1791, contending
against a highly popular work, he opposed the theory
that a State has the right to do what it pleases, declaring
it had no right to do wrong.* In his old age he had not
again to encounter the empty hypothesis of Thomas Paine,
but the substantial enactment of the "Representatives" of
the people of the United States. The hypothesis was
trying to become a fact. The South had passed the infamous Gag-Law, which a symbolical man from New
Hampshire had presented, though it originated with
others.† By that law the mouth of the North was completely stopped in Congress, so that not one word could be
said about the matter of slavery.

The North was quite willing to have it stopped, for it
did not care to speak against slavery, and the gag did not
stop the mouth of the Northern purse. You may take
away from the North its honour, if you can find it; may
take away its rights; may imprison its free citizens in the

* *Answer to Paine's Rights of Man* (London, 1793), originally published
in the Columbian Centinel. The London Edition bears the name of *John
Adams* on the title-page.
† Mr. Atherton.

jails of Louisiana and the Carolinas; yes, may invade the
"Sacred soil of the North," and kidnap a man out of
Boston itself, within sight of Faneuil Hall, and the North
will not complain; will bear it with that patient shrug,
waiting for yet further indignities. Only when the
Northern purse is touched, is there an uproar. If the
postmaster demands silver for letters, there is instant
alarm; the repeal of a tariff rouses the feelings, and an
embargo once drove the indignant North to the perilous
edge of rebellion! Mr. Adams loved his dollars as well as
most New England men; he looked out for their income
as well; guarded as carefully against their outgo; though
conscientiously upright in all his dealings, kind and hos-
pitable, he has never been proved generous, and generosity
is the commonest virtue of the North; is said to have been
"close," if not mean. He loved his dollars as well as most
men, but he loved justice more; honour more; freedom
more; the Unalienable Rights of man far more.

He looked on the Constitution as an instrument for the
defence of the Rights of man. The government was to
act as the people had told how. The Federal government
was not sovereign; the State government was not sovereign;* neither was a court of ultimate appeal;—but the
People was sovereign; had the right of Eminent Domain
over Congress and the Constitution, and making that, had
set limits to the government. He guarded therefore
against all violation of the Constitution, as a wrong done
to the people; he would not overstep its limits in a bad
cause; not even in a good one. Did Mr. Jefferson obtain
Louisiana by a confessed violation of the Constitution,
Mr. Adams would oppose the purchase of Louisiana, and
was one of the six senators who voted against it. Making
laws for that Territory, he wished to extend the trial by
jury to all criminal prosecutions, while the law limited
that form of trial to capital offences. Before that Territory had a representative in Congress, the American
government wished to collect a revenue there. Mr. Adams
opposed that too. It was "assuming a dangerous power;"
it was government without the consent of the governed,
and therefore an unjust government. "All exercise of

---

* See *Oration at Quincy*, 1831, p. 12, *et seq.* (Boston, 1831.)

human authority must be under the limitation of right and wrong." All other power is despotic, and "in defiance of the laws of nature and of God."*

This love of freedom led him to hate and oppose the tyranny of the strong over the weak, to hate it most in its worst form; to hate American Slavery, doubtless the most infamous form of that tyranny now known amongst the nations of Christendom, and perhaps the most disgraceful thing on earth. Mr. Adams called slavery a vessel of dis- honour so base that it could not be named in the Consti- tution with decency. In 1805, he wished to lay a duty on the importation of slaves, and was one of five senators who voted to that effect. He saw the power of this institution— the power of money and the power of votes which it gives to a few men. He saw how dangerous it was to the Union; to American liberty, to the cause of man. He saw that it trod three millions of men down to the dust, counting souls but as cattle. He hated nothing as he hated this; fought against nothing so manfully. It was the lion in the path- way of freedom, which frightened almost all the politicians of the North and the East and the West, so that they forsook that path; a lion whose roar could wellnigh silence the forum and the bar, the pulpit and the press; a lion who rent the Constitution, trampled under foot the Decla- ration of Independence, and tore the Bible to pieces. Mr. Adams was ready to rouse up this lion, and then to beard him in his den. Hating slavery, of course he op- posed whatever went to strengthen its power; opposed Mr. Atherton's Gag-law; opposed the annexation of Texas; opposed the Mexican war; and, wonderful to tell, actually voted against it, and never took back his vote.

When Secretary of State, this same feeling led him to oppose conceding to the British the right of searching American vessels supposed to be concerned in the slave- trade, and when Representative to oppose the repeal of the law giving "protection" to American sailors. It appeared also in private intercourse with men. No matter what was a man's condition, Mr. Adams treated him as an equal.

This devotion to freedom and the unalienable rights of

* The *Social Compact*, etc., etc. (Providence, 1842). p. 24.

man, was the most important work of his life. Compared with some other political men, he seems inconsistent, because he now opposes one evil, then its opposite evil. But his general course is in this direction, and, when viewed in respect to this idea, seems more consistent than that of Mr. Webster, or Calhoun, or Clay, when measured by any great principle. This appears in his earlier life. In 1802, he became a member of the Massachusetts Senate. The majority of the General Court were federalists. It was a time of intense political excitement, the second year of Mr. Jefferson's administration. The custom is well known —to take the whole of the Governor's Council from the party which has a majority in the General Court. On the 27th of May, 1802, Mr. Adams stood up for the rights of the minority. He wanted some anti-federalists in the Council of Governor Strong, and as Senator threw his first vote to secure that object. Such was the first legislative action of John Quincy Adams. In the House of Representatives, in 1831, the first thing he did was to present fifteen petitions for the abolition of slavery in the District of Columbia, though, from constitutional scruples, opposed to granting the petitions. The last public act of his life was this:—The question was before the House on giving medals to the men distinguished in the Mexican war; the minority opposing it wanted more time for debate; the previous question was moved, Mr. Adams voted for the last time,—voted "No," with unusual emphasis; the great loud No of a man going home to God full of "The unalienable right of resistance to oppression," its emphatic word on his dying lips. There were the beginning, the middle, and the end, all three in the same spirit, all in favour of mankind; a remarkable unity of action in his political drama.

Somebody once asked him, What are the recognized principles of politics? Mr. Adams answered that there were none: the recognized precepts are bad ones, and so not principles. But, continued the inquirer, is not this a good one—To seek "The greatest good of the greatest number?" No, said he, that is the worst of all, for it looks specious while it is ruinous. What shall become of the minority, in that case? This is the only principle,—"To seek the greatest good of all."

I do not say there were no exceptions to this devotion to freedom in a long life; there are some passages in his history which it is impossible to justify, and hard to excuse. In early life he was evidently ambitious of place, and rank, and political power. I must confess, it seems to me, at some times, he was not scrupulous enough about the means of attaining that place and power. He has been much censured for his vote in favour of the Embargo, in 1807. His vote, howsoever unwise, may easily have been an honest vote. To an impartial spectator at this day, perhaps it will be evidently so. His defence of it I cannot think an honest defence, for in that he mentions arguments as impelling him to his vote which could scarcely have been present to his mind at the time, and, if they were his arguments then, were certainly kept in silence—they did not appear in the debate,* they were not referred to in the President's message.†

I am not to praise Mr. Adams simply because he is dead; what is wrong before is wrong after death. It is no merit to die; shall we tell lies about him because he is dead? No, the Egyptian people scrutinized and judged their kings after death—much more should we our fellow-citizens, intrusted with power to serve the State. "A lavish and undistinguishing eulogium is not praise." I know what coals of terrible fire lie under my feet, as I speak of this matter, and how thin and light is the coat of ashes deposited there in forty years; how easily they are blown away at the slightest breath of "Hartford Convention," or the "Embargo," and the old flame of political animosity blazes forth anew, while the hostile forms of

* See Pickering's *Letter to Governor Sullivan, on the Embargo.* Boston, 1808. John Quincy Adams's *Letter to the Hon. H. G. Otis*, etc. Boston, 1808. Pickering's *Interesting Correspondence*, 1808. *Review of the Correspondence between the Hon. John Adams and the late William Cunningham*, etc., 1824. But see, also, Mr. Adams's "Appendix" to the above letter, published *sixteen* years after the vote on the embargo. Baltimore, 1824. Mr. Pickering's *Brief Remarks on the Appendix.* August, 1824.

† Reference is here made to British "*Orders in Council*" of Nov. 22nd, 1807. They were not officially made known to the American Congress till Feb. 7th, 1808. They were, however, published in the National Intelligencer, the morning on which the message was sent to the Senate, Dec. 18th, 1807, but were not mentioned in that document nor in the debate.

" federalists " and " democrats " come back to light. I
would not disquiet those awful shades, nor bring them up
again. But a word must be said. The story of the
embargo is well known: the President sent his message to
the Senate recommending it, and accompanied with several
documents. The message was read and assigned to a
committee; the ordinary rule of business was suspended;
the bill was reported by the committee; drafted, debated,
engrossed, and completely passed through all its stages,
the whole on the same day, in secret session, and in about
four hours! Yet it was a bill that involved the whole commerce of the country, and prostrated that commerce, seriously affecting the welfare of hundreds of thousands of men.
Eight hundred thousand tons of shipping were doomed to
lie idle and rot in port. The message came on Friday.
Some of the Senators wanted yet further information and
more time for debate, at least for consideration,—till
Monday. It could not be! Till Saturday, then. No;
the bill must pass now, no man sleeping on that question.
Mr. Adams was the most zealous for passing the bill. In
that " debate," if such it can be called, while opposing a
postponement for further information and reflection, he
said, " The President has recommended the measure on his
high responsibility; I would *not consider*, I would *not
deliberate*; I would *act*. Doubtless the *President possesses
such further information as will justify the measure!*"*
To my mind, that is the worst act of his public life; I
cannot justify it. I wish I could find some reasonable
excuse for it. What had become of the " sovereignty of
the people," the " unalienable right of resistance to
oppression?" Would *not consider*; would *not deliberate*;
would *act* without doing either; leave it all to the " high
responsibility" of the President, with a " doubtless " he
has " further information" to justify the measure! It
was a shame to say so; it would have disgraced a Senator

* I copy this from the first letter of Mr. Pickering. Mr. Adams wrote
a letter (to H. G. Otis) in reply to this of Mr. Pickering, but said nothing
respecting the words charged upon him; but in 1824, in an Appendix to
that letter, he denies that he expressed the " sentiment" which Mr.
Pickering charged him with. But he *does not deny the words themselves*.
They rest on the authority of Mr. Pickering, his colleague in the Senate,
a strong party man, it is true, perhaps not much disposed to conciliation,
but à man of most unquestionable veracity. The " sentiment" speaks for
itself.

in St. Petersburg.   Why not have the "further information" laid before the Senate?   What would Mr. Adams
have said, if President Jackson, Tyler, or Polk, had sent
such a message, and some Senator or Representative had
counselled submissive action, without considering, without
deliberation?   With what appalling metaphors would he
describe such a departure from the first duty of a statesman; how would the tempestuous eloquence of that old
patriot shake the Hall of Congress till it rung again, and
the nation looked up with indignation in its face!   It is
well known what Mr. Adams said in 1834, when Mr. Polk,
in the House of Representatives, seemed over-laudatory of
the President: "I shall never be disposed to interfere
with any member who shall rise on this floor and pronounce a panegyric upon the chief magistrate.

'No, let the candied tongue lick absurd pomp,
And crook the pregnant hinges of the knee
Where thrift may follow fawning.'"

Yet the future of Mr. Polk was not so obvious in 1834, as
the reward of Mr. Adams in 1808.

This act is particularly glaring in Mr. Adams.   The
North often sends men to Washington who might have
done it without any great inconsistency; men, too, not so
remarkable for infirmity in the head, as for that less
pardonable weakness in the knees and the neck; men that
bend to power "right or wrong."   Mr. Adams was not
afflicted with that weakness, and so the more to be censured
for this palpable betrayal of a trust so important.   I wish
I could find some excuse for it.   He was forty years old;
not very old, but old enough to know better.   His defence
made the matter worse.   The Massachusetts Legislature
disapproved of his conduct; chose another man to succeed
him in the Senate.   Then Mr. Adams resigned his seat,
and soon after was sent minister to Russia, as he himself
subsequently declared,* "in consequence of the support he
had for years given to the measures of Mr. Jefferson's
administration against Great Britain."   But his father
said of that mission of his son, "Aristides is banished
because he is too just."†   It is easy to judge of the temper

* Adams's *Remarks in the House of Representatives*, Jan. 5, 1846.
† *Correspondence between the Hon John Adams and the late William
Cunningham, Esq.*   Boston, 1823.   Letter xliii. p. 150.

of the times, when such words as those of the father could
be said on such an occasion, and that by a man who had
been President of the United States! When a famine
occurs, disease appears in the most hideous forms; men
go back to temporary barbarism. In times of political strife,
such diseases appear of the intellectual and moral powers.
No man who did not live in those times can fully understand the obliquity of mind and moral depravity which
then displayed themselves amongst those otherwise without
reproach. Says Mr. Adams himself, referring to that
period, " Imagination in her wildest vagaries can scarcely
conceive the transformation of temper, the obliquities of
intellect, the perversions of moral principle, effected by
junctures of nigh and general excitement." However, it
must be confessed that this, though not the only instance
of injustice, is the only case of servile compliance with the
Executive to be found in the whole life of the man. It
was a grievous fault, but grievously did he answer it; and
if a long life of unfaltering resistance to every attempt at
the assumption of power is fit atonement, then the expia-
tion was abundantly made.

About the same time, Mr. Adams was chairman of a
committee of the Senate, appointed to consider the case of
a Senator from Ohio. His conduct, on that occasion, has
been the theme of violent attack, and defence as violent.
To the calm spectator, at this day, his conduct seems
unjustifiable, inconsistent with the counsels of justice,
which, though moving with her " Pace of snail," looks
always towards the right, and will not move out of her
track, though the heavens fall.

While Mr. Adams was President, Hayti became free;
but he did not express any desire that the United States
should acknowledge her independence, and receive her
minister at Washington,— an African plenipotentiary.
In his message,* he says, "There are circumstances that
have hitherto forbidden the acknowledgment," and mentions "additional reasons for withholding that acknowledgment." In the instructions to the American functionary, sent to the celebrated Congress of Panama, it is
said, the President "is not prepared now to say that
Hayti ought to be recognized as an independent sovereign

* March 15th, 1826.

power;" he "does not think it would be proper at this
time to recognize it as a new State." He was unwilling
to consent to the independence of Cuba, for fear of an
insurrection of her slaves, and the effect at home. The
duty of the United States would be "To defend themselves
against the contagion of such near and dangerous examples," that would "constrain them . . . . to employ all
means necessary to their security." That is, the President
would be constrained to put down the blacks in Cuba, who
were exercising "the unalienable right of resistance to
oppression," for fear the blacks in the United States would
discover that they also were men, and had "unalienable
rights!" Had he forgotten the famous words, "Resistance to tyrants is obedience to God?" The defence of
such language on such an occasion is, that Mr. Adams's
eyes were not yet open to the evil of slavery. That is a
good defence, if true. To me it seems a true defence.
Even great men do not see everything. In 1800, Fisher
Ames, while delivering the eulogy on General Washington,
censured even the British government, beeause, "in the
wilds of Africa it obstructed the commerce in slaves!"
No man is so wise as mankind. It must be confessed that
Mr. Adams, while Secretary of State, and again, while
President, showed no hostility to the institution of slavery.
His influence all went the other way. He would repress
the freedom of the blacks, in the West Indies, lest American slavery should be disturbed, and its fetters broke;
he would not acknowledge the independence of Hayti, he
would urge Spain to make peace with her descendants, for
the same reason—"not for those new republics," but lest
the negroes in Cuba and Porto Rico should secure their
freedom. He negociated with England, and she paid the
United States more than a million of dollars* for the
fugitive slaves who took refuge under her flag during the
late war. Mr. Adams had no scruples about receiving
the money during his administration. An attempt was
repeatedly made by his secretary, Mr. Clay, through Mr.
Gallatin, and then through Mr. Barbour, to induce
England to restore the "fugitive slaves who had taken
refuge in the Canadian provinces," who, escaping from

* See Mr. Adams's *Message*, Dec. 2, 1828. The exact sum was
$1,197,422.18.

the area of freedom, seek the shelter of the British crown.[*]
Nay, he negociated a treaty with Mexico, which bound
her to deliver up fugitive slaves, escaping from the United
States—a treaty which the Mexican Congress refused to
ratify! Should a great man have known better? Great
men are not always wise. Afterwards, public attention
was called to the matter; humble men gave lofty counsel;
Mr. Adams used different language, and recommended
different measures. But long before that, on the 7th of
December, 1804, Mr. Pickering, his colleague in the
Senate of the United States, offered a resolution, for the
purpose of amending the Constitution, so as to apportion
representatives, and direct taxes among the States, according to their free inhabitants.

But there are other things in Mr. Adams's course and
conduct, which deserve the censure of a good man. One
was, the attempt to justify the conduct of England, in her
late war with China, when she forced her opium upon the
barbarians with the bayonet. To make out his case, he
contended that "In the celestial empire . . . . the patriarchal system of Sir Robert Filmer, flourished in all its
glory," and the Chinese claimed superior dignity over all
others; they refused to hold equal and reciprocal commercial intercourse with other nations, and "it is time
this enormous outrage upon the rights of human nature,
and the first principles of the laws of nations, should
cease."[†] It is true, the Chinese were "barbarians;" true,
the English carried thither the Bible and Christianity, at
least their own Christianity. But, even by the law of
nations, letting alone the law of nature, the barbarians
had a right to repel both Bible and Christianity, when
they came in a contraband shape—that of opium and
cannon balls. To justify this outrage of the strong against
the weak, he quite forgets his old antipathy to England,
his devotion to human freedom, and the sovereignty of the
people, calling the cause of England "a righteous cause."

* See Mr. Clay's Letter to Mr. A. H. Everett, April 27th, 1825; to
Mr. Middleton, respecting the intervention of the Emperor of Russia,
May 10th, and Dec. 26th, 1825; to Mr. Gallatin, May 10th, and June
19th, 1826, and Feb. 24th, 1827. *Executive Documents*, Second Session
of the 20th Congress, Vol. I.

† Report of Mr. Adams's *Lecture on the Chinese War*, in the Boston
Atlas, for Dec. 4th and 5th, 1841.

He defended the American claim to the whole of Oregon, up to 54° 40'. He did not so much undertake to make out a title to either, by the law of nature or of nations, but cut the matter short, and claimed the whole of Oregon, on the strength of the first chapter of Genesis. This was the argument: God gave mankind dominion over all the earth;* between Christian nations, the command of the Creator lays the foundation of all titles to land, of titles to territory, of titles to jurisdiction. Then in the Psalms,† God gives the "uttermost part of the earth for a possession" to the Messiah, as the representative of all mankind, who held the uttermost parts of the earth in chief. But the Pope, as head of the visible church, was the representative of Christ, and so, holding under him, had the right to give to any king or prelate, authority to subdue barbarous nations, possess their territory, and convert them to Christianity. In 1493, the Pope, in virtue of the above right, gave the American continent to the Spanish monarchs, who, in time, sold their title to the people of the United States. That title may be defective, as the Pope may not be the representative of Christ, and so the passage in the Psalms will not help the American claim, but then the United States will hold under the first clause in the Testament of God, that is, in Genesis. The claim of Great Britain is not valid, for she does not want the land for the purpose specified in that clause of the Testament, to "replenish the earth and subdue it." She wants it, "that she may keep it open as a hunting-ground," while the United States want it, that it may grow into a great nation, and become a free and sovereign republic.‡

This strange hypothesis, it seems, lay at the bottom of his defence of the British in their invasion of China. It would have led him, if consistent, to claim also the greater part of Mexico. But, as he did not publicly declare his opinion on that matter, no more need be said concerning it.

Such was the most prominent idea in his history; such

* Genesis i. 26–28. † Psalms ii. 6–8.
‡ See Mr. Adams's *Speech on Oregon*, Feb. 9th, 1846. Arguments somewhat akin to this, may be found also in the oration delivered at Newburyport, before cited.

the departures from it. Let us look at other events in his
life. While President, the most important object of his
administration was the promotion of internal improvements, especially the internal communication between the
States. For this purpose the government lent its aid in
the construction of roads and canals, and a little more than
four millions of dollars were devoted to this work in his
administration. On the 4th of July, 1828, he helped
break ground for the Chesapeake and Ohio canal, thinking
it an important event in his life. He then said there were
three great steps in the progress of America. The first
was the Declaration of Independence and the achievement
thereof; the second, the union of the whole country under
the Constitution; but the third was more arduous than
both of the others: "It is," said he, "the adaptation of
the powers, physical, moral, and intellectual, of the whole
Union, to the improvement of its own condition; of its
moral and *political* condition, by wise and liberal institutions; by the cultivation of the understanding and the
heart; by academies, schools, and learned institutions; by
the pursuit and patronage of learning and the arts; of its
physical condition, by associated labour to improve the
bounties and supply the deficiencies of nature; to stem the
torrent in its course; to level the mountain with the plain;
to disarm and fetter the raging surge of the ocean."*
He faithfully adhered to these words in his administration.

He was careful never to exceed the powers which the
Constitution prescribed for him. He thought the acquisition of Louisiana was "accomplished by a flagrant violation of the Constitution,"† and himself guarded against
such violations. He revered the God of Limits, who, in
the Roman mythology, refused to give way or remove,
even for Jupiter himself. No man was ever more conscientious on that ground. To him the Constitution meant
something; his oath to keep it meant something.

No great political event occurred in his administration;
the questions which now vex the country had not arisen.
There was no quarrel between freedom and slavery; no
man in Congress ventured to denounce slavery as a crime;

* *Address on breaking ground for the Chesapeake and Ohio Canal.*
† *Jubilee of the Constitution*, p. 99.

the African slave-trade was thought wrong, not the slavery which caused it. Party lines, obliterated under Mr. Monroe's administration, were viewed and marked with a good deal of care and exactness; but the old lines could not be wholly restored. Mr. Adams was not the President of a section of the country; not the President of a party, but of the nation. He favoured no special interest of a class, to the injury of another class. He did not reward his friends, nor punish his foes; the party of the spoils, patent or latent at all times, got no spoils from him. He never debauched his country by the removal and appointment of officers. Had he done otherwise, done as all his successors have done, used his actual power to promote his own ambition, no doubt he might have been re-elected. But he could not stoop to manage men in that way. No doubt he desired a re-election, and saw the method and means to effect that; but conscience said, "It is not right." He forbore, lost his election, and gained—we shall soon see what he gained.

On the 19th of July, 1826, at a public dinner at Edgefield Court-house, South Carolina, Mr. McDuffie said, "Mr. Adams came into power upon principles utterly subversive of the republican system; substituting the worst species of aristocracy, that of speculating politicians and office-hunters, in the place of a sound and wholesome republican democracy." When Mr. Adams retired from office, he could remember, with the virtuous Athenian, that no man had put on mourning for him because unjustly deprived of his post. Was an office-holder or an office-wanter a political friend of Mr. Adams, that did not help him; a foe, that did not hinder. He looked only to the man's ability and integrity. I wish it was no praise to say these things; but it is praise I dare not apply to any other man since Washington. Mr. Adams once said, "There is no official act of the chief magistrate, however momentous, or however minute, but it should be traceable to a dictate of duty, pointing to the welfare of the people." That was his executive creed.

As a public servant, he had many qualities seldom united in the same person. He was simple, and unostentatious; he had none of the airs of a great man; seemed humble, modest, and retiring ; caring much for the substance of manhood, he let the show take care of itself. He carried the simplicity of a plain New England man into the President's house, spending little in its decorations—about one fourth, it is said, of the amount of his successor. In his house-keeping, public or private, there was only one thing much to be boasted of and remarked upon : strange to say, that was the master of the house. He was never eclipsed by his own brass and mahogany. He had what are called democratic habits, and served himself in preference to being served by others. He treated all that were about him with a marked deference and courtesy, carrying his respect for human rights into the minutest details of common life.

He was a model of diligence, though not, perhaps, very systematic. His State papers, prepared while he was Minister, Secretary, or Member of Congress, his numerous orations and speeches, though not always distinguished for that orderly arrangement of parts which is instinctive with minds of a high philosophical character, are yet astonishing for their number, and the wide learning they display. He was well acquainted with the classic and most modern languages ; at home in their literature. He was surprisingly familiar with modern history ; perhaps no political man was so thoroughly acquainted with the political history of America, and that of Christian Europe for the last two hundred years. He was widely read and profoundly skilled in all that relates to diplomacy, and to international law. He was fond of belleslettres, and commented on Shakspeare more like a professor than a layman in that department. Few theologians in America, it is said, were so widely read in their peculiar lore as he. He had read much, remembered much, understood much. However, he seems to have paid little attention to physical science, and perhaps less to metaphysical. His speeches and his conversation, though neither brilliant, nor rich in ideas, astonished young men with an affluence of learning, which seemed marvellous in one all his life devoted to practical affairs. But this is a trifle : to achieve that, nothing is needed but health, diligence, memory, and a long life. Mr. Adams had all these requisites.

He had higher qualities : he loved his country, perhaps

no man more so; he had patriotism in an heroic degree, yet was not thereby blinded to humanity. He thought it a vital principle of human society, that each nation should contribute to the happiness of all; and, therefore, that no nation should "regulate its conduct by the exclusive or even the paramount consideration of its own interest."* Yet he loved his country, his whole country; and when she was in the wrong he told her so, because he loved her. This, said he, would be a good sentiment: "Our country! May she be always successful; but, whether successful or not, may she be always in the right." He saw the faults of America, saw the corruption of the American government. He did not make gain by this in private, but set an honest face against it.

He was a conscientious man. This peculiarity is strongly marked in most of his life. He respected the limit between right and wrong. He did not think it unworthy of a statesman to refer to moral principles, to the absolutely right. I do not mean to say, that, in his whole life, there was no departure from the strict rule of duty. I have mentioned already some examples, but kept one more for this place: he pursued persons with a certain vindictiveness of spirit. I will not revive again the old quarrels, nor dig up his hard words, long ago consigned to oblivion; it would be unjust to the living. He was what is called a good hater. If he loved an idea, he seemed to hate the man who opposed it. He was not content with replying; he must also retort, though it manifestly weakened the force of the reply. In his attacks on persons he was sometimes unjust, violent, sharp, and vindictive; sometimes cruel, and even barbarous. Did he ever forgive an enemy? Every opponent was a foe, and he thrashed his foes with an iron hoof and winnowed them with a storm. The most awful specimens of invective which the language affords can be found in his words— bitter, revengeful, and unrelenting. I am sorry to say these things; it hurts my feelings to say them, yours not less to hear them. But it is not our fault they are true; it would be mine, if, knowing they were true, I did not on this occasion point them out in warning words. Mr. Adams says that Roger Williams was conscientious and conten-

* *Lecture on China.*

M 2

tious; it is equally true of himself. Perhaps Mr. Adams had little humour, but certainly a giant's wit; he used it tyrannously and like a giant. Wit has its place in debate; in controversy it is a legitimate weapon, offensive and defensive. After one has beaten the single barley-corn of good sense out of a whole waggon-load of chaff, the easiest way to be rid of the rubbish is to burn it up with the lightning of wit; the danger is, that the burning should begin before the separation is made; that the fire consume the good and bad indifferently. When argument is edged and pointed with wit, it is doubly effective; but when that edge is jagged with ill-will, poisoned, too, with personal spleen, then it becomes a weapon unworthy of a man. Sometimes Mr. Adams used his wit as fairly as his wisdom; and bags of wind, on which Hercules might have stamped and beaten a twelvemonth, but in vain—at a single puncture from that keen wit gave up their ghost and flattened into nothing; a vanity to all men, but a vexation of spirit to him who had blown them so full of his own soul. But sometimes, yes, often, Mr. Adams's wit performs a different part: it sits as a judge, unjust and unforgiving, " often deciding wrong, and when right from wrong motives." It was the small dagger with which he smote the fallen foe. It is a poor praise for a famous man, churchman, or statesman, to beat a blackguard with his own weapons. It must be confessed, that, in controversy, Mr. Adams's arrows were sharp and deftly delivered; but they were often barbed, and sometimes poisoned.

True, he encountered more political opposition than any man in the nation. For more than forty years he has never been without bitter and unrelenting enemies, public and private. No man in America, perhaps, ever had such provocations; surely, none had ever such opportunities to reply without retorting. How much better would it have been, if, at the end of that long life and fifty years' war, he could say he had never wasted a shot; had never sinned with his lips, nor once feathered his public arrow with private spleen! Wise as he was, and old, he never learned that for undeserved calumny, for personal insult and abuse, there is one answer, Christian, manly, and irrefutable—the dignity of silence. A just man can afford to wait till the storm of abuse shall spend its rage and vanish under the rainbow, which itself furnishes and leaves behind. The retorting speech of such a man may be silvern or iron ; his silence, victorious and golden.

It is easy to censure Mr. Adams for such intemperance of speech and persecution of persons ; unfortunately, too easy to furnish other examples of both. We know what he spoke—God only what he repressed. Who knows out of how deep a fulness of indignation such torrents gush ? Tried by the standard of other men, his fellow politicians of America and Europe, he was no worse than they, only abler.* The mouse and the fox have as great a proportionate anger as the lion, though the one is ridiculous and the other terrific. Mr. Adams must be tried by his own standard, the rule of right, the standard of conscience and of Christianity ; then surely he did wrong. For such a man the vulgarity of the offence is no excuse.

With this and the other exceptions he appears a remarkably conscientious man in his public life. He may often have erred, as all men, without violating his own sense of right.

While he was President he would not consent to any "public manifestation of honours personal to himself." He would not accept a present, for his Bible taught him what experience continually enforces, that a gift blinds the eyes of wise men and perverts their judgment. While at St. Petersburg, the Russian Minister of the Interior, then an old man, felt uneasy on account of the presents accepted during his official service, and, calculating the value of all gifts received, returned it to the imperial treasury. This fact made an impression on Mr. Adams, and led to a resolution which he faithfully kept. When a bookseller sent him a costly Bible, he kept the book, but paid its full value. No bribes, no pensions, in any form, ever soiled justice in his hands. He would never be indebted to any body of men, lest they might afterwards sway him from the right path.

Because he was a conscientious man he would never be the servant of a party, and never was. It was of great advantage to him that he was absent while the two chief parties were forming in the United States. He came into

* See his defence of this in his *Address to his Constituents at Braintree*, Sept. 17th, 1842. Boston, 1842, p. 56, *et seq.*

the Massachusetts Legislature as a federalist, but some
anti-federalists also voted for him.   His first vote showed
he was not limited by the common principles of a party.
He was chosen to the Senate of the United States, not by
a party vote.   At first he acted mainly with the federalists, though not always voting with his colleague ; but in
1807 acted with the administration in the matter of the
Embargo.   This was the eventful crisis of his life ; this
change in his politics, while it gave him station and political power, yet brought upon him the indignation of his
former friends ; it has never been forgotten nor forgiven.
Be the outward occasion and inward motive what they
may, this led to the sundering of friendships long cherished and deservedly dear ; it produced the most bitter
experience of his life.   Political men would naturally undertake to judge his counsel by its probable and obvious
consequences, the favour of the Executive, rather than
attribute it to any latent motive of patriotism in his heart.

While at the head of the nation he would not be the
President of a party, but of the people ; when he became a
representative in Congress he was not the delegate of a
party, but of justice and the eternal right, giving his constituents an assurance that he would hold himself in alle-
giance to no party, national or political.   He has often
been accused of hatred to the South ; I can find no trace
of it.   "I entered Congress," says he, "without one sentiment of discrimination between the North and South."
At first he acted with Mr. Jackson, to arrest the progress
of nullification, for the democracy of South Carolina was
putting in practice what the federalists of New England
have so often been alleged to have held in theory, and
condemned on that allegation.   Here he was consistent.
In 1834, he approved the spirit of the same President in
demanding justice of France ; but afterwards he did not
hesitate to oppose, and perhaps abuse him.

He had a high reverence for religion ; none of our public men more.   He aimed to be a Christian man.   Signs
of this have often been sought in his habits of church-
going, of reading the Bible ; they may be found rather in
the general rectitude of his life, public and private, and in
the high motives which swayed him, in his opposition to
slavery, in the self-denial which cost him his re-election.

In his public acts he seems animated by the thought that he stood in the presence of God. Though rather unphilosophical in his theology, resting to a great degree on the authority of tradition and the letter, and attaching much value to forms and times, he yet saw the peculiar excellence of Christianity,—that it recognized "Love as the paramount and transcendent law of human nature." I do not say that his life indicates the attainment of a complete religious repose, but that he earnestly and continually laboured to achieve that. You shall find few statesmen, few men, who act with a more continual and obvious reference to religion as a motive, as a guide, as a comfort. He was, however, no sectarian. His devotion to freedom appeared, where it seldom appears, in his notions about religion. He thought for himself, and had a theology of his own, rather old-fashioned, it is true, and not very philosophical or consistent, it may be, and in that he was not very singular; but he allowed others to think also for themselves, and have a theology of their own. Mr. Adams was a Unitarian. It is no great merit to be a Unitarian, or a Calvinist, or a Catholic, perhaps no more merit to be one than the other. But he was not ashamed of his belief when Unitarianism was little, despised, mocked at, and called "Infidelity" on all sides. When the Unitarian church at Washington, a small and feeble body, met for worship in an upper room—not large, but obscure, over a public bathing-house—John Quincy Adams, the Secretary of State and expecting to be President, came regularly to worship with them. It was not fashionable; it was hardly respectable, for the Unitarians were not then, as now, numerous and rich: but he went and worshipped. It was no merit to think with any sect, it was a great merit to dare be true to his convictions. In his theology, as in politics, he feared not to stand in a minority. If there ever was an American who loved the praise of God more than the praise of men, I believe Mr. Adams was one.

His devotion to freedom, his love of his country, his conscientiousness, his religion, are four things strong and noticeable in his character. You shall look long amongst our famous men before you find his equal in these things.*

* In a public address, Mr. Adams once quoted the well-known words of Tacitus (Annal VI. 39), *Par negotiis neque supra,*—applying them to

Somebody says, no man ever used all his intellectual faculties as far as possible. If any man is an exception to this rule, it is Mr. Adams. He was temperate and diligent; industrious almost to a fault, though not orderly or systematic. His diplomatic letters, his orations, his reports and speeches, all indicate wide learning, the fruit of the most remarkable diligence. The attainments of a well-bred scholar are not often found in the American Congress, or the President's house. Yet he never gives proof that he had the mind of a great man. In his special department of politics he does not appear as a master. He has no great ideas with which to solve the riddles of commerce and finance; has done little to settle the commercial problems of the world,—for that work there is needed not only a retrospective acquaintance with the habits and history of men, but the foresight which comes from a knowledge of the nature of things and of man. His chief intellectual excellence seems to have been memory; his great moral merit, a conscientious and firm honesty; his practical strength lay in his diligence. His counsels seem almost always to have come from a knowledge of human history, seldom to have been prompted by a knowledge of the nature of man. Hence he was a critic of the past, or an administrator of the present, rather than a prophetic guide for the future. He had many facts and precedents, but few ideas. Few examples of great political foresight can be quoted from his life; and therein, to his honour be it spoken, his heart seems to have out-travelled his head. The public affairs of the United States seem generally to be conducted by many men of moderate abilities, rather than by a few men of great genius for politics.

Mr. Adams wrote much. Some of his works are remarkable for their beauty, for the graceful proportions of their style, and the felicity of their decoration. Such are his celebrated Lectures on Rhetoric and Oratory, which are sufficiently learned and sagacious, not very philoso-

a distinguished man lately deceased. A lady wrote to inquire whence they came. Mr. Adams informed her, and added, they could not be adequately translated in less than seven words in English. The lady replied that they might be well translated in five—*Equal to, not above, duty;* but better in three—JOHN QUINCY ADAMS.

phical, but written in an agreeable style, and at the present day not wholly without value. His review of the works of Fisher Ames, I speak only of the rhetoric, is, perhaps, the finest of his compositions. Some of his productions are disorderly, ill-compacted, without "joints or con-texture," and homely to a fault : this oration is a growth out of a central thought, marked by an internal harmony ; that, a composition, a piece of carpentry distinguished by only an outward symmetry of members ; others are neither growth nor composition, only a mass of materials huddled and lumped together. Most of his later productions, with the exception of his congressional speeches, are hard, cold, and unfinished performances, with little order in the thoughts, and less beauty in the expression. His extemporaneous speeches have more of both ; they are better finished than his studied orations. He could judge and speak with fury, though he wrote with phlegm. His illustrations are usually drawn from literature, not from nature or human life ; his language is commonly cold, derived from the Roman stream which has been filtered through books, rather than from the deep and original well of our Saxon home. His published letters are compact, written in a cold style, without playfulness or wit, with no elegance, and, though mostly business letters, they are not remarkable for strength or distinctness. His diligence appears in verse as well as prose. He wrote much that rhymed tolerably ; little that was poetical. The same absence of nature, the same coldness and lack of inspiration, mark his poetry and prose. But in all that he wrote, with the exceptions mentioned above, though you miss the genial warmth, the lofty thought, the mind that attracts, embraces, warms, and inspires the reader, you find always a spirit of humanity, of justice, and love to God.

Mr. Adams was seldom eloquent. Eloquence is no great gift. It has its place among subordinate powers, not among the chief. Alas for the statesman or preacher who has only that to save the State withal ! Washington had none of it, yet how he ruled the land ! No man in America has ever had a political influence so wide and permanent as Mr. Jefferson ; yet he was a very indifferent writer, and never made a speech of any value. The acts

of Washington, the ideas of Jefferson, made eloquence
superfluous. True, it has its value : if a man have at
command the electricity of truth, justice, love, the sentiments and great ideas thereof, it is a good thing to be
able with Olympian hand to condense that electric fire into
bolted eloquence ; to thunder and lighten in the sky. But
if a man have that electric truth, it matters little whether
it is Moses that speaks, or only Aaron; whether or not
Paul's bodily presence be weak and his speech contemptible : it is Moses' thought which thunders and lightens
out of Sinai; it is Paul's idea that is powerful and builds
up the church. Of true eloquence, the best thoughts put
in the best words, and uttered in the best form, Mr. Adams
had little, and that appeared mainly in the latter part of
his life. Hundreds have more. What passes for eloquence
is common in America, where the public mouth is always
a-going. His early orations are poor in their substance
and faulty in their form. His ability as an orator developed late ; no proofs of it appear before he entered the
House of Representatives, at a good old age. In his
manner of speaking there was little dignity and no grace,
though sometimes there was a terrible energy and fire.
He was often a powerful speaker—by his facts and figures,
by his knowledge, his fame, his age, and his position, but
most of all by his independent character. He spoke
worthily of great men, of Madison or Lafayette, kindling
with his theme, and laying aside all littleness of a party.
However, he was most earnest and most eloquent not when
he stood up the champion of a neglected truth, not when
he dwelt on great men now venerable to us all, but when
he gathered his strength to attack a foe. Incensed, his
sarcasm was terrific ; colossal vanity, aspiring to be a
Ghenghis Khan, at the touch of that Ithuriel spear shrank
to the dimensions of Tom Thumb. His invective is his
masterpiece of oratoric skill. It is sad to say this, and to
remember that the greatest works of ancient or of modern
rhetoric, from the thundering Philippics of Desmosthenes
down to the sarcastic and crazy rattle of Lord Brougham,
are all of the same character, are efforts against a personal
foe ! Men find hitherto the ablest acts and speech in the
same cause,—not positive and creating, but critical and
combative,—in war.

If Mr. Adams had died in 1829, he would have been remembered for awhile as a learned man; as an able diplomatist, who had served his country faithfully at home and abroad; as a President spotless and incorruptible, but not as a very important personage in American history. His mark would have been faint and soon effaced from the sands of time. But the last period of his life was the noblest. He had worn all the official honours which the nation could bestow; he sought the greater honour of serving that nation, who had now no added boon to give. All that he had done as Minister abroad, as Senator, as Secretary, and President, is little compared with what he did in the House of Representatives; and while he stood there, with nothing to hope, with nothing to fear, the hand of Justice wrote his name high up on the walls of his country. It was surprising to see at his first attendance there, men, who, while he was President, had been the loudest to call out "Coalition, Bargain, Intrigue, Corruption," come forward and express the involuntary confidence they felt in his wisdom and integrity, and their fear, actual though baseless, that his withdrawal from the Committee on Manufactures would "endanger the very Union itself."* Great questions soon came up: nullification was speedily disposed of; the Bank and the tariff got ended or compromised; but slavery lay in the consciousness of the nation, like the one dear but appalling sin in a man's heart. Some wished to be rid of it, northern men and southern men. It would come up; to justify that, or excuse it, the American sentiment and idea must be denied and rejected utterly; the South, who had long known the charms of Bathsheba, was ready for her sake to make away with Uriah himself. To remove that monstrous evil, gradually but totally, and restore unity to the nation, would require a greater change than the adoption of the Constitution. To keep slavery out of sight, yet in existence, unjustified, unexcused, unrepented of, a contradiction in the national consciousness, a political and deadly sin, the sin against the Holy Spirit of American Liberty, known but not confessed, the public secret of the people—that would lead to suppressing petitions, suppressing debate in Congress and out of Congress, to silencing the pulpit, the press, and the people.

* *Remarks* of Mr. Cambreleng.

Under these circumstances, Mr. Adams went to Congress, an old man, well known on both sides the water, the presidential laurels on his brow, independent and fearless, expecting no reward from men for services however great. In respect to the subject of slavery, he had no ideas in advance of the nation; he was far behind the foremost men. He "deprecated all discussion of slavery or its abolition, in the House, and gave no countenance to petitions for the abolition of slavery in the District of Columbia or the territories." However, he acquired new ideas as he went on, and became the congressional leader in the great movement of the American mind towards universal freedom.

Here he stood as the champion of human rights; here he fought, and with all his might. In 1836, by the celebrated resolution, forbidding debate on the subject of slavery, the South drove the North to the wall, nailed it there into shameful silence. A "Northern man with Southern principles," before entering the President's chair, declared, that if Congress should pass a law to abolish slavery in the District of Columbia, he would exercise his veto to prevent the law.* Mr. Adams stood up manfully, sometimes almost alone, and contended for freedom of speech. Did obstinate men of the North send petitions relative to slavery, asking for its abolition in the District or elsewhere? Mr. Adams was ready to present the petitions. Did women petition? It made no difference with him. Did slaves petition? He stood up there to defend their right to be heard. The South had overcome many an obstacle; but that one fearless soul would not bend, and could not be broken. Spite of rules of order, he contrived to bring the matter perpetually before Congress, and sometimes to read the most offensive parts of the petitions. When Arkansas was made a State, he endeavoured to abolish slavery in its domain; he sought to establish international relations with Hayti, and to secure the right of suffrage for the coloured citizens of the District of Columbia. The laws which forbid blacks to vote in the Northern States he held " in utter abhorrence."

He saw from afar the plots of southern politicians, plots for extending the area of slavery, for narrowing the area

* Mr. Van Buren.

of freedom, and exposed those plots. You all remember the tumult it excited when he rose in his place holding a petition from slaves; that the American Congress was thrown into long and disgraceful confusion. You cannot have forgotten the uproar which followed his presenting a petition to dissolve the Union!* I know few speeches more noble and manly than his on the right of petition,— occasioned by that celebrated attempt to stifle debate, and on the annexation of Texas. Some proposed to censure him, some clamoured, "expel him," some cried out, "burn the petitions!" and "him with them," screamed yet others. Some threatened to have him indicted by the grand jury of the district, " or be made amenable to *another tribunal,*" hoping to see " an incendiary brought to condign punishment." "My life on it," said a southern legislator, "if he presents that petition from slaves, we shall yet see him within the walls of the penitentiary." Some in secret threatened to assassinate him in the streets. They mistook their man ; with justice on his side he did "not fear all the grand juries in the universe." He would not curl nor cringe, but snorted his defiance in their very face. In front of ridicule, of desertion, obloquy, rage, and brutal threats, stood up that old man, bald and audacious; and the chafed rock of Cohasset stands not firmer mid the yesty waves, nor more triumphant spurns back into the ocean's face the broken billows of the storm. That New England knee bent only before his God. That unpretending man— the whole power of the nation could not move him from his post.

Men threatened to increase the slave power. Said one of the champions of slavery with prophetic speech, but fatal as Cassandra's in the classic tale, Americans "would come up in thousands to plant the lone star of the Texan banner on the Mexican capital . . . The boundless wealth of captured towns and rifled churches, and a lazy, vicious, and luxurious priesthood, would soon enable Texas to pay her soldiery and redeem her State debt, and push her

* See the *Debates of the House*, January 23rd and following, 1837 ; or Mr. Adams's own account of the matter in his *Letters to his Constituents,* etc. (Boston, 1837.) See, too, his *Series of Speeches on the Right of Petition and the Annexation of Texas*, January 14th and following, 1838. (Printed in a pamphlet. Washington, 1838.)

victorious arms to the very shores of the Pacific. And
would not all this extend the bounds of slavery? Yes,
the result would be, that, before another quarter of a century, the extension of slavery would not stop short of the
Western ocean." Against this danger Mr. Adams armed
himself, and fought in the holiest cause—the cause of
human rights.

I know few things in modern times so grand as that old
man standing there in the House of Representatives, the
compeer of Washington, a man who had borne himself
proudly in kings' courts, early doing service in high places,
where honour may be won; a man who had filled the
highest office in any nation's gift; a President's son,
himself a President, standing there the champion of the
neediest of the oppressed: the conquering cause pleased
others; him only, the cause of the conquered. Had he
once been servile to the hands that wielded power? No
thunderbolt can scare him now! Did he once make a
treaty and bind Mexico to bewray the wandering fugitive
who took his life in his hand and fled from the talons of
the American eagle? Now he would go to the stake
sooner than tolerate such a deed! When he went to the
Supreme Court, after an absence of thirty years, and arose
to defend a body of friendless negroes torn from their home
and most unjustly held in thrall; when he asked the judges
to excuse him at once both for the trembling faults of age
and the inexperience of youth, the man having laboured
so long elsewhere that he had forgotten the rules of court;
when he summed up the conclusion of the whole matter,
and brought before those judicial but yet moistening eyes
the great men whom he had once met there—Chase,
Cushing, Martin, Livingston, and Marshall himself; and
while he remembered them that were "gone, gone, all
gone," remembered also the Eternal Justice that is never
gone,—why the sight was sublime. It was not an old
patrician of Rome who had been consul, dictator, coming
out of his honoured retirement at the Senate's call, to stand
in the forum to levy new armies, marshal them to victory
afresh, and gain thereby new laurels for his brow;—but it
was a plain citizen of America, who had held an office far
greater than that of consul, king, or dictator, his hand
reddened by no man's blood, expecting no honours, but

coming in the name of Justice to plead for the slave, for
the poor barbarian negro of Africa, for Cinque and Grabbo,
for their deeds comparing them to Harmodius and Aristo-
geiton, whose classic memory made each bosom thrill.
That was worth all his honours,—it was worth while to live
fourscore years for that.

When he stood in the House of Representatives, the
champion of the rights of a minority, of the rights of man,
he stood colossal. Frederick the Great seems doubly so,
when, single-handed, "that son of the Dukes of Branden-
burg" contended against Austria, France, England,
Russia, kept them all at bay, divided by his skill, and
conquered by his might. Surely he seems great, when
measured merely by his deeds. But, in comparison,
Frederick the Great seems Frederick the little: for Adams
fought not for a kingdom, nor for fame, but for Justice
and the Eternal Right; fought, too, with weapons tem-
pered in a heavenly stream!*

He had his reward. Who ever missed it? From
mythological Cain, who slew his brother, down to Judas
Iscariot, and Aaron Burr; from Jesus of Nazareth, down
to the least man that dies or lives—who ever lost his
reward? None. No; not one. Within the wicked
heart there dwells the avenger, with unseen hands, to
adjust the cord, to poison the fatal bowl. In the impene-
trable citadel of a good man's consciousness, unseen by
mortal eyes, there stands the palladium of justice, radiant
with celestial light; mortal hands may make and mar,—
this they can mar not, no more than they can make.
Things about the man can others build up or destroy; but
no foe, no tyrant, no assassin, can ever steal the man out
of the man. Who would not have the consciousness of
being right, even of trying to be right, though affronted
by a whole world, rather than conscious of being wrong,
and hollow, and false, have all the honours of a nation on
his head? Of late years, no party stood up for Mr.
Adams, "The madman of Massachusetts," as they called

---

* " Acer et indomitus, quo spes, quoque ira vocasset,
    Ferre manum, et nunquam temerando parcere ferro;
    Successus urgere suos ; instare favori
    Numinis ; impellens quicquid sibi summa petenti
    Obstaret, gaudensque viam fecisse ruina."

him, on the floor of Congress; but he knew that he had,
and in his old age, done one work,—he had contended for
the unalienable rights of man, done it faithfully. The
government of God is invisible, His justice the more
certain,—and by that Mr. Adams had his abundant reward.

But he had his poorer and outward rewards, negative
and positive. For his zeal in behalf of freedom he was
called "a monarchist in disguise," "an alien to the true
interests of his country," "a traitor." A slaveholder from
Kentucky published to his constituents that he "was sincerely desirous to check that man, for if he could be
removed from the councils of the nation, or silenced upon
the exasperating subject to which he had devoted himself,
none other, I believe, could be found hardy enough or bad
enough to fill his place." It was worth something to
have an enemy speak such praise as that; but the slaveholder was wrong in his conjecture; the North has yet
other sons not less hardy, not more likely to be silenced.
Still more praise of a similar sort:—at a fourth of July
dinner at Walterborough, in South Carolina, this sentiment was proposed and responded to with nine cheers:
"May we never want a democrat to trip up the heels of a
federalist, or a hangman to prepare a halter for John
Quincy Adams." Considering what he had done and
whence those rewards proceeded, that was honour enough
for a yet greater man.

Let me turn to things more grateful. Mr. Adams,
through lack of genial qualities, had few personal friends,
yet from good men throughout the North there went up a
hearty thanksgiving for his manly independence, and
prayers for his success. Brave men forgot their old
prejudices, forgot the "Embargo," forgot the "Hartford
Convention," forgot all the hard things which he had ever
said, forgot his words in the Senate, forgot their dis-
appointments, and said—"For this our hearts shall honour
thee, thou brave old man!" In 1843, when, for the first
time, he visited the West, to assist at the foundation of a
scientific institution, all the West rose up to do him reverence. He did not go out to seek honours, they came to
seek him. It was the movement of a noble people, feeling
a noble presence about them no less than within. When

Cicero, the only great man whom Rome never feared, returned from his exile, all Italy rose up and went out to meet him; so did the North and the West welcome this champion of freedom, this venerable old man. They came not to honour one who had been a President, but one who was a man. That alone, said Mr. Adams, with tears of joy and grief filling his eyes, was reward enough for all that he had done, suffered, or undertaken. Yes, it was too much; too much for one man as the reward of one life!

You all remember the last time he was at any public meeting in this city. A man had been kidnapped in Boston, kidnapped at noon-day, "on the high road between Faneuil Hall and old Quincy," and carried off to be a slave! New England hands had seized their brother, sold him into bondage for ever, and his children after him. In the presence of slavery, as of arms, the laws are silent, —not always men. Then it appears who are men, who not! A meeting was called to talk the matter over, in a plain way, and look in one another's faces. Who was fit to preside in such a case? That old man sat in the chair in Faneuil Hall; above him was the image of his father, and his own; around him were Hancock and the other Adams,—Washington, greatest of all; before him were the men and women of Boston, met to consider the wrongs done to a miserable negro slave; the roof of the old Cradle of Liberty spanned over them all. Forty years before, a young man and a Senator, he had taken the chair at a meeting called to consult on the wrong done to American seamen, violently impressed by the British from an American ship of war, the unlucky Chesapeake; some of you remember that event. Now, an old man, clothed with half a century of honours, he sits in the same hall, to preside over a meeting to consider the outrage done to a single slave; a greater outrage—alas, not done by a hostile, not by an alien hand! One was the first meeting of citizens he ever presided over, the other was the last; both for the same object—the defence of the Eternal Right.

But I would not weary you. His death was noble; fit ending for such a life. He was an old man, the last that had held a diplomatic office under Washington. He had uttered his oracles; had done his work. The highest honours of the nation he had worthily worn; but, as his townsmen tell us,—caring little for the President, and much for the man,—that was very little in comparison with his character. The good and ill of the human cup he had tasted, and plentifully, too, as son, husband, father. He had borne his testimony for freedom and the rights of mankind; he had stood in Congress almost alone; with a few gallant men had gone down to the battle-field, and if victory escaped him, it was because night came on.

He saw others enter the field in good heart, to stand in the imminent deadly breach; he lived long enough for his own welfare, for his own ambition; long enough to see the seal broken,—and then, this aged Simeon, joyful in the consolation, bowed his head and went home in peace. His feet were not hurt with fetters; he died with his armour on; died like a Senator in the capitol of the nation; died like an American, in the service of his country; died like a Christian, full of immortality; died like a man, fearless and free!

You will ask, What was the secret of his strength? Whence did he gain such power to stand erect where others so often cringed and crouched low to the ground? It is plain to see: he looked beyond time, beyond men; looked to the eternal God, and, fearing Him, forgot all other fear. Some of his failings he knew to be such, and struggled with them though he did not overcome. A man, not over-modest, once asked him what he most of all lamented in his life, and he replied, "My impetuous temper and vituperative speech; that I have not always returned good for evil, but in the madness of my blood have said things that I am ashamed of before my God!" As the world goes, it needed some greatness to say that.

When he was a boy, his mother, a still woman, and capable, deep-hearted, and pious, took great pains with his culture; most of all with his religious culture. When, at the age of ten, he was about to leave home for years of absence in another land, she took him aside to warn him of temptations which he could not then understand. She bade him remember religion and his God—his secret, silent prayer. Often in his day there came the earthquake of party strife; the fire, the storm, and the whirlwind of passion; he listened—and God was not there; but there came, too, the remembrance of his mother's whispered words; God came in that memory, and earthquake and storm, the fire and the whirlwind were powerless, at last, before that still small voice. Beautifully did she write to her boy of ten, "Great learning and superior abilities will be of little value . . . unless virtue, honour, truth, and integrity, are added to them. Remember that you are accountable to your Maker for all your words and your actions." "Dear as you are to me," says this more than Spartan, this Christian mother, "Dear as you are to me, I would much rather you should have found your grave in the ocean you have crossed, or that any untimely death cross you in your infant years, than see you an immoral, profligate, or graceless child. Let your observations and comparisons produce in your mind an abhorrence of domination and power—the parents of slavery, ignorance, and barbarism. May you be led to an imitation of that disinterested patriotism and that noble love of your country which will teach you to despise wealth, titles, pomp, and equipage, as mere external advantages, which cannot add to the internal excellence of your mind, or compensate for the want of integrity and virtue." She tells him in a letter, that her father, a plain New England clergyman, of Braintree, who had just died, "left you a legacy more valuable than gold or silver; he left you his blessing, and his prayers that you might become a useful citizen, a guardian of the laws, liberty, and religion of your country. . . . . Lay this bequest up in your memory and practise upon it; believe me, you will find it a treasure that neither moth nor rust can destroy."

If a child have such a mother, there is no wonder why he stood fearless, and bore a charmed life which no opposition could tame down. I wonder more that one so born and by such a mother bred, could ever once bend a servile knee; could ever indulge that fierce and dreadful hate; could ever stoop to sully those hands which hers had joined in prayer. It ill accords with teachings like her own. I wonder that he could ever have refused to "deliberate." Religion is a quality that makes a man independent; disappointment will not render such an one sour, nor oppression drive him mad, nor elevation bewilder;

N 2

power will not dazzle, nor gold corrupt; no threat can silence and no fear subdue.

There are men enough born with greater abilities than Mr. Adams, men enough in New England, in all the walks of man. But how many are there in political life who use their gifts so diligently, with such conscience, such fearless deference to God?—nay, tell us one. I have not spared his faults; I am no eulogist, to paint a man with undiscriminating praise. Let his follies warn us, while his virtues guide. But look on all his faults, and then compare him with our famous men of the North or the South; with the great whigs or the great democrats. Ask which was the purest man, the most patriotic, the most honest; which did his nation the smallest harm and the greatest good; which for his country and his kind denied himself the most. Shall I examine their lives, public and private, strip them bare and lay them down beside his life, and ask which, after all, has the least of blemish and the most of beauty? Nay, that is not for me to do or to attempt.

In one thing he surpassed most men,—he grew more liberal the more he grew old, ripening and mellowing, too, with age. After he was seventy years old, he welcomed new ideas, kept his mind vigorous, and never fell into that crabbed admiration of past times and buried institutions, which is the palsy of so many a man, and which makes old age nothing but a pity, and gray hairs provocative of tears. This is the more remarkable in a man of his habitual reverence for the past, in one who judged oftener by the history than by the nature of man.

Times will come when men shall look to that vacant seat. But the thunder is silent, the lightning gone; other men must take his place and fill it as they can. Let us not mourn that he has gone from us; let us remember what was evil in him, but only to be warned of ambition, of party strife, to love more that large charity which forgives an enemy, and, through good and ill, contends for mankind. Let us be thankful for the good he has said and done, be guided by it and blessed. There is a certain affluence of intellectual power granted to some men, which provokes admiration for a time, let the man of myriad gifts use his talent as he may. Such merely cubic greatness of mind is matter of astonishment rather than a fit subject for esteem and praise. Of that, Mr. Adams had little, as so many of his contemporaries had more. In him what most commands respect is, his independence, his love of justice, of his country and his kind. No son of New England has been ever so distinguished in political life. But it is no great thing to be President of the United States; some men it only makes ridiculous. A worm on a steeple's top is nothing but a worm, no more able to fly than while creeping in congenial mud; a mountain needs no steeple to lift its head and show the world what is great and high. The world obeys its great men, stand where they may.

After all, this must be the greatest praise of Mr. Adams: in private he corrupted no man nor woman; as a politician he never debauched the public morals of his country, nor used public power for any private end; in public and private he lived clean and above board; he taught a fearless love of truth and the right, both by word and deed. I wish I could add, that was a small praise. But, as the times go, as our famous men are, it is a very great fame, and there are few competitors for such renown; I must leave him alone in that glory. Doubtless, as he looked back on his long career, his whole life, motives as well as actions, must have seemed covered with imperfections. I will seek no further to disclose his merits, or "draw his frailties from their dead abode."

He has passed on, where superior gifts and opportunities avail not, nor his long life, nor his high station, nor his wide spread fame; where enemies cease from troubling, and the flattering tongue also is still. Wealth, honour, fame, forsake him at the grave's mouth. It is only the living soul, sullied or clean, which the last angel bears off in his arms to that world where many that seem first shall be last, and the last first; but where justice shall be lovingly done to the great man full of power and wisdom who rules the State, and the feeblest slave whom oppression chains down in ignorance and vice—done by the all-seeing Father of both President and slave, who loves both with equal love. The venerable man is gone home. He shall have his praise. But who shall speak it worthily? Mean men and little, who shrank from him in life, who

never shared what was manliest in the man, but mocked at
his living nobleness, shall they come forward and with
mealy mouths, to sing his requiem, forgetting that his
eulogy is their own ban?   Some will rejoice at his death;
there is one man the less to fear, and they who trembled
at his life may well be glad when the earth has covered up
the son she bore.   Strange men will meet with mutual
solace at his tomb, wondering that their common foe is
dead, and they are met!   The Herods and Pilates of contending parties may be made friends above his grave, and
clasping hands may fancy that their union is safer than
before; but there will come a day after to-day!   Let us
leave him to his rest.

The slave has lost a champion who gained new ardour
and new strength the longer he fought; America has lost
a man who loved her with his heart; Religion has lost a
supporter; Freedom an unfailing friend, and Mankind a
noble vindicator of our unalienable rights.

It is not long since he was here in our own streets;
three winter months have scantly flown: he set out for his
toil—but went home to his rest.   His labours are over.
No man now threatens to assassinate; none to expel; none
even to censure.   The theatrical thunder of Congress, noisy
but harmless, has ended as it ought, in honest tears.
South Carolina need ask no more a halter for that one
northern neck she could not bend nor break.   The tears of
his country are dropped upon his urn; the muse of history
shall write thereon, in letters not to be effaced, THE ONE
GREAT MAN SINCE WASHINGTON, WHOM AMERICA HAD NO
CAUSE TO FEAR.

To-day that venerable form lies in the Capitol,—the
disenchanted dust.   All is silent.   But his undying soul,
could we deem it still hovering o'er its native soil, bound
to take leave, yet lingering still, and loath to part, that
would bid us love our country, love man, love justice,
freedom, right, and above all, love God.   To-morrow that
venerable dust starts once more to join the dear presence
of father and mother, to mingle his ashes with their ashes,
as their lives once mingled, and their souls again.   Let his
native State communicate her last sad sacrament, and give
him now, it is all she can, a little earth for charity.

But what shall we say as the dust returns?

"Where slavery's minions cower
  Before the servile power,
    He bore their ban;
And, like the aged oak,
That braved the lightning's stroke,
When thunders round it broke,
    Stood up a man.

"Nay, when they stormed aloud,
  And round him like a cloud,
    Came thick and black,—
He single-handed strove,
And, like Olympian Jove,
With his own thunder drove
    The phalanx back.

"Not from the bloody field,
  Borne on his battered shield,
    By foes o'ercome ;—
But from a sterner fight,
In the defence of Right,
Clothed with a conqueror's might,
    We hail him home.

"His life in labours spent,
  That 'Old man eloquent'
    Now rests for aye ;—
His dust the tomb may claim ;—
His spirit's quenchless flame,
His 'venerable name,' *
Pass not away." †

* *Clarum et venerabile nomen.*
† The above lines are from the pen of the Rev. John Pierpont.

VII.

A DISCOURSE OCCASIONED BY THE DEATH OF THE
LATE PRESIDENT TAYLOR.—PREACHED AT THE
MELODEON, JULY 14, 1850.

LAST Sunday, on a day near the national anniversary,
something was said of the relation which the American
citizen bears to the State, and of the duties and rights
which belong to that relation. Since then an event has
occurred which suggests another topic of a public nature,
and so I invite your attention to a discourse of the general
position and duties of an American ruler, and in special of
the late President Taylor. It is no pleasant task to rise
to speak so often on such themes as this; but let us see what
warning or guidance we can gather from this occasion.

In order that a man should be competent to become a
complete political ruler and head of the American people,
he ought to be distinguished above other men in three
particulars.
First, he ought to have just political ideas in advance of
the people, ideas not yet organized into institutions in the
State. Then he will be a leader in ideas.
Next, he ought to have a superior power of organizing
those ideas, of putting them into institutions in the State.
Then he will be a leader in the matter of organizing ideas.
Then he ought to have a superior power of administering
the institutions after they are made. Then he will be a
leader in the matter of administering institutions.
An eminent degree of these three qualities constitutes
genius for statesmanship, genius, too, of a very high order.
A man who really and efficiently leads in politics must
possess some or all of these qualities; without them, or
any of them, he can only seem to lead. He and the

people both may think he is the leader, and call him so; but he that shall lead others aright must himself be on the right road and in advance of them. To perform the functions of a leader of men, the man must be eminently just, also, true to the Everlasting Right, the Law of God; otherwise he can never possess in the highest degree, or in a competent degree, the power of ideas, of organization, of administration. A man eminently just, and possessing these three qualities, is a leader by nature; if he is also put into the conventional position of leader, then he bears the same relation to the people, which the captain of a ship, skilful and competent, would bear to the ship's company who were joint owners with him, and had elected him to his office, expecting that he would serve them as captain while he held the office of captain.

The complete and perfect leader must be able to originate just political ideas, to organize them justly, to administer the organization with justice. But these three powers are seldom united in the same man; so, practically, the business of leading, and therefore of ruling, is commonly distributed amongst many persons; not concentrated in one man's hands. I think we have as yet had no statesman in America who has enjoyed each and all of these three talents in an eminent degree. No man is so rich as mankind. Any one of them is a great gift, entitling the man to distinction; but the talent for administration is not very rare. It is not difficult to find a man of good administrative ability with no power to invent, none to organize the inventions of other men. How many men can work all day with oxen yoked to a plough; how few could invent a plough or tame wild cattle. It is not hard to find men capable of managing political machinery, of holding the national plough and conducting the national team, when both are in the field, and there is the old furrow to serve as guide. That is all we commonly look for in an American politician. He is to follow the old constitutional furrow, and hold the old plough, and scatter a little democratic or whig seed, furnished by his party, not forgetting to give them the handsel of the crop. That is all we commonly look for in an American politician, leaving it for some bright but obscure man in the mass of the people to discover a new idea, and to devise the mode of its organization. Then the politician, perched aloft on his high place and conspicuous, holds the string of the kite which some unknown men have thought out, made up, and hoisted with great labour; he appears to be the great man, because he sits and holds the string, administering the kite, and men look up and say, "See there, what a great man he is! Is not this the foremost man of the age?"

In this way the business of ruling the nation is made a matter of mere routine, not of invention or construction. The ruler is to tend the public mill; not to make it, or to mend it; not to devise new and better mills, not even to improve the old one. We may be thankful if he does not abuse and leave it worse than he found it. He is not to gather the dam, only to shut the gate at the right time, and at the right time open it; to take sufficient toll of all comers, and now and then make a report of the grinding, or of what he sees fit to communicate to the owners of the mill. As it is a part of the written Constitution of the land that all money bills shall originate with the House of Representatives, so it is a part of the unwritten custom that political ideas in advance of the people shall not originate with the nominal rulers of the nation, but elsewhere. One good thing results from this: we are not much governed, but much let alone. The American form of government has some great merits; this I esteem the greatest; that it lets the people alone so much. In forming ourselves into a State, we agreed with one another not to meddle and make politically with individuals so much as other nations had done.

It is a long time since we have had a man of large genius for politics at the head of affairs in America. I think we could not mention more than one who had any genius for just political ideas in advance of the people. Skilful administrators we have had in great abundance in politics as in other matters. Nature herself seems democratic in her action here, and all our great movements appear to be brought about by natural power diffused amongst many men of talent, not by natural power condensed into a single man of genius. So long as this is the case, the present method of letting alone is the best one. The American nation has marched on without much pioneering on the part of its official rulers, no one of them for a long time being much in advance of the million; and, while it is so, it is certainly best that the million are very much left to themselves. But if we could have a man as much in advance of the people in all these three qualities, and especially in the chief quality—as the skilful projector of a cotton mill is in advance of the girls who tend the looms, in all that relates to the projection of a cotton mill, —then we should know what it was to have a real leader, a ruler who could be the school-master of the nation, not ruling over our bodies by fear, but in the spirit of love, setting us lessons which we could not have devised, nor even understand without his help; one who preserves all the good of the old, and adds thereto much new good not seen before, and so instructs and helps forward the people. But, as the good God has not sent such a man, and he is not to be made by men, only found, nor in the least helped in any of those three qualities by all the praise we can pour on him; so it comes to pass that an ordinary ruler is a person of no very great consequence. His importance is official and not personal, and as only the person dies, not the office, the death of such an one is not commonly an affair of much significance. Suppose after Mr. Tyler or Mr. Polk had taken the oath of office, he had appointed a common clerk, a man of routine and experience, as his factotum, with power to affix the presidential name to necessary documents, and then had quietly and in silence departed from this life, how much would the nation have lost? A new and just political idea; an organization thereof? No such thing. If the public press had kept the secret, we should not have found out their death till this time. The obscure clerk could tend the mill as well as his famous master, who would not be missed.

Louis XIV. said, "The State! That is I." He was the State. So when the ruler dies, the State is in peril. If the King of Prussia, the Emperor of Russia or Austria, or the Pope of Rome were to die, there would be a revolution, and nobody knows what would come of it; for there the ruler is master of the people, who are subjects, not citizens, and the old master dying, it is not easy to yoke the people to the chariot of a new one. Here the people are the State; and though the power of General Taylor was

practically greater than that of any monarch in Europe,
save Nicholas, William, and Ferdinand, yet at his death
all the power passes into the hands of his successor, with
no noise, no tumult, not even the appearance of a street
constable.   I think that was a sublime sight—the rule
over twenty millions of people, jealous of their rights,
silently, by due course of law, passes into the hands of
another man at dead of night, and the next morning the
nation is just as safe, just as quiet and secure as before, no
fear of change perplexing them.   That was a sublime
sight—one of the fair things which comes of a democracy.
Here the ruler is servant, and the people master; so the
death of a President like Mr. Van Buren, or any of his
successors, Harrison or Tyler or Polk, would really have
been a very unimportant event; not so momentous as the
death of one of the ablest doctors in Boston, for should the
physician die, your chance of life is diminished by that
fact.   If Dr. Channing had died at the age of forty, before
he wrote his best works, his death would have been a
greater calamity than that of any or all of the four Presidents just named, as soon as their inaugural address was
delivered; for Dr. Channing had some truths to tell, which
there was nobody else to deliver at that time.   No President since Jefferson, I think, has done the nation so much
good as the opening of the Erie Canal in New York, or
the chief railroads in Massachusetts, or the building up of
any one of the half dozen large manufacturing towns in
New England.   Mr. Cunard, in establishing his line of
Atlantic steamers, did more for America than any President for five-and-twenty years.   The discovery of the
properties of sulphuric ether, the devising of the magnetic
telegraph, was of more advantage to this nation, than the
service of any President for a long time.   I think I could
mention a few men in Boston, any one of whom has been
of more service than four or five Presidents; and, accordingly, the death of any one of those would be a greater
calamity than the demise of all those Presidents the day
after election.   With us the President is only one spoke
in the wheel, and, if that is broken, we always have a spare
spoke on hand, and the wheel is so made that, without
stopping the mill, the new spoke drops into the place of
the old one and no one knows the change till told thereof.

If Mr. Polk had really been the ablest man in the land, a creator and an organizer, his death would have been a public calamity, and the whole nation would have felt it, as Boston or New York would feel the loss of one of its ablest manufacturers or merchants, lawyers or doctors. That would deprive us of the services of a man which could not be supplied. We have always spare men of routine, but not spare men of genius. Dr. Channing has been missed ever since his death, and the churches of Boston, poor enough before, are the poorer for his absence. So has John Quincy Adams, old as he was, been missed in the House of Representatives. The enemy of freedom may well rejoice that his voice is still. But who misses General Harrison or Mr. Polk? What interest languishes in consequence of their departure? What idea, what right, lost thereby a defender? If Sir Robert Peel were to die, the British nation would feel the loss.

We attach a false importance to the death of a President. Great calamities were apprehended at the death of General Harrison. But what came? Whigs went out of office and democrats went into office. Had Jefferson died before the Declaration of Independence, or Washington any time after it, or before the termination of his official service, or John Adams before the end of the war, that would have been a great calamity; for I know not where we should have found another Jefferson, to see so distinctly, and write down so plain the great American idea, or another Washington to command an army without money, without provisions, without hats and shoes, as that man did. The death of Samuel Adams, in 1760, would have been a terrible misfortune to America. But the death of General Harrison only made a change in the Cabinet, not in the country; it affected the politicians more than the people.

We are surrounded in the world with nations ruled by kings, who are the masters of the people; hard masters too! When they die the people mourn, not always very wisely, not always sincerely, but always with ceremony. The mourning for George IV. and William IV. in England, I doubt not, was more splendid and imposing than that for Edward the Confessor and Oliver Cromwell; and that for Louis XV. outdid that for Henry IV. In a monarchy, men always officially mourn their king, whether it be King Log, or King Snake, or King Christian; we follow the example of those States. If some of the men, whose death would be the greatest calamity, should die, the newspapers would not go into mourning; we should not have a day of fasting set apart; no minister would think it "An inscrutable providence;" only a few plain country people would come together and take up the dust, disenchanted of the genius which gave it power over other and animated clay, to lay it down in the ground. There would be no Catafalques in the street; but the upper mountain-tops would miss that early sun which kissed their foreheads, while all below the world was wrapped in drowsy mist, and the whole race of man would be losers by the fading out of so much poetry, or truth, or justice, love and faith.

The office of President of the United States is undeniably one of great importance. If you put in it a great man, one with ability to invent, to organize and to administer, he has a better opportunity to serve mankind than most kings of Europe. I know of no position in the world more desirable for a really great man, a man with a genius for statesmanship, a million-minded man, than to take this young, daring, hopeful nation, so full of promise, so ready for work, and lead them forward in the way of political righteousness, giving us ideas, persuading us to build institutions thereof, and make the high thought of a man of genius the common life of a mighty nation, young as yet and capable of taking any lesson of national nobility which the most gifted man can devise; to be the ruler, not over Russian serfs, but American freemen, citizens, not subjects; to be the schoolmaster for twenty millions, and they such promising pupils, loving hard lessons; and the men that set them, the most enterprising race of persons in the world, who have already learned something of Christianity and the idea of personal freedom,—why that is a noble ambition. I do not wonder that a man of great powers should covet this great position, and feel a noble dissatisfaction and unrest until he found himself there, gravitating towards it as naturally as the Mississippi to the ocean. Put in it such men as I point to, one with the intellect of a Webster, the conscience of a Channing, the philanthropy of much humbler men; let him aim at the welfare of the nation and mankind; let him have just political ideas in advance of the nation, and, in virtue thereof, ability to solve the terrible social and political questions of this age; careless of his popularity and reputation, but careful of his conscience and his character, let him devote himself to the work of leading this people, and what an office is that of President of the United States in the middle of the nineteenth century! He would make this nation a society for mutual improvement twenty millions strong; not King Log, not King Stork, but King Good-man, King Christian if you will, he would do us a service, dignifying an office which was itself a dignity.

But if it be so noble for such a man, working with such an aim, for such an end; when a little man is in that office, with no ideas in advance of the people, and incapable of understanding such as have them; with no ability to organize the political ideas not yet organized, and applied to life; a man of routine; not ruling for the nation, but the ruler of a party and for a party, his ambition only to serve the party; an ordinary man, surrounding himself with other ordinary men; with ordinary habits, ordinary aims, ordinary means, and aiming at the ordinary ends of an adventurer; careless of his conscience and character, but careful of his party-popularity and temporary reputation,— why the office becomes painful to think of; and the officer, his state is not kingly, it is vulgar, and mean, and low! So the lighthouse on the rocks of Boston harbour is a pleasant thing to see and to imagine, with its great lamp looking far out to sea, and shining all night long, a star of special providence; seen afar off, when stormy skies shut other stars from sight, it assures the mariner of his whereabouts, guides the whaler and the Indiaman safe into port and peace, bringing wealth to the merchant, and a husband to the lingering wife, almost a widow in the cheating sea's delay and her own heart-sickness from hope so long deferred. But take away the great lamp, leaving all else; put in its place a little tallow candle of twenty to the pound, whose thin glitter could not be seen a mile off, spite of the burnished reflectors at its side, and which requires constant picking and trimming to keep the flame alive, and at its best estate flickers with every flutter of

the summer wind,—what would the lighthouse be to look
upon or to imagine? What a candlestick for what a
candle! Praise it as much as you will; flatter it in the
newspapers; vote it "adequate" and the "tallest beacon
in the world;" call it the "Pharos of America;" it is all
in vain; at the best, it can only attract moths and mosquitoes on a serene night; and, when the storm thunders
on that sepulchral rock, it is no light at all; and the
whaler may be split asunder, and the Indiaman go to the
grave, and the wealth of the merchant be scattered as
playthings for the sea, and the bones of the mariner may
blanch the bottom of the deep, for all the aid which that
thin dazzle can furnish, spite of its lofty tower and loftier
praise!

To rule a bank, a factory, or a railroad, when the officer
is chosen for business and not charity, to command a
packet-ship or a steamboat, you will get a man of real
talent in his line of work; one that has some history, who
has made his proof-shot, and shown that he has some
mettle in him. But to such a pass has the business of
ruling a nation arrived, that, of all the sovereigns of
Christian Europe, it is said not more than two, Nicholas
of Russia, and Oscar of Sweden, would have been distinguished if born in private stations. The most practical
and commercial nation in the world, possessing at this
moment a power more eminently great than that of the
Roman empire in its palmy time, has for a ruler a quite
ordinary woman, who contributes neither ideas nor organ-
izations, and probably could not administer wisely the
affairs of a single shire in the island. In this respect, the
highest stations of political life seem to have become as
barren as the Dead Sea. In selecting our rulers in America, it is long since we have had a man of large powers,
even of the sort which the majority of men appreciate in a
contemporary. I have sometimes thought men were selected who were thought not strong enough to hurt us
much, forgetting that a weak man may sometimes hurt us
as much more than a strong one would.

After all this preliminary, let me now say something of
the late President Taylor, only further premising that I
am here to tell the truth about him, so far as I know it,

and nothing more or less. I am not responsible for the facts of the case, only for the correct statement thereof. There have been men who were not disposed to do him justice; there were men enough to flatter and overpraise him while alive, and there will probably be enough of such now that he is dead. Much official panegyric has there been already, and much more is in prospect. I think I need not be called on for any contribution of that sort. I wish to weigh him in an even balance, neither praising nor blaming without cause. To eulogize is one thing; to deal justly, another and quite different.

ZACHARY TAYLOR was born on the 24th of November, 1784, in Orange county, Virginia. His father, Richard Taylor, was a soldier during a part of the Revolutionary War, had a colonel's commission in 1779, and appears to have been a valuable officer and a worthy man. In 1785 he removed to Kentucky, where he resided until his death. He was a farmer, a man of property and influence in Kentucky, then a new country. He was one of the framers of the Constitution of that State; several times in the Legislature, and the first collector of the port of Louisville, then a port of entry.

Zachary, the third son, followed the business of farming until he was more than twenty-three years of age. During his childhood he received such an education as you can imagine in a new and wild country like Kentucky sixty years ago. However, it is said his father took great pains with his education, and he enjoyed the instruction of a schoolmaster from Connecticut, who is still living. Hence it is plain the best part of his education must have come, not from the schoolmaster, but from the farm, the woods, and the connection with his parents and their associates. What a man learns at school, even in Boston, is but a small part of his education. In General Taylor's case, it is probable that things had much more to do with his culture than words. Men nursed on Greek and Latin would probably have called him an uneducated man; with equal justice he might call many a scholar an uneducated man. To speak and write with grammatical accuracy is by no means the best test of education.

Fondness for a military life is natural in a man born and

bred as he was, living in a country where the vicinity of the Indians made every man a Quaker or a soldier.

About 1808, volunteers were raised in the West to oppose the expected movements of Aaron Burr, a traitor to his country, a bold, bad man, who had been the candidate of the federalists for the Presidency; perhaps the worst man we had had in politics up to that time. Mr. Taylor joined one of the companies of volunteers. In 1808 he was appointed Lieutenant in the army of the United States, joined the forces, was soon sent to New Orleans, was seized with the yellow fever, and returned home.

In 1810 he was married to Miss Margaret Smith, of Maryland.

In 1811 he was employed in expeditions against the Indians in the North-west of the United States. Here he was under the command of General Harrison.

In 1812 he was made Captain, and had the command of a block-house and stockade called Fort Harrison, on the Wabash river, soon after the declaration of war against England. This place was attacked by a strong body of Indians. Captain Taylor, with less than fifty men, defended it with vigour and success. In consequence of his services on that occasion, he was promoted to the rank of Brevet Major. During the rest of the war, he continued in service on the frontiers, and seems to have done his duty faithfully as a soldier.

After the war was over, in 1815, the army was diminished to a peace establishment, and Major Taylor reduced to the rank of Captain. In consequence of this, he withdrew from the army; but, after a few months, returned, and was then, or subsequently, restored to his former rank as Major. For several years he was employed in such various military services, in the west and south-west, as must be performed in a time of peace. In 1819 he was made Lieutenant-Colonel. In 1832 he became Colonel, and in that year, with a command of four hundred men, he served under General Atkinson, in the expedition against the Sacs and other Indians led by the celebrated Black Hawk. Afterwards he was intrusted with the command of Fort Crawford, where he remained till 1836, when he was ordered to Florida, to fight against the Seminole Indians.

It was here that he made use of the bloodhounds to hunt

the poor savages from their hiding-places in the woods. You know what Mr. Pitt once said of the Spanish use of this weapon in the sixteenth century; but the animals imported from Cuba, where they had been trained to hunt runaway slaves, were of no value when put upon the track of red men. I do not know who originated the scheme of employing the bloodhounds. It has often been ascribed to General Taylor; and with good reason, I believe, has it been denied that he was the author of that plan. It was of no great honour to the nation, let who would invent it; and few men will be sorry that it did not turn out well.

It was thought Colonel Taylor displayed a good deal of skill in contending with the Indians in Florida, and, accordingly, he was made Brevet Brigadier-General, in 1838. After finishing the conquest of the Indians, he left Florida, in 1840. It is said that fighting against the Indians is a good school for a soldier. General Taylor served long at this work, and served faithfully. In the Florida war, his conduct as General is said to have been noble.

In 1840 he was made Commander of that portion of the American army in the south-west of the United States, and in 1841 removed his family from Kentucky to Baton Rouge, in Louisiana, which has since been his home. In 1845 he was ordered to Texas, and had command of the " Army of Occupation," and subsequently of the " Army of Invasion." In the war against Mexico, it is thought by competent judges that he displayed a good deal of military skill. He was beloved by his soldiers, and seems to have won their confidence, partly by success, partly by military talent, but also in part by his character, which was frank, honest, just and unpretending. I have heard of no instance in the whole war in which cruelty is chargeable upon him. Several anecdotes are related of his kindness, generosity, and openness of heart. No doubt they are true. War is a bloody trade; it makes one shudder to think of it in its terrible details; but the soldier is not necessarily a malignant or a cruel man; that bloody and profane command, so well known, uttered in the heat of conflict, when the battle seemed to waver, does not imply any peculiar cruelty or ill-will. It is only one of the accidents of war, which shows more clearly what its substance is.

I am no judge of warlike operations and of military skill, and therefore shall not pretend to pass judgment on matters which I know I do not understand; I shall not inquire as to the military value of the laurels he won at Resaca de la Palma, at Monterey, and at Buena Vista. But, in our judgment, we ought to remember one circumstance: that is, the inferiority of the Mexicans. They were beaten, I think, in every considerable battle throughout the whole war; no matter who commanded. General Scott landed at Vera Cruz, captured the city, and the far-famed Castle of St. Juan d'Ulloa, garrisoned by four thousand three hundred and ninety soldiers; and the American loss amounted to thirteen men killed, and sixty-three hurt! General Scott took possession of the great port of the nation, with less than twenty thousand soldiers, with only about fifteen thousand troops; marched nearly two hundred miles into the interior, fighting his way, and garrisoning the road behind him, sometimes even subsisting his army in the country which he conquered as he went on; and finally took the capital, a city with nearly two hundred thousand inhabitants, with less than six thousand soldiers. Suppose an army of that size were to land at Newburyport, with the intention of marching to Worcester, not two hundred miles, but only fifty or sixty, how many do you think would ever reach the spot? Why, suppose the American men did nothing, there are women enough in Massachusetts to throw every soldier into the Merrimac!

I do not believe that this inferiority of the Mexican arises so much from the superior bravery of the Americans; almost any male animal will fight on small provocation; your Mexican male, as well as your American, on as small provocation, and as desperately. But the American soldier was always well armed, furnished with everything that modern science makes terrible in war; well clad, well fed, well paid, he went voluntarily to the work. The Mexicans were ill armed, ill clad, ill fed, often not paid at all, and sometimes brought to fight against their will.

The difference does not end here: the main reliance of the Mexican government, the regular soldiers, the Presidiales, were men who seemed to have most of the vices of old garrison soldiers, with most of the faults of new recruits; or, as another has said, himself a soldier in the war,

"All the vices engendered in a garrison life; all the cowardice which their constant defeats by the Indians had created; all the laziness contracted in an idle monotonous existence, and very little military skill." The new levies came unwillingly, and were often only "food for powder." On the American side was a small body of veteran soldiers, low and coarse men—it is the policy of America to have the rank and file of our army in peace composed usually of such—but full of brute courage; accustomed to all sorts of hardships and exposure; under a discipline rigorous and almost perfect; wonted to danger, and weaned from fear; careless of life almost to desperation; full of confidence in their commander, and of contempt for their foe. The volunteers brought with them the characteristic ardour of Americans, their confidence of success, their contempt of toil and of danger; familiar with fire-arms from their youth, they soon learned the discipline of the camp.

You see what a difference this makes between the two armies; but the chief superiority of the American soldiers was this—they came from a country where there is a complete national unity of action. So the government could trust the army, and the army the government; the soldiers had confidence in their commander, confidence in their country, confidence in their cause; while the Mexicans had no national unity of action, the people little confidence in the government, the government as little in the people; the nation but little trust in the army, and the army little in the nation; the soldiers had great fear of the enemy, little faith in their officers, and the officers little in their men. Did you ever see a swarm of bees when the queen bee was dead, and moths had invaded the hive? The Mexicans were much in the same state. The result was what had readily been foreseen: at the battle of Buena Vista, on the one side, there were twenty-one thousand five hundred and fifty-three Mexicans; on the other, four thousand seven hundred and fifty-nine American soldiers, of which only four hundred and seventy-six were regulars. Yet the American loss, in killed, wounded and missing, was but seven hundred and forty-six, while that of the Mexican army was nearly two thousand men lost. If the Mexicans had done the same proportionate execution, every American would have been killed long before night.

All these things ought to be taken into account, in making up our mind about the difficulty of the enterprise. Still, after this allowance is made, it must be confessed the American invasion of Mexico was a remarkable undertaking, distinguished for its boldness, not to say its rashness, and almost unparalleled in the history of modern wars. It certainly did require great coolness, courage, and prudence, on the part of General Taylor, to conduct his part of the expedition. He had those qualities; but it has not yet been proved, or shown to be probable, that he had the nobler qualities which make a great General. The kind of warfare he was engaged in does not bring to light the high qualities of a man like Gustavus Adolphus, Frederick the Great, or Napoleon. Perhaps General Taylor had them, but they did not appear.

The Mexican war was unfortunate for the administration which carried it on, for the political party which caused the war. The success of General Taylor attracted the attention of the people, and the obscure soldier took popular rank before the President of the United States. Unconsciously the vicarious suitor, courting public favour for his master, won good graces for himself. The political party which began the war was eclipsed by the triumph of its own soldier; and the slave-power which projected the war seems likely to be ruined by the success of the enterprise.

It has been said, that he was averse to the Mexican war which he fought in; I know not whether this be true or false. But, if true, it deserves to be remembered in his defence, that the soldier is only an active tool, as much the instrument of his employer as the spade of the workman whose foot crowds it into the ground. The soldier, high or low, must obey the men who have the official right to command him, his free-will merging in that of his superior. If General Taylor had thought the Mexican war unjust and wicked, and in consequence had resigned his commission, he would have been covered with obloquy and contempt in the eyes of military men, and the officials of government. Most of the newspapers of the land would have attacked him, called him a coward, a traitor and a fanatic; their condemnation would have been worth as

much as their praise is now. In estimating his character
we ought to remember this fact, for few men do more than
their office demands of them, or more than public opinion
can approve.

Such was the success of General Taylor in war, at the
head of a few thousand men, that public attention was
turned towards him, and in a few months the obscure
frontier soldier was the most prominent man in the nation.
In 1848 he received the nomination of the Whig Convention at Philadelphia for President, and in due time was
elected.

His election was certainly one of the most remarkable
that ever took place in America. It is worth while to
look at it for a moment. There was nothing very remarkable in the man to entitle him to that eminent distinction;
if there were, the nation was very slow in finding it out.
He was a farmer till about twenty-four years old; then a
common Lieutenant four years more. In the next twenty
years he got no higher than to the rank of a "Frontier
Colonel;" he attained that dignity, in fact, at the age of
forty-eight. He was not made General till the fifty-fifth
year of his age. But for the Mexican war, I suppose he
would, at this day, be as obscure as any other General in
the United States' army; nobody would think he was the
"Second Washington," "first in war, first in peace, and
first in the hearts of his countrymen," as his creatures
have declared. Other military men have been chosen
to the presidency. But Washington was much more than
a soldier; in "a time that tried men's souls" to the utmost,
he had carried the nation through eight years of most
perilous warfare, more by his character than any eminent
military skill, and so had become endeared to the hearts of
the people as no American had ever been before. General
Jackson, at first educated as a lawyer, was a man of large
talents, distinguished as a Governor, as a Senator, and as
a Judge of the Supreme Court of Tennessee, before he was
elected President, or nominated for that office. General
Harrison, a man of small abilities, surely not more than a
third-rate politician in Ohio, was yet familiar with the
routine of political affairs. He had been a member of the
Legislature of Ohio, of both branches of the Congress of
the United States, and Minister to Colombia. General

Taylor, with an education very imperfect, had passed his life, from twenty-four to sixty-four, on the frontiers and in the army; had never held any civil office; had seldom voted, and, though an excellent officer in the sphere of duty he had occupied, did not appear to be the most promising man in the nation to select for its highest and most difficult office. The defence of a log-house in 1812 against a troop of Indians, the conquest of Black Hawk, the rout of the Seminoles, the gaining of half-a-dozen battles in Mexico, at the head of a few thousand soldiers, does not seem exactly an adequate schooling to prepare a common man to lead and rule twenty million Americans with the most complicated government in the world. It certainly was surprising that he should be nominated for that office; and more so, that the nomination should be confirmed by the people. It is not surprising that the distinguished Senator of Massachusetts should call this "A nomination not fit to be made;" the wonder is, he deemed it fit to be confirmed. In selecting him for our chief, the nation went hap-hazard, and made a leap in the dark. No prudent man in Boston would hire a cook or a coachman with such inadequate recommendations as General Taylor had to prove his fitness for his place. Had a sensible man on election day asked the nation, "What do you know about the man you vote for?" the people would have been sadly puzzled to seek for an answer. The reasons which led to his election were partly special, and partly of a general and popular character. It is instructive for us to look at them, now that we can do it coolly.

I suppose this was the special cause of his nomination: The leaders of the whig party thought they could not elect either of their most prominent men. If they went before the people with nothing but their idea,—The protection of property by a tariff, and a Representative of that idea, however able and well trained, they feared defeat; such as they had met with in the last campaign, when the democratic party, with a man almost unknown to the people, a tricky lawyer from Tennessee, had yet carried the day against one of the oldest and ablest politicians in the country. So the whig leaders availed themselves of the temporary popularity of a successful General to give an accidental triumph to their party, and apparently to their idea. That I think was the specific reason which led the politicians to nominate him. Doubtless there were other private reasons, weighty to certain individuals, that need not be touched upon.

But the general reasons, which gave him weight with the mass of the people and secured his election, ought to be stated for our serious reflection.

1. There was no one of the great leaders of either party whom the people had much confidence in. I am sorry to say so, but I do not think there is much in any of them to command the respect of a nation, and make us swear fealty to those men. There were two candidates of the whig party; from one of them you might expect a compromise; from the other you were not certain even of that. The democratic candidate had not a name to conjure with. The free soil candidate—was he a man to trust in such times as these? Did you see your king and chief in any one of those four men? Was any one of them fit to be the political schoolmaster of this nation? What "ground and lofty tumbling" have we had from all four of them?

2. General Taylor was not mixed up with the grand or petty intrigues of the parties, their quarrels and struggles for office. Men knew little about him; if little good, certainly little not good; little evil in comparison with any of the others. Sometimes you take a man whom you do not know, in preference to an old acquaintance whom you have known too long and too well to trust.

3. Then General Taylor had shown himself a rough, honest, plain, straightforward man, and withal mild and good-natured. Apparently, there was much in him to attract and deserve the good-will of the nation. His likeness went abroad through the country like a proclamation; it was the rude, manly, firm, honest, good-natured, homely face of a backwoodsman. His plain habits, plain talk, and modest demeanour reminded men of the old English ballad of "The King and the Miller," and the like, and won the affections of honest men. I doubt not the fact that General Harrison had once lived in a log-cabin, and, other things failing, did drink "hard cider," gave him thousands of votes. The candidate was called "Old Rough and Ready," and there was not a clown in field or city but could understand all that was meant by

those terms.   Even his celebrated horse contributed to his
master's election, and drew votes for the President by the
thousand.

4. Then he was a successful soldier.   The dullest man
in the Alleghany mountains, or in the low lanes of New
York and Boston, or the silliest behind the counters of a
city shop, can understand fighting, and remember who
won a battle.   It is wholly needless for such to inquire
what the battle was fought for.   Hence military success is
always popular with the multitude, and will be, I suppose,
for some ages in America as everywhere else.   Our churches
know no God but the "Lord of hosts," "A man of
war!"

5. Then he was a southern man, and all our masters
must be from the South, or of it, devoted to its peculiar
institution.   If he had been born in Barnstable county,
and owned a little patch of yellow sand at Cape Cod, and
had the freeman's hatred of slavery, even Churubusco
and Buena Vista would not have given him the votes of
the Convention, and his war-horse might have lived till
this day, he would not have carried his master to the presidency.   He was a slaveholder, as seven Presidents had
been before him, holding office for eight-and-forty-years.
There are some men at the North, chiefly in the country
towns, who think it is not altogether right for a man to steal
his brother; such men were to be propitiated.   So it was
diligently rumoured abroad in the North, that the candidate was "opposed to slavery," that he would "probably
emancipate his slaves as soon as he was elected."   I am
told that some persons who heard such a story actually
believed it; I think nobody who told it believed any such
thing.   The fact that he was a slaveholder, that he had
lately purchased one hundred and fourteen men, women,
and children, and kept them at hard work for his advantage, showed the value of such a story; and the opposite
statement, publicly and industriously circulated at the
South, that he loved slavery, desired its extension, and
hated the Wilmot Proviso, shows the honesty of some of
the men at the North, who, knowing these facts, sought to
keep them secret.

These seem to have been the chief reasons which procured his nomination and election.   It is easy to see that

such a man, though as honest as Washington, must be eminently unfit for the high office of President of the United States. He knew little or nothing of the political history of the country, or of the political questions then up for solution; little or nothing of the political men. He had the honesty to confess it. He declared that he was not fit for the office, not acquainted with the political measures of the day, and only consented to be brought from his obscurity when great men told him he was the only man that could " save the Union." He was no statesman, and knew nothing of politics, less than the majority of the more cultivated mechanics, merchants and farmers. He was a soldier, and knew something of fighting, at least of fighting Indians and Mexicans. If you should take a man of the common abilities, intellectual and moral, the common education, a farmer from Northfield, a skipper from Provincetown, a jobber from Boston, a bucket-maker from Hingham, and appoint him Chief Justice of the Supreme Court of Massachusetts, with the duty of selecting all his associate Judges, I think he would be about as competent for the office as General Taylor for the post he was elected to. In such a case as I have supposed, the new "Judge" must depend on other men, who will tell him what to do; his only safety would be in relying on their advice. Then they would be the Chief Justice, not he.

Under such circumstances, the leaders of one party nominated him. I must confess such an act, committed by such men, seems exceedingly rash. It was done by the very men who ought, above all others, to have known better. This is one of the many things we have had, which show thinking men how little we can rely on our political chiefs. The nomination once made, the election followed. The wise men told the multitude: " You must vote for him," and the multitude voted. You know how angry men were if you did not believe in his fitness for the office; how it became a test of " patriotism" to believe in him. Now the good man is cold in death, how base all that seems !

When such a man, under such circumstances, comes into such an office, you do not know whether the deeds which receive his official sanction, the papers published under his name, the speeches he delivers, and the messages he sends,

are his or not his. It is probable that he has little to do
with them; they are his officially, not personally; he
writes State papers by their signature. Some of his
speeches were undoubtedly made for him. You know it
once happened that a speech, alleged to have been made by
him at a public meeting, was sent on by telegraph, and
published by the party organ, in one of our great cities,
and he was taken sick before the meeting was held, and
could not speak at all. That speech betrayed the trick of
the administration: it was a speech he had never heard of.
From this one act judge of many more. In his arduous
office, he must choose advisers; but he wants advisers to
advise him to choose advisers. Much will depend on his
first step; that must needs be in the dark.

Since this is so, I shall pass over his brief administration
with very few words. I do not know how much it was the
administration of General Taylor, or how far it was that
of his Cabinet. I do not know who made the Cabinet.
The messages, in his official term, were as good as usual;
but who made the messages? One thing is clear: he
promised to be the President of the country, not of a
party; to remove no man from office except for reasons
not political. Neither promise was kept. It was plain
that other elements interfered and counteracted the honest
intentions of that honest man. General Jackson rewarded
his "friends" and punished his "enemies," men who
voted against him. Mr. Jefferson had done the same.
But I doubt if the administration of either of these men
was so completely a party administration as that of General
Taylor. Men were continually removed from office purely
for political reasons. The general character of his appointments to office you can judge of better than I. It seems
to me the removal of subordinate officers from their station
on account of their vote is one great evil in the manage-
ment of our institutions. Of what consequence is it
whether the postmaster at Eastham or West-Newton, the
keeper of the lighthouse at Cape Anne, or the Clay Pounds
of Truro, or the district attorney in Boston, or the
tide-waiters at Nantucket are " good whigs," or not good
whigs?

What shall I say of the character of the man who has

left this high office; of him on the whole? Some men can be as eloquent on a ribbon as on a Raphael. They find no difficulty in calling General Taylor " the Second Washington." I like the first Washington too much to call any one by that name lightly. General Harrison was the " Second Washington" ten years ago. General Jackson ten years before that. I think there is another " Second Washington" getting ready; and before the century ends we shall perhaps have five or six of this family. But the world does not breed great men every day. I must confess it, I have not seen anything very great in General Taylor, though I have diligently put my eye to the magnifying glasses of his political partisans; neither have I seen anything uncommonly mean and little in him, though I have also looked through the minifying glasses of his foes. To be a frontier soldier for forty years, to attain the rank of Colonel at the age of forty-eight, after twenty-four years of service, to become a Brigadier-General at fifty-four, is no great thing. To defend a log-house, to capture Black Hawk, to use bloodhounds in war, and to extirpate the Seminole Indians from the ever-glades of Florida, to conquer the Mexicans at Churubusco and Monterey, does not require very high qualities of mind and heart. But in all the offices he ever held, he appears to have done his official duty openly and honestly. He was a good officer, a plain, blunt, frank, open, modest man. No doubt he was " rough and ready;" his courage was never questioned. His integrity is above suspicion. All this is well known. But is all this enough to make a great man in the middle of this century; a great man in America, and for such an office? Judge for yourselves.

I sincerely believe that he was more of a man than his political supporters thought him; that he had more natural sagacity, more common sense, more firmness of purpose, and very much more honesty than they expected or desired. Rumours reach me that he was not found quite so manageable as his "friends" and admirers had hoped; that he had some conscience and a will of his own. It seems to me that he honestly intended to be an honest and impartial ruler, the President of his country; that he took Washington for his general model; that he never sought the office, and at first did not desire it; but when

he came to it endeavoured to deserve well of his country
and do well by mankind. But, with the best intentions,
what could such a man do, especially with such foes, and
more especially with such friends.

It is said he was a religious man : sometimes that means
that a man loves God and loves men; sometimes that he is
superstitious, formal, hypocritical, that he does not love
men, and is afraid of God, or of a devil. I do not know
in which sense the word is used in reference to him. But
it appears to me that he was a man of veracity, honest,
upright, and downright too ; a good father, a good husband, a good friend, faithful to his idea of duty; very
plain, very unpretending, mild and yet firm, good-natured,
free, and easy. There were many that loved him; a rare
circumstance among politicians. He was a temperate man,
also, remarkably temperate ; and such temperance as his is
not a very common virtue in high political and social
stations in America, as we all know too well.

These are all the good qualities I can make out his title
to. I suppose there are some ten thousand men in Massachusetts that are his equals in all these qualities, as
honest, as able, and as patriotic as he. It is hardly worth
while to worship those qualities in a President which are
not rare in farmers, and traders, and butchers, and mechanics.

There are two things which seem to me decidedly wrong
in his public career. His partisans at the North claimed
that he was hostile to slavery. I never could find any
reason for that opinion : at the South his friends insisted
that he was the decided friend of slavery. When his
opinion was asked on this matter, he remained steadily and
pertinaciously silent. To me this does not seem honest or
manly.

Then he was a slaveholder, not by compulsion, as some
pretend they hold men in bondage, not by inheritance.
He was a slaveholder from choice, and only three years
ago bought one hundred and fourteen human beings and
kept them as his slaves. This fact must be considered in
estimating the character and value of the man. I know
that Money is the popular god of America; that slaveholding is one of the canonical forms of worshipping that
god, sanctioned by the Constitution and the laws and the

legislature of the land, by its literature and by its churches. I know men in Boston who would have no more scruple in buying and selling a black man as a slave, or a white man if they could catch and keep him, than they would have of buying a cow at Brighton. There are men in Massachusetts that have grown rich by the slave-trade. It does not hurt their reputation; it is no impeachment of their religious character. Now I do not expect a frontier colonel, busy in fighting Indians half his life, dogging them with Cuban bloodhounds, to be more enlightened on such a matter than merchants, manufacturers, lawyers, ministers and professors of theology in New England. It may be that he had the same opinion as Professor Stuart, that slavery was allowed in the New Testament and sanctioned in the Old Testament; such a good thing that Paul and James said never a word against it. We should not judge such a man as you would judge a Unitarian Minister in Boston or Doctors of Divinity at Andover. Born as he was, bred as he had been, living in a camp, sustained by the public opinion of the Press, the State and the Church, it would not be surprising if it had never occurred to him that it was wrong to steal men. But the fact is to be taken into the account in determining the elevation of his character.

It is now plain that he found the office of President a heavy burden; that it cost him his life. It seems to me the conduct of some of our public men towards him was ungenerous, not to say unjust and shameful. An honest man, he looked for honest foes and honest friends; but his hardest battles were fought after he had ceased to be a soldier.

Well, he has gone to his rest and his recompense. To his family the affliction is sudden, painful and terrible. What vicissitudes in their life—from the obscurity of their former home to the glaring publicity of that high station; then, in so brief a time, the honoured and well-beloved head is silent and cold for ever! The nation may well drop its tears of sympathy for those whom its election has robbed of a father and a husband; the ghastly honours of the office are poor recompense for the desolation it has brought into a quiet and once happy home.

He has gone to his reward. He leaves the government

in the hands of an obscure man, whom the nation knows very little of, whom no one would ever have thought of making President; a man selected certainly for no eminence of faculty, intellectual or moral. There is some cause to fear, perhaps some little for hope.* Two very important questions are now before the nation: Shall we extend over the territory conquered from Mexico the awful blight which now mildews the material welfare of the South, and curses with a threefold ban the intellect, the conscience and the religion of the land ? Shall Congress pass that

---

* The above was written in July, 1851. Since then the ground of hope has wholly vanished; the ground for fear remains alone. The following statement may suggest a thought the other side of the ocean, if no shame on this side among politicians and their priests :

Elisha Brazealle, a planter of Jefferson county in the State of Mississippi, was taken sick, and as he lay oppressed with a loathsome disease, a slave of his, a bright mulatto or quadroon, nursed him, and, as was believed, through her nursing, saved him from death. He was a man of feeling and did not forget her kindness, but took her to Ohio and there educated her. She made rapid progress, and soon became his wife. He made, or caused to be made, a legal and sound deed of emancipation, and had it legally and formally recorded in Ohio and Mississippi. Lawyers, in both States, said she was free, safe, and that no power in the South or elsewhere, could legally deprive her or her children of freedom.

Mr. Brazealle returned to Mississippi with his wife; they had a son, and named him John Munroe Brazealle. After some years, Mr. Brazealle sickened and died, leaving a will, in which he recited the deed of emancipation, declared his intention to ratify it, and devised all his property to his son, acknowledging him in the will to be such.

Some poor and distant relations of his in North Carolina, whom he did not know, and for whom he did not care, hearing of his death, went on to Mississippi and claimed the property devised by Mr. Brazealle to his son. They instituted a suit for the recovery of the property. The case came before William L. Sharkey, "Chief Justice of the High Court of Errors and Appeals" for that State. It is reported in Howard's Mississippi Reports, Vol. II., p. 837, et seq. Judge Sharkey declared the act of emancipation "An offence against morality, pernicious and detestable as an example," set aside the will, gave to those distant relations the property which Mr. Brazealle had devised to his son, and, in addition, declared that son and his mother to be slaves. Here is his own language :—

"The state of the case shows conclusively that the contract had its origin in an offence against morality, pernicious and detestable as an example." . . . . "The consequence [of the decision] is, that the negroes John Munroe and his mother are still slaves, and a part of the estate of Elisha Brazealle." "John Munroe, being a slave, cannot take the property as devised; and I apprehend it is equally clear that it cannot be held in trust for him."

While these volumes are in the press, I learn that Mr. Fillmore has appointed Judge Sharkey to the honourable and lucrative post of Consul to Havana.

infamous fugitive slave measure, known as Mr. Mason's bill, with Mr. Webster's indorsement on it? I know not how his death will affect these things. Who knows the intentions of the late President? or those of his successor? He has power to bless, he may use it only to curse the land. Let us wait and see. The fact that the "Great Compromiser" now represents the Administration in the Senate, the rumour of the appointment of the Senator of Boston to the highest place in the Cabinet, are things of ill omen for freedom, and bid us fear the worst. However, it may be that this event will affect the politicians more than the people.

Last Tuesday night General Taylor ceased to be mortal. His soul went home to God. He that fought against the Mexican and the Indian has gone to meet the God of the red man as well as the white. He who claimed to own the body and the soul of more than a hundred of his fellow-creatures, enriched by the unrequited toil, which they unwillingly gave him when stung by the lash of his hireling overseers, has gone home to the Father of negro slaves, who is no respecter of persons; gone where the servant is free from his master. Black and white, conqueror and vanquished, the bond and the free, alike come up before the Infinite Father, whose perfect justice is perfect love; and there the question is, "What hast thou done with the talent committed unto thee?" The same question is asked of the President; the same of the slave; yea, it will one day be asked of you and me!

"An old man, wearied with the storms of State," now only asks a little earth for charity. Costly heathen pageants there will be in these streets to his memory, and politicians will, I suppose, hold their drunken and profane debauch over his grave, as over the tomb of that far-famed friend of freedom who died two years ago. But he has ceased to be mortal. The memory of his battle-fields faded from before his dying sight. Power rests no longer in his hands; victory perches on another banner. His ear is still, and his heart is cold. How hollow sounds the voice of former flattery! His riches go to other men; his slaves will be called by his name no more; the scourge that goads them to unpaid toil is now owned by another man. His fame goes back to such as gave; the accident

of an accident succeeds him in the presidential chair : only
the man, not the officer, goes home to God, with what of
goodness and piety he had won. His manhood is all that he
can carry out of the world ; elected or rejected, a conqueror
or conquered, it is now the same to him ; and it may be the
humblest female slave who only earned the bread which her
master only ate, and got an enforced concubinage for pay,
takes rank in heaven far before the man whom the nation
honoured with its highest trust, and for whom the official
Senate and low-browed Church send out their hollow
groans.

> " The glories of our birth and State
>   Are shadows, not substantial things.
>   There is no armour against fate :
>   Death lays his icy hand on kings.
>   Sceptre and crown
>   Must tumble down,
>   And in the dust be equal made,
>   With the poor crooked scythe and spade.
>
> " Some men with swords may reap the field,
>   And plant fresh laurels where they kill ;
>   But their strong arms at last must yield,
>   They tame but one another still.
>   Early or late
>   They stoop to fate,
>   And must give up their murmuring breath
>   When they, pale captives, creep to death.
>
> " The garlands wither on his brow :
>   Then boast no more his mighty deeds,
>   Upon death's purple altar now,
>   See where the victor victim bleeds.
>   All heads must come
>   To the cold tomb,
>   Only the actions of the just
>   Smell sweet and blossom in the dust."

If he could speak to us from his present position,
methinks he would say : Countrymen and friends ! You
see how little it availed you to agitate the land and put a
little man in a great place. It is not the hurrah of parties
that will " save the Union," it is not " great men." It is
only Justice. Remember that Atheism is not the first
principle of a Republic ; remember there is a law of God,
the higher law of the universe, the Everlasting Right ; I
thought so once, and now I know it. Remember that you
are accountable to God for all things ; that you owe justice

to all men, the black not less than the white; that God will demand it of you, proud, wicked nation, careful only of your gold, forgetful of God's high law! Before long each of you shall also come up before the Eternal. Then and there it will not avail you to have compromised truth, justice, love, but to have kept them. Righteousness only is the salvation of a State; that only of a man.

VIII.

SPEECH AT A MEETING OF THE CITIZENS OF BOS-
TON, IN FANEUIL HALL, MARCH 25, 1850, TO
CONSIDER THE SPEECH OF MR. WEBSTER.

Mr. President and Fellow Citizens : It is an important occasion which has brought us together. A great
crisis has occurred in the affairs of the United States.
There is a great question now before the people. In any
European country west of Russia and east of Spain, it
would produce a revolution, and be settled with gunpowder.
It narrowly concerns the material welfare of the nation.
The decision that is made will help millions of human
beings into life, or will hinder and prevent millions from
being born. It will help or hinder the advance of the
nation in wealth for a long time to come. It is a question
which involves the honour of the people. Your honour
and my honour are concerned in this matter, which is presently to be passed upon by the people of the United States.
More than all this, it concerns the morality of the people.
We are presently to do a right deed, or to inflict a great
wrong on others and on ourselves, and thereby entail an
evil upon this continent which will blight and curse it for
many an age.

It is a great question, comprising many smaller ones :—
Shall we extend and foster Slavery, or shall we extend and
foster Freedom ? Slavery, with its consequences, material,
political, intellectual, moral ; or Freedom, with the consequences thereof ?

A question so important seldom comes to be decided
before any generation of men. This age is full of great
questions, but this of Freedom is the chief. It is the same
question which in other forms comes up in Europe. This
is presently to be decided here in the United States by the

servants of the people, I mean, by the Congress of the nation; in the name of the people; for the people, if justly decided; against them, if unjustly. If it were to be left to-morrow to the naked votes of the majority, I should have no fear. But the public servants of the people may decide otherwise. The political parties, as such, are not to pass judgment. It is not a question between whigs and democrats; old party distinctions, once so sacred and rigidly observed, here vanish out of sight. The party of Slavery or the party of Freedom is to swallow up all the other parties. Questions about tariffs and banks can hardly get a hearing. On the approach of a battle, men do not talk of the weather.

Four great men in the Senate of the United States have given us their decision; the four most eminent in the party politics of the nation—two great whigs, two great democrats. The Shibboleth of their party is forgotten by each; there is a strange unanimity in their decision. The Herod of free-trade and the Pilate of protection are "made friends," when freedom is to be crucified. All four decide adverse to freedom; in favour of slavery; against the people. Their decisions are such as you might look for in the politicians of Austria and Russia. Many smaller ones have spoken on this side or on that. Last of all, but greatest, the most illustrious of the four, so far as great gifts of the understanding are concerned, a son of New England, long known, and often and deservedly honoured, has given his decision. We waited long for his words; we held our peace in his silence; we listened for his counsel. Here it is; adverse to freedom beyond the fears of his friends, and the hopes even of his foes. He has done wrong things before, cowardly things more than once; but this, the wrongest and most cowardly of them all: we did not look for it. No great man in America has had his faults or his failings so leniently dealt with; private scandal we will not credit, public shame we have tried to excuse, or, if inexcusable, to forget. We have all of us been proud to go forward and honour his noble deeds, his noble efforts, even his noble words. I wish we could take a mantle big and black enough, and go backward and cover up the shame of the great man who has fallen in the midst of us, and hide him till his honour and his conscience shall return. But no, it cannot be; his deed is done in the face of the world, and nothing can hide it.

We have come together to-night in Faneuil Hall, to talk the matter over, in our New England way; to look each other in the face; to say a few words of warning, a few of counsel, perhaps something which may serve for guidance. We are not met here to-night to "calculate the value of the Union," but to calculate the worth of freedom and the rights of man; to calculate the value of the Wilmot Proviso. Let us be cool and careful, not violent, not rash; true and firm, not hasty or timid.

Important matters have brought our fathers here many times before now. Before the Revolution, they came here to talk about the Molasses Act, or the Sugar Act, or the Stamp Act, the Boston Port Bill, and the long list of grievances which stirred up their manly stomachs to the Revolution; afterwards, they met to consult about the Embargo, and the seizure of the Chesapeake, and many other matters. Not long ago, only five years since, we came here to protest against the annexation of Texas. But before the Revolution or after it, meetings have seldom been called in Faneuil Hall on such solemn occasions as this. Not only is there a great public wrong contemplated, as in the annexation of Texas, but the character and conduct of a great public servant of the people come up to be looked after. This present conduct of Mr. Webster is a thing to be solemnly considered. A similar thing once happened before. In 1807, a senator from Massachusetts was disposed to accept a measure the President had advised, because he had "recommended" it "on his high responsibility." "I would *not consider*," said the senator, "I would *not deliberate*, I would *act*." * He did so; and with little deliberation, with small counsel, as men thought at the time, he voted for the Embargo, and the Embargo came. This was a measure which doomed eight hundred thousand tons of shipping to rot at the wharf. It touched the pockets of New England and all the North. It affected the daily meals of millions of men. There was indignation, deep and loud indignation; but it was political in its nature and personal in its form; the obnoxious measure was purely political, not obviously immoral and

* Mr. John Quincy Adams.

unjust. But, long as John Quincy Adams lived, much as he did in his latter years for mankind, he never wholly wiped off the stain which his conduct then brought upon him. Yet it may be that he was honest in his vote; it may have been an error of judgment, and nothing more; nay, there are men who think it was no error at all, but a piece of political wisdom.

A senator of Massachusetts has now committed a fault far greater than was ever charged upon Mr. Adams by his most inveterate political foes. It does not directly affect the shipping of New England and the North: I wish it did. It does not immediately concern our daily bread; if it were so, the contemplated wrong would receive a speedy adjustment. But it concerns the liberty of millions of men yet unborn.

Let us look at the matter carefully.

Here is a profile of our national action on the subject now before the people.

In 1774, we agreed to import no more slaves after that year, and never finally repealed this act of agreement.

In 1776, we declared that all men are created equal, and endowed by their Creator with certain unalienable rights, among which are life, liberty, and the pursuit of happiness.

In 1778, we formed the Confederacy, with no provision for the surrender of fugitive slaves.

In 1787, we shut out slavery from the North-West Territory for ever, by the celebrated proviso of Mr. Jefferson.

In 1788, the Constitution was formed, with its compromises and guarantees.

In 1808, the importation of slaves was forbidden. But,

In 1803, we annexed Louisiana, and slavery along with it.

In 1819, we annexed Florida, with more slavery.

In 1820, we legally established slavery in the territory west of the Mississippi, south of 36 deg. 30 min.

In 1845, we annexed Texas, with three hundred and twenty-five thousand five hundred and twenty square miles, as a slave State.

In 1848, we acquired, by conquest and by treaty, the vast territory of California and New Mexico, containing five hundred and twenty-six thousand and seventy-eight square miles. Of this, two hundred and four thousand

three hundred and eighty-three square miles are south of
the slave line—south of 36 deg. 30 min.   Here is territory
enough to make more than thirty slave States of the size
of Massachusetts.

At the present day, it is proposed to have some further
action on the matter of slavery.   Connected with this subject, four great questions come up to be decided :—

1. Shall four new slave States at any time be made out
of Texas ?   This is not a question which is to be decided at
present, yet it is one of great present importance, and furnishes an excellent test of the moral character and political
conduct of politicians at this moment.   The other questions
are of immediate and pressing concern.   Here they are:—

2. Shall Slavery be prohibited in California ?

3. Shall Slavery be prohibited in New Mexico ?

4. What laws shall be passed relative to fugitive slaves ?

Mr. Webster, in this speech, defines his position in regard to each of these four questions.

I. In regard to the new States to be made hereafter out
of Texas, he gives us his opinion, in language well studied,
and even with an excess of caution.   Let us look at it, and
the resolution which annexed Texas.   That declares that
" new States   .   .   .   not exceeding four in number, in
addition to said State of Texas   .   .   .   may hereafter,
by the consent of said State, be formed out of the territory
thereof, which shall be entitled to admission under the
provisions of the Federal Constitution.   And such States
.   .   .   shall be admitted with or without slavery, as the
people of each State asking admission may desire."

I will not stop to consider the constitutionality of the
joint resolution which annexed Texas.   Mr. Webster's
opinion on that subject is well known.   But the resolution
does two things : 1. It confers a power, the power to make
four new States on certain conditions ; a qualified power,
restricted by the terms of the act.   2nd. It imposes an
obligation, namely, the obligation to leave it to the people
of the new State to keep slaves or not, when the State is
admitted.   The words *may be,* etc., indicate the confer-
ring of a power : the words *shall be,* etc., the imposing of
an obligation. ' But as the power is a qualified power, so
is the obligation a qualified obligation ; the *shall be* is
dependent on the *may be,* as much as the *may be* on the

shall. Admitting in argument what Mr. Webster has denied, that Congress had the constitutional right to annex Texas by joint resolution, and also that the resolution of one Congress binds the future Congress, it is plain Congress may admit new States from Texas, on those conditions, or refuse to admit them. This is plain, by any fair construction of the language. The resolution does not say, they *shall* be formed, only "*may* be formed," and "*shall* be entitled to admission, under the provisions of the Federal Constitution"—not in spite of those provisions. The provisions of the Constitution, in relation to the formation and admission of new States, are well known, and sufficiently clear. Congress is no more bound to admit a new slave State formed out of Texas, than out of Kentucky. But Mr. Webster seems to say that Congress is bound to make four new States out of Texas, when there is sufficient population to warrant the measure, and a desire for it in the States themselves, and to admit them with a Constitution allowing slavery. He says, "Its guaranty is, that new States shall be made out of it, . . . and that such States . . . may come in as slave States," etc. Quite the contrary. It is only said they "*may be* formed," and admitted "under the provisions of the Constitution." The *shall be* does not relate to the fact of admission.

Then he says, there is "a solemn pledge," "that if she shall be divided into States, those States may come in as slave States." But there is no "solemn pledge" that they *shall come* in at all. I make a "solemn pledge" to John Doe, that if ever I give him any land, it shall be a thousand acres in the meadows on Connecticut River; but it does not follow from this that I am bound to give John Doe any land at all. This solemn pledge is worth nothing, if Congress says to new States, You shall not come in with your slave Constitution. To make this "stipulation with Texas" binding, it ought to have provided that "new States . . . shall be formed out of the territory thereof . . . such States shall be entitled to admission, in spite of the provisions of the Constitution." Even then it would be of no value; for as there can be no moral obligation to do an immoral deed, so there can be no constitutional obligation to do an unconstitutional deed. So much for the first question. You see that Mr. Webster proposes to do what we never stipulated to do, what is not "so nominated in the bond." He wrests the resolution against freedom, and for the furtherance of the slave power.

II. and III. Mr. Webster has given his answer to the second and third questions, which may be considered as a single question, Shall slavery be legally forbidden by Congress in California and New Mexico? Mr. Webster is opposed to the prohibition by Congress. Here are his words : "Now, as to California and New Mexico, I hold slavery to be excluded from those territories by a law even superior to that which admits and sanctions it in Texas. I mean the law of nature, of physical geography, the law of the formation of the earth." . . . "I will say further, that if a resolution or a law were now before us to provide a territorial government for New Mexico, I would not vote to put any prohibition into it whatever. The use of such a prohibition would be idle, as it respects any effect it would have upon the territory : and I would not take pains to re-affirm an ordinance of nature, nor to re-enact the will of God." "The gentlemen who belong to the Southern States would think it a taunt, an indignity ; they would think it an act taking away from them what they regard as a proper equality of privilege " . . . "a plain theoretic wrong," "more or less derogatory to their character and their rights."

"African slavery," he tells us, "cannot exist there." It could once exist in Massachusetts and New Hampshire. Very little of this territory lies north of Mason and Dixon's line, the northern limit of Maryland; none above the parallel of forty-two degrees ; none of it extends fifty miles above the northern limit of Virginia ; two hundred and four, thousand three hundred and fifty-three square miles of it lie south of the line of the Missouri Compromise, south of 36° 30'. Almost all of it is in the latitude of Virginia and the Carolinas. If slavery can exist on the west coast of the Atlantic, I see not why it cannot on the east of the Pacific, and all the way between. There is no reason why it cannot. It will, unless we forbid it by positive laws, laws which no man can misunderstand. Why, in 1787, it was thought necessary to forbid slavery in the North-West Territory, which extends from the Ohio River to the forty-ninth parallel of north latitude.

Not exclude slavery from California and New Mexico, because it can never exist there! Why, it was there once, and Mexico abolished it by positive law. Abolished, did I say! We are not so sure of that; I mean, not sure that the Senate of the United States is sure of it. Not a month before Mr. Webster made this very speech, on the 13th and 14th of last February, Mr. Davis, the Senator from Mississippi, maintained that slavery is not abolished in California and New Mexico. He denies that the acts abolishing slavery in Mexico were made by competent powers; denies that they have the force of law. But even if they have, he tells us, "Suppose it be conceded that by law it was abolished—could that law be perpetual? Could it extend to the territory after it became the property of the United States? Did we admit territory from Mexico, subject to the Constitution and laws of Mexico? Did we pay fifteen million dollars for jurisdiction over California and New Mexico, that it might be held subordinate to the laws of Mexico?" The Commissioners of Mexico, he tells us, did not think that "we were to be bound by the edicts and statutes of Mexico." They pressed this point in the negotiation, " the continuation of their law for the exclusion of slavery;" and Mr. Trist told them he could not make a treaty on that condition; if they would "offer him the land covered a foot thick with pure gold, upon the single condition that slavery should be excluded therefrom, I could not entertain the offer for a moment." Does not Mr. Webster know this? He knows it too well.

But Mr. Davis goes further. He does not think slavery is excluded by legislation stronger than a joint resolution. This is his language: " I believe it is essential, on account of the climate, productions, soil, and the peculiar character of cultivation, that we shall, during its first settlement, have that slavery [African slavery] in a part, at least, of California and New Mexico." Now on questions of " A law of nature and physical geography," the Senator from Mississippi is as good authority as the Senator from Massachusetts, and a good deal nearer to the facts of the case.

In the House of Representatives, Mr. Clingman, of North Carolina, amongst others, wants New Mexico for slave soil. Pass the Wilmot Proviso over this territory, and the question is settled, disposed of for ever. Omit to

pass it, and slavery will go there, and you may get it out
if you can. Once there, it will be said that the "Compromises of the Constitution" are on its side, and we have
no jurisdiction over the slavery which we have established
there.

Hear what Mr. Foote said of a similar matter on the
26th of June, 1848, in his place in the Senate: "Gentlemen have said this is not a practical question, that slaves
will never be taken to Oregon. With all deference to
their opinion, I differ with them totally. I believe, if
permitted, slaves would be carried there, and that slavery
would continue, at least, as long as in Maryland or Virginia.
['The whole of Oregon' is north of forty-two degrees.]
The Pacific coast is totally different in temperature from
the Atlantic. It is far milder. . . . Green peas are
eaten in the Oregon city at Christmas. Where is the
corresponding climate to be found on this side the continent? Where we sit—near the thirty-ninth? No, sir;
but to the south of us." "The latitude of Georgia gives,
on the Pacific, a tropical climate." "The prohibition of
slavery in the laws of Oregon was adopted for the express
purpose of excluding slaves." "A few had been brought
in; further importations were expected; and it was with a
view to put a stop to them, that the prohibitory act was
passed."

Now, Mr. Foote of Mississippi—"Hangman Foote," as
he has been called—understands the laws of the formation
of the earth as well as the distinguished senator from
Massachusetts. Why, the inhabitants of that part of the
North-West Territory, which now forms the States of
Indiana and Illinois, repeatedly asked Congress to allow
them to introduce slaves north of the Ohio; and but for
the ordinance of '87, that territory would now be covered
with the mildew of slavery !

But I have not yet adduced all the testimony of Mr.
Foote. Last year, on the 23rd of February, 1849, he
declared: "No one acquainted with the vast mineral resources of California and New Mexico, and who is aware of
the peculiar adaptedness of slave labour to the development of mineral treasures, can doubt for a moment, that
were slaves introduced into California and New Mexico,
being employed in the mining operations there in progress,

their labour would result in the acquisition of pecuniary profits not heretofore realized by the most successful cotton or sugar planter of this country?" Does not Mr. Webster know this? Perhaps he did not hear Mr. Foote's speech last year; perhaps he has a short memory, and has forgotten it. Then let us remind the nation of what its Senator forgets. Not know this—forget it? Who will credit such a statement? Mr. Webster is not an obscure clergyman, busy with far different things, but the foremost politician of the United States.

But why do I mention the speeches of Mr. Foote, a year ago? Here is something hardly dry from the printing-press. Here is an advertisement from the "Mississippian" of March 7th, 1850, the very day of that speech. The "Mississippian" is published at the city of Jackson, in Mississippi.

"CALIFORNIA,
"THE SOUTHERN SLAVE COLONY.

"Citizens of the slave States, desirous of emigrating to California with their slave property, are requested to send their names, number of slaves, and period of contemplated departure, to the address of 'SOUTHERN SLAVE COLONY, Jackson, Miss. . . . .

"It is the desire of the friends of this enterprise to settle in the richest mining and agricultural portions of California, and to have the uninterrupted enjoyment of slave property. It is estimated that, by the 1st of May next, the members of this Slave Colony will amount to about five thousand, and the slaves to about ten thousand. The mode of effecting organization, &c., will be privately transmitted to actual members.

"Jackson (Miss.), Feb. 24, 1850.   "dtf."

What does Mr. Webster say in view of all this? "If a proposition were now here for a government for New Mexico, and it was moved to insert a provision for the prohibition of slavery, I would not vote for it." Why not vote for it? There is a specious pretence, which is publicly proclaimed, but there is a real reason for it which is not mentioned!

In the face of all these facts, Mr. Webster says that these men would wish "to protect the everlasting snows of Canada from the pest of slavery by the same overspreading wing of an act of Congress." Exactly so. If we ever annex Labrador—if we "re-annex" Greenland, and Kamskatka, I would extend the Wilmot Proviso, there, and exclude slavery for ever and for ever.

But Mr. Webster would not "re-affirm an ordinance of

nature," nor "re-enact the will of God." I would. I would re-affirm nothing else, enact nothing else. What is justice but the "ordinance of nature?" What is right but "the will of God?" When you make a law, "Thou shalt not kill," what do you but "re-enact the will of God?" When you make laws for the security of the "unalienable rights" of man, and protect for every man the right to life, liberty, and the pursuit of happiness, are you not re-affirming an ordinance of nature? Not re-enact the will of God? Why, I would enact nothing else. The will of God is a theological term; it means truth and justice, in common speech. What is the theological opposite to "The will of God?" It is "The will of the devil." One of the two you must enact—either the will of God, or of the devil. The two are the only theological categories for such matters. *Aut Deus aut Diabolus.* There is no other alternative, " Choose you which you will serve."

So much for the second and third questions. Let us now come to the last thing to be considered. What laws shall be enacted relative to fugitive slaves? Let us look at Mr. Webster's opinion on this point.

The Constitution provides—you all know that too well —that every person "held to service or labour in one State, . . . escaping into another, shall be delivered up." By whom shall he be delivered up? There are only three parties to whom this phrase can possibly apply. They are,

1. Individual men and women : or,
2. The local authorities of the States concerned ; or,
3. The Federal Government itself.

It has sometimes been contended that the Constitution imposes an obligation on you, and me, and every other man, to deliver up fugitive slaves. But there are no laws or decisions that favour that construction. Mr. Webster takes the next scheme, and says, "I always thought that the Constitution addressed itself to the Legislatures of the States, or to the States themselves." "It seems to me that the import of the passage is, that the State itself . . . shall cause him [the fugitive] to be delivered up. That is my judgment." But the Supreme Court, some years ago, decided otherwise, that " The business of seeing that these fugitives are delivered up resides in the power of Congress and the national judicature." So the matter stands now. But it is proposed to make more stringent laws relative to the return of fugitive slaves. So continues Mr. Webster —" My friend at the head of the judiciary committee has a bill on the subject now before the Senate, with some amendments to it, which I propose to support, with all its provisions, to the fullest extent."

Everybody knows the act of Congress of 1793, relative to the surrender of fugitive slaves, and the decision of the Supreme Court in the " Prigg Case," 1842. But everybody does not know the bill of Mr. Webster's "friend at the head of the judiciary committee." There is a bill providing " for the more effectual execution of the third clause of the second section of the fourth article of the Constitution of the United States." It is as follows :—

" Be it enacted by the Senate and House of Representatives of the United States of America, in Congress assembled, That when a person held to service or labour, in any State or territory of the United States, under the laws of such State or territory, shall escape into any other of the said States or territories, the person to whom such service or labour may be due, his or her agent, or attorney, is hereby empowered to seize or arrest such fugitive from service or labour, and to take him or her before any Judge of the Circuit or District Courts of the United States, or before any commissioner or clerk of such courts, or marshal thereof, or before any postmaster of the United States, or collector of the customs of the United States, residing or being within such State wherein such seizure or arrest shall be made ; and, upon proof to the satisfaction of such judge, commissioner, clerk, postmaster, or collector, as the case may be, either by oral testimony or affidavit taken before and certified by any person authorized to administer an oath under the laws of the United States, or. of any State, that the person so seized or arrested, under the laws of the State or territory, from which he or she fled, owes service or labour to the person claiming him or her, it shall be the duty of such judge, commissioner, clerk, marshal, postmaster, or collector, to give a certificate thereof to such claimant, his or her agent or attorney, which certificate shall be a sufficient warrant for taking and removing such fugitive from service or labour to the State or territory from which he or she fled.

" Sec. 2. *And be it further enacted,* That when a person held to service or labour, as mentioned in the first section of this act, shall escape from such service or labour, therein-mentioned, the person to whom such service or labour may be due, his or her agent or attorney, may apply to any one of the officers of the United States named in said section, other than a marshal of the United States, for a warrant to seize and arrest such fugitive ; and upon affidavit being made before such officer (each of whom, for the purposes of this act, is hereby authorized to administer an oath or affirmation), by such claimant, his or her agent, that such person does, under the laws of the State or territory from which he or she fled, owe service or labour to such claimant, it shall be and is hereby made the duty of such officer, to and before whom such application and affidavits are made to issue his warrant to any marshal of any of the courts of the United States, to seize and arrest such alleged fugitive, and to bring him or her forthwith, or on a day to be named in such warrant, before the officer issuing such warrant, or either of the other officers mentioned in said first section, except the marshal to whom the said warrant is directed, which said warrant or authority, the said marshal is hereby authorized and directed in all things to obey.

"Sec. 3. *And be it further enacted,* That upon affidavit made as aforesaid, by the claimant of such fugitive, his agent or attorney, after such certificate has been issued, that he has reason to apprehend that such fugitive shall be rescued by force from his or their possession, before he can be taken beyond the limits of the State in which the arrest is made, it shall be the duty of the officer making the arrest, to retain such fugitive in his custody, and to remove him to the State whence he fled, and there to deliver him to said claimant, his agent or attorney. And to this end, the officer aforesaid is hereby authorized and required to employ so many persons as he may deem necessary to overcome such force, and to retain them in his service, so long as circumstances may require. The said officer and his assistants, while so employed, to receive the same compensation, and to be allowed the same expenses as are now allowed by law, for transportation of criminals, to be certified by the judge of the district within which the arrest is made, and paid out of the treasury of the United States: *Provided,* That before such charges are incurred, the claimant, his agent, or attorney, shall secure to said officer payment of the same, and in case no actual force be opposed, then they shall be paid by such claimant, his agent or attorney.

"Sec. 4. *And be it further enacted,* When a warrant shall have been issued by any of the officers under the second section of this act, and there shall be no marshal or deputy marshal within ten miles of the place where such warrant is issued, it shall be the duty of the officer issuing the same, at the request of the claimant, his agent, or attorney, to appoint some fit and discreet person, who shall be willing to act as marshal, for the purpose of executing said warrant; and such persons so appointed shall, to the extent of executing such warrant, and detaining and transporting the fugitive named therein, have all the power and the authority, and he, with his assistants, entitled to the same compensation and expenses, provided in this act, in cases where the services are performed by the marshals of the courts.

"Sec. 5. *And be it further enacted,* That any person who shall knowingly and wilfully obstruct or hinder such claimant, his agent, or attorney, or any person or persons assisting him, her, or them, in so serving or arresting such fugitive from service or labour, or shall rescue such fugitive from such claimant, his agent, or attorney, when so arrested, pursuant to the authority herein given or declared, or shall aid, abet, or assist such person so owing service or labour, to escape from such claimant, his agent, or attorney, or shall harbour or conceal such person, after notice that he or she was a fugitive from labour, as aforesaid, shall, for either of the said offences, forfeit and pay the sum of one thousand dollars, which penalty may be recovered by, and for the benefit of, such claimant, by action of debt in any court proper to try the same, saving, moreover, to the person claiming such labour or service, his right of action for, on account of, the said injuries, or either of them.

"Sec. 6. *And be it further enacted,* That when such person is seized and arrested, under and by virtue of the said warrant, by such marshal, and is brought before either of the officers aforesaid, other than said marshal, it shall be the duty of such officer to proceed in the case of such person, in the same way that he is directed and authorized to do, when such person is seized and arrested by the person claiming him, or by his or her agent, or attorney, and is brought before such officer or attorney, under the provisions of the first section of this act."

This is the bill known as "Mason's Bill," introduced by Mr. Butler, of South Carolina, on the 16th of January last. This is the bill which Mr. Webster proposes to support, "with all its provisions to the fullest extent." It is a bill of abominations, but there are "some amendments to it," which modify the bill a little. Look at them. Here they are. The first provides in addition to the fine of one thousand dollars for aiding and abetting the escape of a fugitive, for harbouring and concealing him, that the offender "shall also be imprisoned twelve months." The second amendment is as follows—"And in no trial or hearing under this act shall the testimony of such fugitive be admitted in evidence."

These are Mr. Mason's amendments, offered on the 23rd of last January. This is the bill, "with some amendments," which Mr. Webster says, "I propose to support, with all its provisions, to the fullest extent." Mr. Seward's bill was also before the Senate—a bill granting the fugitive slave a trial by jury in the State where he is found, to determine whether or not he is a slave. Mr. Webster says not a word about this bill. He does not propose to support it.

Suppose the bill of Mr. Webster's friend shall pass Congress, what will the action of it be? A slave-hunter comes here to Boston, he seizes any dark-looking man that is unknown and friendless, he has him before the postmaster, the collector of customs, or some clerk or marshal of some United States' court, and makes oath that the dark man is his slave. The slave-hunter is allowed his oath. The fugitive is not allowed his testimony. The man born free as you and I, on the false oath of a slave-hunter, or the purchased affidavit of some one, is surrendered to a southern State, to bondage life-long and irremediable. Will you say, the postmaster, the collector, the clerks and marshals in Boston would not act in such matters? They have no option; it is their official business to do so. But they would not decide against the unalienable rights of man—the right to life, liberty, and the pursuit of happi-

ness. That may be, or may not be. The slave-hunter
may have his "fugitive" before the collector of Boston, or
the postmaster of Truro, if he sees fit. If they, remembering their Old Testament, refuse to "bewray him that
wandereth," the slave-hunter may bring on his officer
with him from Georgia or Florida; he may bring the
custom-house officer from Mobile or Wilmington, some
little petty postmaster from a town you never heard of in
South Carolina or Texas, and have any dark man in Boston
up before that "magistrate," and on his decision have the
fugitive carried off to Louisiana or Arkansas, to bondage
for ever. The bill provides that the trial may be had
before any such officer, "residing or being" in the State
where the fugitive is found!

There were three fugitives at my house the other night.
Ellen Craft was one of them. You all know Ellen Craft is
a slave: she, with her husband, fled from Georgia to
Philadelphia, and is here before us now. She is not so
dark as Mr. Webster himself, if any of you think freedom
is to be dealt out in proportion to the whiteness of the
skin. If Mason's bill passes, I might have some miserable
postmaster from Texas or the District of Columbia, some
purchased agent of Messrs. Bruin and Hill, the great slave-
dealers of the Capitol, have him here in Boston, take Ellen
Craft before the caitiff, and on his decision hurry her off to
bondage as cheerless, as hopeless, and as irremediable as
the grave!

Let me interest you in a scene which might happen.
Suppose a poor fugitive, wrongfully held as a slave—let it
be Ellen Craft—has escaped from Savannah in some
northern ship. No one knows of her presence on board;
she has lain with the cargo in the hold of the vessel.
Harder things have happened. Men have journeyed
hundreds of miles bent double in a box half the size of a
coffin, journeying towards freedom. Suppose the ship
comes up to Long Wharf, at the foot of State Street.
Bulk is broken to remove the cargo; the woman escapes,
emaciated with hunger, feeble from long confinement in a
ship's hold, sick with the tossing of the heedless sea, and
still further etiolated and blanched with the mingling
emotions of hope and fear. She escapes to land. But her
pursuer, more remorseless than the sea, has been here

beforehand; laid his case before the official he has brought with him, or purchased here, and claims his slave. She runs for her life, fear adding wings. Imagine the scene—the flight, the hot pursuit through State Street, Merchants' Row—your magistrates in hot pursuit. To make the irony of nature still more complete, let us suppose this shall take place on some of the memorable days in the history of America—on the 19th of April, when our fathers first laid down their lives "in the sacred cause of God and their country;" on the 17th of June, the 22nd of December, or on any of the sacramental days in the long sad history of our struggle for our own freedom! Suppose the weary fugitive takes refuge in Faneuil Hall, and here, in the old Cradle of Liberty, in the midst of its associations, under that eye of Samuel Adams, the blood-hounds seize their prey! Imagine Mr. Webster and Mr. Winthrop looking on, cheering the slave-hunter, intercepting the fugitive fleeing for her life. Would not that be a pretty spectacle?

Propose to support that bill to the fullest extent, with all its provisions! Ridiculous talk! Does Mr. Webster suppose that such a law could be executed in Boston? that the people of Massachusetts will ever return a single fugitive slave, under such an act as that? Then he knows his constituents very little, and proves that he needs "Instruction."*

"Slavery is a moral and religious blessing," says somebody in the present Congress. But it seems some thirty thousand slaves have been blind to the benefits—moral and religious benefits—which it confers, and have fled to the free States. Mr. Clingman estimates the value of all the fugitive slaves in the North at $15,000,000. Delaware loses $100,000 in a year in this way; her riches taking to themselves not wings, but legs. Maryland lost $100,000 in six months. I fear Mr. Mason's bill and Mr. Webster's speech will not do much to protect that sort of "property" from this kind of loss. Such action is prevented "by a law even superior to that which admits and sanctions it in Texas."

Such are Mr. Webster's opinions on these four great questions. Now, there are two ways of accounting for

* Alas, a single year taught me the folly of this confidence in Boston!

this speech, or, at least, two ways of looking at it. One is, to regard it as the work of a statesman seeking to avert some great evil from the whole nation. This is the way Mr. Webster would have us look at it, I suppose. His friends tell us it is a statesmanlike speech—very statesmanlike. He himself says, *Vera pro gratis**—true words in preference to words merely pleasing. *Etsi meum ingenium non moneret necessitas cogit*—Albeit my own humour should not prompt the counsel, necessity compels it. The necessity so cogent is the attempt to dissolve the Union, in case the Wilmot Proviso should be extended over the new territory. Does any man seriously believe that Mr. Webster really fears a dissolution of this Union undertaken and accomplished on this plea, and by the Southern States? I will not insult the foremost understanding of this continent by supposing he deems it possible. No, we cannot take this view of his conduct.

The other way is to regard it as the work of a politician, seeking something beside the permanent good of a great nation. The lease of the Presidency is to be disposed of for the next four years by a sort of auction. It is in the hands of certain political brokers, who "operate" in presidential and other political stock. The majority of those brokers are slaveholders or pro-slavery men; they must be conciliated, or they will "not understand the nod" of the candidate—I mean of the man who bids for the lease. All the illustrious men in the national politics have an eye on the transaction, but sometimes the bid has been taken for persons whose chance at the sale seemed very poor. General Cass made his bid some time ago. I think his offer is recorded in the famous "Nicholson Letter." He was a Northern man, and bid Non-intervention—the unconstitutionality of any intervention with slavery in the new territory. Mr. Clay made his bid, for old Kentucky "never tires," the same old bid that he has often made—a Compromise. Mr. Calhoun did as he has always done. I will not say he made any bid at all; he was too sick for that, too sick for any thought of the Presidency. Perhaps at this moment the angel of death is dealing with that famed and remarkable man. Nay, he may already have gone where "The servant is free from his master, and the

* Motto of Mr. Webster's speech.

weary are at rest;" have gone home to his God, who is the Father of the great politician and the feeblest-minded slave. If it he so, let us follow him only with pity for his errors, and the prayer that his soul may be at rest. He has fought manfully in an unmanly cause. He seemed sincerely in the wrong, and spite of the badness of the cause to which he devoted his best energies, you cannot but respect the man.

Last of all, Mr. Webster makes his bid for the lease of "that bad eminence," the Presidency. He bids higher than the others, of course, as coming later; bids Non-intervention, Four new slave States in Texas, Mason's Bill for Capturing Fugitive Slaves, and Denunciation of all the Anti-slavery movements of the North, public and private. That is what he bids, looking to the southern side of the board of political brokers. Then he nods northward, and says, The Wilmot Proviso is my "thunder;" then timidly glances to the South and adds, But I will never use it.

I think this is the only reasonable way in which we can estimate this speech—as a bid for the Presidency. I will not insult that mighty intellect by supposing that he, in his private heart, regards it in any other light. Mr. Calhoun might well be content with that, and say, "Organ-ize the territories on the principle of that gentleman, and give us a free scope and sufficient time to get in—we ask nothing but that, and we never will ask it."

Such are the four great questions before us; such Mr. Webster's answers thereunto; such the two ways of looking at his speech. He decides in advance against freedom in Texas, against freedom in California, against freedom in New Mexico, against freedom in the United States, by his gratuitous offer of support to Mr. Mason's bill. His great eloquence, his great understanding, his great name, give weight to all his words. Pains are industriously taken to make it appear that his opinions are the opinions of Boston. Is it so? [Cries of No, No.] That was rather a feeble cry. Perhaps it is the opinion of the prevailing party in Boston. [No, No.] But I put it to you, Is it the opinion of Mas-sachusetts? [Loud cries of No, No, No.] Well, so I say, No; it is not the opinion of Massachusetts.

Before now, servants of the people and leaders of the

people have proved false to their employers, and betrayed their trust. Amongst all political men who have been weighed in the balance, and found wanting, with whom shall I compare him? Not with John Quincy Adams, who, in 1807, voted for the embargo. It may have been the mistake of an honest intention, though I confess I cannot think so yet. At any rate, laying an embargo, which he probably thought would last but a few months, was a small thing compared with the refusal to restrict slavery, willingness to enact laws to the disadvantage of mankind, and the voluntary support of Mason's iniquitous bill. Besides, Mr. Adams lived a long life; if he erred, or if he sinned in this matter, he afterwards fought most valiantly for the rights of man.

Shall I compare Mr. Webster with Thomas Wentworth, the great Earl of Strafford, a man "whose doubtful character and memorable end have made him the most conspicuous character of a reign so fertile in recollections?" He, like Webster, was a man of large powers, and once devoted them to noble uses. Did Wentworth defend the "Petition of Right?" So did Webster many times defend the great cause of liberty. But it was written of Strafford, that "in his self-interested and ambitious mind," patriotism "was the seed sown among thorns!" "If we reflect upon this man's cold-blooded apostacy on the first lure to his ambition, and on his splendid abilities, which enhanced the guilt of that desertion, we must feel some indignation at those who have palliated all his iniquities, and embalmed his memory with the attributes of patriot heroism. Great he surely was, since that epithet can never be denied without paradox to so much comprehension of mind, such ardour and energy, such courage and eloquence, those commanding qualities of soul, which, impressed upon his dark and stern countenance, struck his contemporaries with mingled awe and hate. . . . But it may be reckoned a sufficient ground for distrusting any one's attachment to the English Constitution, that he reveres the name of Strafford." His measures for stifling liberty in England, which he and his contemporaries significantly called "Thorough," in the reign of Charles I., were not more atrocious, than the measures which Daniel Webster proposes himself, or proposes to support "to the fullest extent." But Strafford paid the forfeit—tasting the sharp and bitter edge of the remorseless axe. Let his awful shade pass by. I mourn at the parallel between him and the mighty son of our own New England. Would God it were not thus.

For a sadder parallel, I shall turn off from the sour features of that great British politician, and find another man in our own fair land. This name carries us back to "the times that tried men's souls," when also there were souls that could not stand the rack. It calls me back to "The famous year of '80;" to the little American army in the highlands of New York; to the time when the torch of American liberty which now sends its blaze far up to heaven, at the same time lighting the northern lakes and the Mexique Bay, tinging with welcome radiance the eastern and the western sea, was a feeble flame flickering about a thin and hungry wick, and one hand was raised to quench in darkness, and put out for ever, that feeble and uncertain flame. Gentlemen, I hate to speak thus. I honour the majestic talents of this great man. I hate to couple his name with that other, which few Americans care to pronounce. But I know no deed in American history, done by a son of New England, to which I can compare this, but the act of Benedict Arnold!

Shame that I should say this of any man; but his own motto shall be mine—VERA PRO GRATIS—and I am not responsible for what he has made the TRUTH; certainly, *meum ingenium non moneret, necessitas cogit!*

I would speak with all possible tenderness of any man, of every man; of such an one, so honoured, and so able, with respect I feel for superior powers. I would often question my sense of justice, before I dared to pronounce an adverse conclusion. But the Wrong is palpable, the Injustice is open as the day. I must remember, here are twenty millions, whose material welfare his counsel defeats: whose honour his counsel stains; whose political, intellectual, moral growth he is using all his mighty powers to hinder and keep back. "*Vera pro gratis. Necessitas cogit. Vellem, equidem, vobis placere, sed multo malo vos salvos esse, qualicunque erga me animo futuri estis.*"

Let me take a word of warning and of counsel from the same author; yes, from the same imaginary speech of

Quintus Capitolinus, whence Mr. Webster has drawn his
motto :—*Ante portas est bellum : si inde non pellitur, jam
intra mœnia erit, et arcem et Capitolium scandet, et in
domos vestras vos persequetur.* The war [against the
extension of Slavery, not against the Volscians, in this
case] is before your very doors : if not driven thence, it
will be within your walls [namely, it will be in California
and New Mexico] ; it will ascend the citadel and the
capitol [to wit, it will be in the House of Representatives
and the Senate] ; and it will follow you into your very
homes [that is, the curse of Slavery will corrupt the morals
of the nation].

*Sedemus desides domi, mulierum ritu inter nos alter-
cantes ; præsenti pace læti, nec cernentes* EX OTIO ILLO
BREVI MULTIPLEX BELLUM REDITURUM. We [the famous
Senators of the United States] sit idle at home, wrangling
amongst ourselves like women [to see who shall get the
lease of the Presidency], glad of the present truce [mean-
ing that which is brought about by a compromise], not
perceiving that for this brief cessation of trouble, a manifold war will follow [that is, the " horrid internecine war"
which will come here, as it has been elsewhere, if justice
be too long delayed] !

It is a great question before us, concerning the existence
of millions of men. To many men in politics, it is merely
a question of party rivalry ; a question of in and out, and
nothing more. To many men in cities, it is a question of
commerce, like the establishment of a bank, or the building of one railroad more or less. But to serious men, who
love man and love their God, this is a question of morals,
a question of religion, to be settled with no regard to party
rivalry, none to fleeting interests of to-day, but to be
settled under the awful eye of conscience, and by the just
law of God.

Shall we shut up Slavery or extend it ? It is for us to
answer. Will you deal with the question now, or leave it
to your children, when the evil is ten times greater ? In
1749, there was not a slave in Georgia ; now, two hundred
and eighty thousand. In 1750, in all the United States,
but two hundred thousand ; now, three millions. In 1950,
let Mr. Webster's counsels be followed, there will be thirty
millions. Thirty millions ! Will it then be easier for

your children to set limits to this crime against human nature, than now for you? Our fathers made a political, and a commercial, and a moral error—shall we repeat it? They did a wrong; shall we extend and multiply the wrong? Was it an error in our fathers; not barely a wrong—was it a sin? No, not in them; they knew it not. But what in them to establish was only an error, in us to extend or to foster is a sin!

Perpetuate Slavery, we cannot do it. Nothing will save it. It is girt about by a ring of fire which daily grows narrower, and sends terrible sparkles into the very centre of the shameful thing. "Joint resolutions" cannot save it; annexations cannot save it—not if we re-annex all the West Indies; delinquent representatives cannot save it; uninstructed senators, refusing instructions, cannot save it—no, not with all their logic, all their eloquence, which smites as an earthquake smites the sea. No, Slavery cannot be saved; by no compromise, no non-intervention, no Mason's Bill in the Senate. It cannot be saved in this age of the world until you nullify every ordinance of nature, until you repeal the will of God, and dissolve the union He has made between righteousness and the welfare of a people. Then, when you displace God from the throne of the world, and instead of His eternal justice, re-enact the will of the Devil, then you may keep Slavery; keep it for ever, keep it in peace. Not till then.

The question is, not if slavery is to cease, and soon to cease, but shall it end as it ended in Massachusetts, in New Hampshire, in Pennsylvania, in New York; or shall it end as in St. Domingo? Follow the counsel of Mr. Webster—it will end in fire and blood. God forgive us for our cowardice, if we let it come to this, that three millions or thirty millions of degraded human beings, degraded by us, must wade through slaughter to their unalienable rights.

Mr. Webster has spoken noble words—at Plymouth, standing on the altar-stone of New England; at Bunker Hill, the spot so early reddened with the blood of our fathers. But at this hour, when we looked for great counsel, when we forgot the paltry things which he has often done and said, " Now he will rouse his noble soul, and be the man his early speeches once bespoke," who dared to fear that Olympian head would bow so low, so deeply kiss the ground? Try it morally, try it intellectually, try it by the statesman's test, world-wide justice ; nay, try it by the politician's basest test, the personal expediency of to-day— it is a speech "not fit to be made," and when made, not fit to be confirmed.

"We see dimly in the distance what is small and what is great,
  Slow of faith how weak an arm may turn the iron helm of fate ;
  But the soul is still oracular ; amid the market's din,
  List the ominous stern whisper from the Delphic cave within—
  'They enslave their children's children, who make compromise with
    sin.' "

IX.

THE STATE OF THE NATION, CONSIDERED IN A SERMON FOR THANKSGIVING DAY.—PREACHED AT THE MELODEON, NOVEMBER 28, 1850.

PROVERBS XIV. 34.

Righteousness exalteth a nation : but sin is a reproach to any people.

WE come together to-day, by the Governor's proclamation, to give thanks to God for our welfare, not merely for our happiness as individuals or as families, but for our welfare as a people. How can we better improve this opportunity, than by looking a little into the condition of the people? And accordingly I invite your attention to a Sermon of the State of this Nation. I shall try to speak of the Condition of the nation itself, then of the Causes of that Condition, and, in the third place, of the Dangers that threaten, or are alleged to threaten, the nation.

First, of our Condition. Look about you in Boston. Here are a hundred and forty thousand souls, living in peace and in comparative prosperity. I think, without doing injustice to the other side of the water, there is no city in the old world, of this population, with so much intelligence, activity, morality, order, comfort, and general welfare, and, at the same time, with so little of the opposite of all these. I know the faults of Boston, and I think I would not disguise them ; the poverty, unnatural poverty, which shivers in the cellar; the unnatural wealth which bloats in the parlour ; the sin which is hid in the corners of the gaol ; and the more dangerous sin which sets up Christianity for a pretence ; the sophistry which lightens

in the newspapers, and thunders in the pulpit :—I know
all these things, and do not pretend to disguise them; and
still I think no city of the old world, of the same population, has so much which good men prize, and so little
which good men deplore.

See the increase of material wealth; the buildings for
trade and for homes; the shops and ships. This year
Boston will add to her possessions some ten or twenty
millions of dollars, honestly and earnestly got. Observe
the neatness of the streets, the industry of the inhabitants,
their activity of mind, the orderliness of the people, the
signs of comfort. Then consider the charities of Boston;
those limited to our own border, and those which extend
further, those beautiful charities which encompass the
earth with their sweet influence. Look at the schools, a
monument of which the city may well be proud, in spite
of their defects.

But Boston, though we proudly call it the Athens of
America, is not the pleasantest thing in New England to
look at; it is the part of Massachusetts which I like the
least to look at, spite of its excellence. Look further, at
the whole of Massachusetts, and you see a fairer spectacle.
There is less wealth at Provincetown, in proportion to the
numbers, but there is less want; there is more comfort;
property is more evenly and equally distributed there than
here, and the welfare of a country never so much depends
upon the amount of its wealth, as on the mode in which its
wealth is distributed. In the State, there are about one
hundred and fifty thousand families—some nine hundred
and seventy-five thousand persons, living with a degree of
comfort, which, I think, is not anywhere enjoyed by such
a population in the old world. They are mainly industrious, sober, intelligent, and moral. Everything thrives;
agriculture, manufactures, commerce. "The carpenter
encourages the goldsmith; he that smites the anvil, him
that smootheth with the hammer." Look at the farms,
where intelligent labour wins bread and beauty both, out
of the sterile soil and climate not over-indulgent. Behold
the shops all over the State; the small shops where the
shoemaker holds his work in his lap, and draws his thread
by his own strong muscles; and the large shops where
machines, animate with human intelligence, hold, with

iron grasp, their costlier work in their lap, and spin out
the delicate staple of Sea Island cotton.   Look at all this;
it is a pleasant sight.   Look at our hundreds of villages,
by river, mountain, and sea; behold the comfortable homes,
the people well fed, well clad, well instructed.   Look at
the school-houses, the colleges of the people; at the higher
seminaries of learning; at the poor man's real college further back in the interior, where the mechanic's and farmer's
son gets his education, often a poor one, still something to
be proud of.   Look at the churches, where, every Sunday,
the best words of Hebrew and of Christian saints are read
out of this Book, and all men are asked, once in the week,
to remember they have a Father in heaven, a faith to swear
by, and a heaven to live for, and a conscience to keep.   I
know the faults of these churches.   I am not in the habit
of excusing them; still I know their excellence, and I will
not be the last man to acknowledge that.   Look at the
roads of earth and iron which join villages together, and
make the State a whole.   Follow the fisherman from his
rocky harbour at Cape Ann; follow the mariner in his
voyage round the world of waters; see the industry, the
intelligence, and the comfort of the people.   I think Massachusetts is a State to be thankful for.   There are faults
in her institutions and in her laws, that need change very
much.   In her form of society, in her schools, in her colleges, there is much which clamours loudly for alteration,
—very much in her churches to be christianized.   These
changes are going quietly forward, and will in time be
brought about.

I love to look on this State, its material prosperity, its
increase in riches, its intelligence and industry, and the
beautiful results that are seen all about us to-day.   I love
to look on the face of the people, in halls and churches, in
markets and factories; to think of our great ideas; of the
institutions which have come of them; of our schools and
colleges, and all the institutions for making men wiser and
better; to think of the noble men we have in the midst
of us, in every walk of life, who eat an honest bread, who
love mankind, and love God, who have consciences they
mean to keep, and souls which they intend to save.

The great business of society is not merely to have farms,
and ships, and shops,—the greater shops and the less,—

but to have men ; men that are conscious of their manhood, self-respectful, earnest men, that have a faith in the living God. I do not think we have many men of genius. We have very few that I call great men; I wish there were more; but I think we have an intelligent, an industrious, and noble people here in Massachusetts, which we may be proud of.

Let us go a step further. New England is like Massachusetts in the main, with local differences only. All the North is like New England in the main; this portion is better in one thing; that portion worse in another thing. Our ideas are their ideas; our institutions are the same. Some of the northern States have institutions better than we. They have added to our experience. In revising their constitutions and laws, or in making new ones, they go beyond us, they introduce new improvements, and those new improvements will give those States the same advantage over us, which a new mill, with new and superior machinery, has over an old mill, with old and inferior machinery. By and by we shall see the result, and take counsel from it, I trust.

All over the North we find the same industry and thrift, and similar intelligence. Here attention is turned to agriculture, there to mining; but there is a similar progress and zeal for improvement. Attention is bestowed on schools and colleges, on academies and churches. There is the same abundance of material comfort. Population advances rapidly, prosperity in a greater ratio. Everywhere new swarms pour forth from the old hive, and settle in some convenient nook, far off in the West. So the frontier of civilization every year goes forward, further from the ocean. Fifty years ago it was on the Ohio; then on the Mississippi; then on the upper Missouri : presently its barrier will be the Rocky Mountains, and soon it will pass beyond that bar, and the tide of the Atlantic will sweep over to the Pacific—yea, it is already there! The universal Yankee freights his schooner at Bangor, at New Bedford, and at Boston, with bricks, timber, frame-houses, and other "notions," and by and by drops his anchor in the smooth Pacific, in the Bay of St. Francis. We shall see there, ere long, the sentiments of New England, the ideas of New England, the institutions of New England;

the school-house, the meeting-house, the court-house, the town-house. There will be the same industry, thrift, intelligence, morality, and religion, and the idle ground that has hitherto borne nothing but gold, will bear upon its breast a republic of men more precious than the gold of Ophir, or the rubies of the East.

Here I wish I could stop. But this is not all. The North is not the whole nation; New England is not the only type of the people. There are other States differing widely from this. In the southern States you find a soil more fertile under skies more genial. Through what beautiful rivers the Alleghanies pour their tribute to the sea! What streams beautify the land in Georgia, Alabama, Louisiana, and Mississippi! There genial skies rain beauty on the soil. Nature is wanton of her gifts. There rice, cotton, and sugar grow; there the olive, the orange, the fig, all find a home. The soil teems with luxuriance. But there is not the same wealth, nor the same comfort. Only the ground is rich. You witness not a similar thrift. Strange is it, but in 1840 the single State of New York alone earned over four million dollars more than the six States of North and South Carolina, Georgia, Alabama, Louisiana, and Mississippi! The annual earnings of little Massachusetts, with her seven thousand and five hundred square miles, are nine million dollars more than the earnings of all Florida, Georgia, and South Carolina! The little county of Essex, with ninety-five thousand souls in 1840, earned more than the large State of South Carolina, with five hundred and ninety-five thousand.

In those States we miss the activity, intelligence, and enterprise of the North. You do not find the little humble school-house at every corner; the frequent meeting-house does not point its taper finger to the sky. Villages do not adorn the margin of the mountain, stream, and sea; shops do not ring with industry; roads of earth and iron are poorer and less common. Temperance, morality, comfort are not there as here. In the slave States, in 1840, there were not quite three hundred and two thousand youths and maidens in all the schools, academies, and colleges of the South; but in 1840, in the free States of the North there were more than two million two hundred and twelve thousand in such institutions! Little Rhode Island has five thousand more girls and boys at school than large South Carolina. The State of Ohio alone has more than seventeen thousand children at school beyond what the whole fifteen slave States can boast. The permanent literature of the nation all comes from the North; your historians are from that quarter—your Sparkses, your Bancrofts, your Hildreths, and Prescotts, and Ticknors; the poets are from the same quarter—your Whittiers and Longfellows, and Lowells, and Bryants; the men of literature and religion—your Channings, and Irvings, and Emersons—are from the same quarter! Preaching—it is everywhere, and sermons are as thick almost as autumnal leaves; but who ever heard of a great or famous clergyman in a Southern State? of a great and famous sermon that rang through the nation from that quarter? No man. Your Edwards of old time, and your Beechers, old and young, your Channing and Buckminster, and the rest, which throng to every man's lips—all are from the North. Nature has done enough for the South; God's cup of blessing runs over—and yet you see the result! But there has been no pestilence at the South more than at the North; no earthquake has torn the ground beneath their feet; no war has come to disturb them more than us. The government has never laid a withering hand on their commerce, their agriculture, their schools and colleges, their literature and their church.

Still, letting alone the South and the North as such, not considering either exclusively, we are one nation. What is a nation? It is one of the great parties in the world. It is a sectional party, having geographical limits; with a party organization, party opinions, party mottoes, party machinery, party leaders, and party followers; with some capital city for its party head-quarters. There has been an Assyrian party, a British, a Persian, an Egyptian, and a Roman party; there is now a Chinese party, and a Russian, a Turkish, a French, and an English party; these are also called nations. We belong to the American party, and that includes the North as well as the South; and so all are brothers of the same party, differing amongst ourselves—but from other nations in this, that we are the American party, and not the Russian nor the English.

We ought to look at the whole American party, the

North and South, to see the total condition of the people. Now at this moment there is no lack of cattle and corn and cloth in the United States, North or South, only they are differently distributed in the different parts of the land. But still there is a great excitement. Men think the nation is in danger, and for many years there has not been so great an outcry and alarm amongst the politicians. The cry is raised, "The Union is in danger!" and if the Union falls, we are led to suppose that everything falls. There will be no more Thanksgiving days; there will be anarchy and civil war, and the ruin of the American people! It is curious to see this material plenty, on the one side, and this political alarm and confusion on the other. This condition of alarm is so well known, that nothing more need be said about it at this moment.

Let me now come to the next point, and consider the Causes of our present condition. This will involve a consideration of the cause of our prosperity and of our alarm.

1. First, there are some causes which depend on God entirely; such as the nature of the country, soil, climate, and the like; its minerals, and natural productions; its seas and harbours, mountains and rivers. In respect to these natural advantages, the country is abundantly favoured, but the North less so than the South. Tennessee, Virginia, and Alabama, certainly have the advantage over Maine, New Hampshire, and Ohio. That I pass by; a cause which depends wholly on God.

2. Then again, this is a wide and new country. We have room to spread. We have not to contend against old institutions, established a thousand years ago, and that is one very great advantage. I make no doubt that in crossing the ocean, our fathers helped forward the civilization of the world at least a thousand years; I mean to say, it would have taken mankind a thousand years longer to reach the condition we have attained in New England, if the attempt had of necessity been made on the soil of the old world and in the face of its institutions.

3. Then, as a third thing, much depends on the peculiar national character. Well, the freemen in the North and South are chiefly from the same race, this indomitable Caucasian stock; mainly from the same composite stock,

the tribe produced by the mingling of Saxon, Danish, and Norman blood. That makes the present English nation, and the American also. This is a very powerful tribe of men, possessing some very noble traits of character; active and creative in all the arts of peace; industrious as a nation never was before; enterprising, practical; fond of liberty, fond also of law, capable of organizing themselves into great masses, and acting with a complete concert and unity of action. In these respects, I think this tribe, which I will call the English tribe, is equal to any race of men in the world that has been or is; perhaps superior to any race that has been developed hitherto. But in what relates to the higher reason and imagination, to the affections and to the soul, I think this tribe is not so eminent as some others have been. North and South, the people are alike of Anglo-Norman descent.

4. Another cause of our prosperity, which depends a great deal on ourselves, is this—the absence of war and of armies. In France, with a population of less than forty millions, half a million are constantly under arms. The same state of things prevails substantially in Austria, Prussia, and in all the German States. Here in America, with a population of twenty millions, there is not one in a thousand that is a soldier or marine. In time of peace, I think we waste vast sums in military preparations, as we did in actual war not long since. Still, when I compare this nation with others, I think we have cause to felicitate ourselves on the absence of military power.

5. Again, much depends on the past history of the race; and here there is a wide difference between the different parts of the country. New England was settled by a religious colony. I will not say that all the men who came here from 1620 to 1650 were moved by religious motives; but the controlling men were brought here by these motives, and no other. Many who cared less for religious ideas, came for the sake of a great moral idea, for the sake of obtaining a greater degree of civil freedom than they had at home. Now the Pilgrims and the Puritans are only a little ways behind us. The stiff ruff, the peaked beard, the "Prophesying book" are only six or seven generations behind the youngest of us. The character of the Puritans has given to New England much of

its present character and condition. They founded schools and colleges; they trained up their children in a stern discipline which we shall not forget for two centuries to come. The remembrance of their trials, their heroism, and their piety affects our preaching to-day, and our politics also. The difference between New England and New York, from 1750 to 1790, is the difference between the sons of the religious colony and the sons of the worldly colony. You know something of New York politics before the Revolution, and also since the Revolution; the difference between New York and New England politics at that time, is the difference between the sons of religious men and the sons of men who cared very much less for religion.

Just now, when I said that all the North is like New England, I meant substantially so. The West is our own daughter. New England has helped people the western part of the State of New York; and the best elements of New England character mingling with others, its good qualities will appear in the politics of that mighty State.

The South, in the main, had a very different origin from the North. I think few if any persons settled there for religion's sake; or for the sake of freedom in the State. It was not a moral idea which sent men to Virginia, Georgia, and Carolina. "Men do not gather grapes of thorns." The difference of the seed will appear in the difference of the crop. In the character of the people of the North and South, it appears at this day. The North is not to be praised, nor the South to be blamed for this; they could not help it: but certainly it is an advantage to be descended from a race of industrious, moral and religious men; to have been brought up under their training, to have inherited their ideas and institutions,—and this is a circumstance which we make quite too little account of. I pass by that.

6. There are other causes which depend on ourselves entirely. Much depends on the political and social organization of the people. There is no denying that government has a great influence on the character of the people; on the character of every man. The difference between the development of England and the development of Spain at this day, is mainly the result of different forms of

government; for three centuries ago the Spaniards were as
noble a race as the English.

A government is carried on by two agencies : the first is
public opinion, and the next is public law,—the fundamental law which is the Constitution, and the subsidiary
laws which carry out the ideas of the Constitution. In a
government like this, public opinion always precedes the
laws, overrides them, takes the place of laws when there
are none, and hinders their execution when they do not
correspond to public opinion.   Thus the public opinion of
South Carolina demands that a free coloured seaman from
the North shall be shut up in gaol, at his employer's cost.
The public opinion of Charleston is stronger than the
public law of the United States on that point, stronger
than the Constitution, and nobody dares execute the laws
of the United States in that matter.   These two things
should always be looked at, to understand the causes of a
nation's condition—the public opinion, as well as the public
law. Let me know the opinions of the men between
twenty-five and thirty-five years of age, and I know what
the laws will be.

Now in public opinion and in the laws of the United
States, there are two distinct political ideas.   I shall call
one the Democratic, and the other the Despotic idea.
Neither is wholly sectional ; both chiefly so. Each is composed of several simpler ideas.   Each has enacted laws
and established institutions. This is the democratic idea :
that all men are endowed by their Creator with certain
natural rights, which only the possessor can alienate ; that
all men are equal in these rights ; that amongst them is
the right to life, liberty, and the pursuit of happiness ;
that the business of the government is to preserve for every
man all of these rights until he alienates them.

This democratic idea is founded in human nature, and
comes from the nature of God who made human nature.
To carry it out politically is to execute justice, which is
the will of God. This idea, in its realization, leads to a
democracy, a government of all, for all, by all.   Such a
government aims to give every man all his natural rights ;
it desires to have political power in all hands, property in
all hands, wisdom in all heads, goodness in all hearts,
religion in all souls. I mean the religion that makes a

man self-respectful, earnest, and faithful to the infinite
God, that disposes him to give all men their rights, and to
claim his own rights at all times; the religion which is
piety within you, and goodness in the manifestation. Such
a government has laws, and the aim thereof is to give
justice to all men; it has officers to execute these laws, for
the sake of justice. Such a government founds schools for
all; looks after those most who are most in need; defends
and protects the feeblest as well as the richest and most
powerful. The state is for the individual, and for all the
individuals, and so it reverences justice, where the rights
of all, and the interests of all, exactly balance. It demands
free speech; everything is open to examination, discussion, "agitation," if you will. Thought is to be free,
speech to be free, work to be free, and worship to be free.
Such is the democratic idea, and such the State which it
attempts to found.

The despotic idea is just the opposite :—That all men
are *not* endowed by their Creator with certain natural
rights which only the possessor can alienate, but that one
man has a natural right to overcome and make use of some
other men for his advantage and their hurt; that all men
are *not* equal in their rights; that all men have *not* a
natural right to life, liberty, and the pursuit of happiness;
that government is *not* instituted to preserve these natural
rights for all.

This idea is founded on the excess of human passions,
and it represents the compromise between a man's idleness
and his appetite. It is not based on facts eternal in human
nature, but on facts transient in human nature. It does
not aim to do justice to all, but injustice to some; to take
from one man what he ought not to lose, and give to
another what he ought not to get.

This leads to aristocracy in various forms, to the government of all by means of a part and for the sake of a part.
In this state of things political power must be in few
hands; property in few hands; wisdom in few heads;
goodness in few hearts, and religion in few souls. I mean
the religion which leads a man to respect himself and his
fellow-men; to be earnest, and to trust in the infinite God;
to demand his rights of other men and to give their rights
to them.

Neither the democratic nor the despotic idea is fully made real anywhere in the world. There is no perfect democracy, nor perfect aristocracy. There are democrats in every actual aristocracy; despots in every actual democracy. But in the Northern States the democratic idea prevails extensively and chiefly, and we have made attempts at establishing a democratic government. In the Southern States the despotic idea prevails extensively and chiefly, and they have made attempts to establish an aristocratic government. In an aristocracy there are two classes: the people to be governed, and the governing class, the nobility which is to govern. This nobility may be moveable, and depend on wealth; or immoveable, and depend on birth. In the Southern States the nobility is immoveable, and depends on colour.

In 1840, in the North there were ten million free men, and in the South five million free men and three million slaves. Three-eighths of the population have no human rights at all—privileges as cattle, not rights as men. There the slave is protected by law, as your horse and your ox, but has no more human rights.

Here, now, is the great cause of the difference in the condition of the North and South; of the difference in the material results, represented by towns and villages, by farms and factories, ships and shops. Here is the cause of the difference in schools, colleges, churches, and in the literature; the cause of the difference in men. The South, with its despotic idea, dishonours labour, but wishes to compromise between its idleness and its appetite, and so kidnaps men to do its work. The North, with its democratic idea, honours labour; does not compromise between its idleness and its appetite, but lays its bones to the work to satisfy its appetite; instead of kidnapping a man who can run away, it kidnaps the elements, subdues them to its command, and makes them do its work. It does not kidnap a freeman, but catches the winds, and chains them to its will. It lays hands on fire and water, and breeds a new giant, which " courses land and ocean without rest," or serves while it stands and waits, driving the mills of the land. It kidnaps the Connecticut and the Merrimac; does not send slave-ships to Africa, but engineers to New Hampshire; and it requires no fugitive slave-law to keep the earth and sea from escaping, or the rivers of New England from running up hill.

This is not quite all! I have just now tried to hint at the causes of the difference in the condition of the people, North and South. Now let me show the cause of the agitation and alarm. We begin with a sentiment; that spreads to an idea; the idea grows to an act, to an institution; then it has done its work.

Men seek to spread their sentiments and ideas. The democratic idea tries to spread; the despotic idea tries to spread. For a long time the nation held these two ideas in its bosom, not fully conscious of either of them. Both came here in a state of infancy, so to say, with our fathers; the democratic idea very dimly understood; the despotic idea not fully carried out, yet it did a great mischief in the State and church. In the Declaration of Independence, writ by a young man, only the democratic idea appears, and that idea never got so distinctly stated before. But mark you, and see the confusion in men's minds. That democratic idea was thus distinctly stated by a man who was a slaveholder almost all his life; and unless public rumour has been unusually false, he has left some of his own offspring under the influence of the despotic and not the democratic idea; slaves and not free men.

In the Constitution of the United States these two ideas appear. It was thought for a long time they were not incompatible; it was thought the great American party might recognise both, and a compromise was made between the two. It was thought each might go about its own work and let the other alone; that the hawk and the hen might dwell happily together in the same coop, each lay her own eggs, and rear her own brood, and neither put a claw upon the other.

In the meantime each founded institutions after its kind; in the Northern States, democratic institutions; in the Southern, aristocratic. What once lay latent in the mind of the nation has now become patent. The thinking part of the nation sees the difference between the two. Some men are beginning to see that the two are completely incompatible, and cannot be good friends. Others are asking us to shut our eyes and not see it, and they think that so long as our eyes are shut, all things will go on peacefully. Such is the wisdom of the ostrich.

At first the trouble coming from this source was a very little cloud, far away on the horizon, not bigger than a man's hand. It seemed so in 1804, when the brave senator from Massachusetts, a Hartford Convention Federalist, a name that calls the blood to some rather pale cheeks now-a-days, proposed to alter the Constitution of the United States, and cut off the North from all responsibility for slavery. It was a little cloud not bigger than a man's hand; now it is a great cloud which covers the whole hemisphere of heaven, and threatens to shut out the day.

In the last session of Congress, ten months long, the great matter was the contest between the two ideas. All the newspapers rung with the battle. Even the pulpits now and then alluded to it; forgetting their decency, that they must preach " only religion," which has not the least to do with politics and the welfare of the State.

Each idea has its allies, and it is worth while to run our eye over the armies and see what they amount to. The idea of despotism has for its allies :—

1. The slaveholders of the South with their dependents; and the servile class who take their ideas from the prominent men about them. This servile class is more numerous at the South than even at the North.

2. It has almost all the distinguished politicians of the North and South; the distinguished great politicians in the Congress of the nation, and the distinguished little politicians in the Congress of the several States.

3. It has likewise the greater portion of the wealthy and educated men in many large towns of the North; with their dependents and the servile men who take their opinions from the prominent class about them. And here, I am sorry to say, I must reckon the greater portion of the prominent and wealthy clergy, the clergy in the large cities. Once this class of men were masters of the rich and educated; and very terrible masters they were in Madrid and in Rome. Now their successors are doing penance for those old sins. " It is a long lane," they say, " which has no turn," and the clerical has had a very short and complete turn. When I say the majority of the clergy in prominent situations in the large cities are to

be numbered among the allies of the despotic idea, and are a part of the great pro-slavery army, I know there are some noble and honourable exceptions, men who do not fear the face of gold, but reverence the face of God.

Then on the side of the democratic idea there are :—

1. The great mass of the people at the North; farmers, mechanics, and the humbler clergy. This does not appear so at first sight, because these men have not much confidence in themselves, and require to be shaken many times before they are thoroughly waked up.

2. Beside that, there are a few politicians at the North who are on this side; some distinguished ones in Congress, some less distinguished ones in the various legislatures of the North.

3. Next there are men, North and South, who look at the great causes of the welfare of nations, and make up their minds historically, from the facts of human history, against despotism. Then there are such as study the great principles of justice and truth, and judge from human nature, and decide against despotism. And then such as look at the law of God, and believe Christianity is sense and not nonsense; that Christianity is the ideal for earnest men, not a pretence for a frivolous hypocrite. Some of these men are at the South; the greater number are in the North ; and here again you see the difference between the son of the Planter and the son of the Puritan.

Here are the allies, the threefold armies of Despotism on the one side, and of Democracy on the other.

Now it is not possible for these two ideas to continue to live in peace. For a long time each knew not the other, and they were quiet. The men who clearly knew the despotic idea, thought, in 1787, it would die "of a rapid consumption :" they said so ; but the culture of cotton has healed its deadly wound, at least for the present. After the brief state of quiet, there came a state of armed neutrality. They were hostile, but under bonds to keep the peace. Each bit his thumb, but neither dared say he bit it at the other. Now the neutrality is over; attempts are made to compromise, to compose the difficulty. Various peace measures were introduced to the Senate last summer; but they all turned out war measures, every one of them. Now there is a trial of strength between the two. Which shall recede? which be extended? Freedom or Slavery? That is the question; refuse to look at it as we will,—refrain or refrain not from "political agitation," that is the question.

In the last Congress it is plain the democratic idea was beaten. Congress said to California, " You may come in, and you need not keep slaves unless you please." It said, " You shall not bring slaves to Washington for sale, you may do that at Norfolk, Alexandria, and Georgetown, it is just as well, and this ' will pacify the North.' " Utah and New Mexico were left open to slavery, and fifty thousand or seventy thousand square miles and ten million dollars were given to Texas lest she should " dissolve the Union," —without money or men! To crown all, the Fugitive Slave Bill became a law.

I think it is very plain that the democratic idea was defeated, and it is easy to see why. The three powers which are the allies of the despotic idea, were ready, and could act in concert—the Southern slaveholders, the leading politicians, the rich and educated men of the Northern cities, with their appendages and servile adherents. But since then, the conduct of the people in the North, and especially in this State, shows that the nation has not gone that way yet. I think the nation never will; that the idea of freedom will never be turned back in this blessed North. I feel sure it will at last overcome the idea of slavery.

I come to this conclusion, firstly, from the character of the tribe: this Anglo-Norman-Saxon tribe loves law, deliberation, order, method; it is the most methodical race that ever lived. But it loves liberty, and while it loves law, it loves law chiefly because it keeps liberty; and without that it would trample law under foot.

See the conduct of England. She spent one hundred millions of dollars in the attempt to wipe slavery from the West Indies. She keeps a fleet on the coast of Africa to put down the slave-trade there—where we also have, I think, a sloop-of-war. She has just concluded a treaty with Brazil for the suppression of the slave-trade in that country, one of her greatest achievements in that work for many years.

See how the sons of the Puritans, as soon as they came to a consciousness of what the despotic idea was, took their charters and wiped slavery clean out, first from Massachusetts, and then from the other States, one after another. See how every Northern State, in revising its Constitution, or in making a new one, declares all men are created equal, that all have the right to life, liberty, and the pursuit of happiness.

Then the religion of the North demands the same thing. Professors may try to prove that the Old Testament establishes slavery; that the New Testament justifies the existence of slavery; that Paul's epistle to Philemon was nothing more than another fugitive slave law, that Paul himself sent back a runaway; but it does not touch the religion of the North. We know better. We say if the Old Testament does that and the New Testament, so much the worse for them both. We say, "Let us look and see if Paul was so benighted," and we can judge for ourselves that the professor was mistaken more than the apostle.

Again, the spirit of the age, which is the public opinion of the nations, is against slavery. It was broken down in England, France, Italy, and Spain; it cannot stand long against civilization and good sense; against the political economy and the religious economy of the civilized world. The genius of freedom stands there, year out, year in, and hurls firebrands into the owl's nest of the prince of darkness, continually,—and is all this with no effect?

Besides that, it is against the law of God. That guides this universe, treating with even-handed justice the great geographical parties, Austrian, Roman, British, or American, with the same justice wherewith it dispenses its blessings to the little local factions that divide the village for a day, marshalling mankind forward in its mighty progress towards wisdom, freedom, goodness towards men, and piety towards God.

Of the final issue I have no doubt; but no man can tell what shall come to pass in the meantime. We see that political parties in the State are snapped asunder: whether the national party shall not be broken up, no man can say. In 1750, on the 28th day of November, no man in Old England or New England could tell what 1780 would bring forth. No man, North or South, can tell to-day

what 1880 will bring to pass. He must be a bold man
who declares to the nation that no new political machinery
shall be introduced, in the next thirty years, to our
national mill. We know not what a day shall bring
forth, but we know that God is on the side of right and
justice, and that they will prevail so long as God is God.

Now, then, to let alone details, and generalize into one
all the causes of our condition, this is the result : we have
found welfare just so far as we have followed the democratic idea, and enacted justice into law. We have lost
welfare just so far as we have followed the despotic idea,
and made iniquity into a statute. So far as we have re-
affirmed the ordinance of nature and re-enacted the will of
God, we have succeeded. So far as we have refused to do
that, we have failed. Of old it was written, " Righteousness exalteth a nation: but sin is a reproach to any
people."

And now a word of our dangers. There seems no
danger from abroad; from any foreign State, unless we
begin the quarrel; none from famine. The real danger,
in one word, is this—That we shall try to enact injustice
into a law, and with the force of the nation to make
iniquity obeyed.
See some of the special forms of injustice which threaten
us, or are already here. I shall put them into the form of
ideas.
1. One, common among politicians, is, that the State is
for a portion of the people, not the whole. Thus it has
been declared that the Constitution of the United States
did not recognise the three million slaves as citizens, or
extend to them any right which it guarantees to other
men. It would be a sad thing for the State to declare
there was a single child in the whole land to whom it
owed no protection. What, then, if it attempts to take
three millions from under its shield? In obedience to
this false idea, the counsel has been given, that we must
abstain from all " Political agitation " of the most important matter before the people. We must leave that to
our masters, for the State is for them, it is not for you and
me. They must say whether we shall " agitate " and

"discuss" these things or not. The politicians are our masters, and may lay their fingers on our lips when they will.

2. The next false idea is,—That government is chiefly for the protection of property. This has long been the idea on which some men legislated, but on the 19th day of this month, the distinguished Secretary of State, in a speech at New York, used these words: "The great object of government is the protection of property at home and respect and renown abroad." You see what the policy must be where the government is for the protection of the hat, and only takes care of the head so far as it serves to wear a hat. Here the man is the accident, and the dollar is the substance for which the man is to be protected. I think a notion very much like this prevails extensively in the great cities of America, North and South. I think the chief politicians of the two parties are agreed in this—that government is for the protection of property, and everything else is subsidiary. With many persons politics are a part of their business ; the state-house and the custom-house are only valued for their relation to trade. This idea is fatal to a good government.

Think of this, that "The great object of government is the protection of property." Tell that to Samuel Adams, and John Hancock, and Washington, and the older Winthrops, and the Bradfords and Carvers! Why! it seems as if the buried majesty of Massachusetts would start out of the ground, and with its Bible in its hand say —This is false!

3. The third false idea is this—That you are morally bound to obey the statute, let it be never so plainly wrong and opposed to your conscience. This is the most dangerous of all the false ideas yet named. Ambitious men, in an act of passion, make iniquity into a law, and then demand that you and I, in our act of prayer, shall submit to it and make it our daily life ; that we shall not try to repeal and discuss and agitate it! This false idea lies at the basis of every despot's throne, the idea that men can make right wrong, and wrong right. It has come to be taught in New England, to be taught in our churches— though seldom there, to their honour be it spoken, except in the churches of commerce in large towns—that if wrong is law, you and I must do what it demands, though con-

science declares it is treason against man and treason against God. The worst doctrines of Hobbes and Filmer are thus revived.

I have sometimes been amazed at the talk of men who call on us to keep the fugitive slave law, one of the most odious laws in a world of odious laws—a law not fit to be made or kept. I have been amazed that they should dare to tell us the law of God, writ on the heavens and our hearts, never demanded we should disobey the laws of men! Well, suppose it were so. Then it was old Daniel's duty at Darius's command to give up his prayer; but he prayed three times a day, with his windows up. Then it was John's and Peter's duty to forbear to preach of Christianity; but they said, "Whether it be right in the sight of God to hearken unto you more than unto God, judge ye." Then it was the duty of Amram and Jochebed to take up their new-born Moses and cast him into the Nile, for the law of king Pharaoh, commanding it, was "constitutional," and "political agitation" was discountenanced as much in Goshen as in Boston. But Daniel did not obey; John and Peter did not fail to preach Christianity; and Amram and Jochebed refused "passive obedience" to the king's decree! I think it will take a strong man all this winter to reverse the judgment which the world has passed on these three cases. But it is "innocent" to try.

However, there is another ancient case, mentioned in the Bible, in which the laws commanded one thing and conscience just the opposite. Here is the record of the law: —"Now both the chief priests and the Pharisees had given a commandment, that if any one knew where he [Jesus] were, he should show it, that they might take him." Of course, it became the official and legal business of each disciple who knew where Christ was, to make it known to the authorities. No doubt James and John could leave all and follow him, with others of the people who knew not the law of Moses, and were accursed; nay, the women, Martha and Mary, could minister unto him of their substance, could wash his feet with tears, and wipe them with the hairs of their head. They did it gladly, of their own free will, and took pleasure therein, I make no doubt. There was no merit in that—"Any man can perform an agreeable duty." But there was found one disciple who could "perform a disagreeable duty." He went, perhaps "with alacrity," and betrayed his Saviour to the marshal of the district of Jerusalem, who was called a centurion. Had he no affection for Jesus? No doubt; but he could conquer his prejudices, while Mary and John could not.

Judas Iscariot has rather a bad name in the Christian world: he is called "the son of perdition," in the New Testament, and his conduct is reckoned a "transgression;" nay, it is said the devil "entered into him," to cause this hideous sin. But all this it seems was a mistake; certainly, if we are to believe our "republican" lawyers and statesmen, Iscariot only fulfilled his "constitutional obligations." It was only "on that point," of betraying his Saviour, that the constitutional law required him to have anything to do with Jesus. He took his "thirty pieces of silver"—about fifteen dollars; a Yankee is to do it for ten, having fewer prejudices to conquer—it was his legal fee, for value received. True, the Christians thought it was "the wages of iniquity," and even the Pharisees— who commonly made the commandment of God of none effect by their traditions—dared not defile the temple with this "price of blood;" but it was honest money. It was as honest a fee as any American commissioner or deputy will ever get for a similar service. How mistaken we are! Judas Iscariot is not a traitor; he was a great patriot; he conquered his "prejudices," performed "a disagreeable duty" as an office of "high morals and high principle;" he kept the "law" and the "Constitution," and did all he could to "save the Union;" nay, he was a saint, "not a whit behind the very chiefest apostles." "The law of God never commands us to disobey the law of man." *Sancte Iscariote ora pro nobis.*

It is a little strange to hear this talk in Boston, and hear the doctrine of passive obedience to a law which sets Christianity at defiance, taught here in the face of the Adamses, and Hancock, and Washington! It is amazing to hear this talk, respecting such a law, amongst merchants. Do they keep the usury laws? I never heard of but one money-lender who kept them,* and he has been a

* The late Mr. John Parker.

long time dead, and I think he left no kith nor kin ! The temperance law,—is that kept ? The fifteen gallon law,— were men so very passive in their obedience to that, that they could not even "agitate?" yet it violated no law of God—was not unchristian. When the government inter- feres with the rumsellers' property, the law must be trod under foot; but when the law insists that a man shall be made a slave, I must give up conscience in my act of prayer, and stoop to the vile law men have made in their act of passion !

It is curious to hear men talk of law and order in Boston, when the other day one or two hundred smooth-faced boys, and youths beardless as girls, could disturb a meet- ing of three or four thousand men, for two hours long ; and the chief of the police, and the mayor of the city stood and looked on, when a single word from their lips might have stilled the tumult and given honest men a hearing.*

Talk of keeping the fugitive slave law ! Come, come, we know better. Men in New England know better than this. We know that we ought not to keep a wicked law, and that it must not be kept when the law of God forbids !

But the effect of a law which men cannot keep without violating conscience, is always demoralizing. There are men who know no higher law than the statute of the State. When good men cannot keep a law that is base, some bad ones will say, "Let us keep no law at all,"—then where does the blame lie ? On him that enacts the outrageous law.

The idea that a statute of man frees us from obligation to the law of God, is a dreadful thing. When that be- comes the deliberate conviction of the great mass of the people, North or South, then I shall despair of human nature ; then I shall despair of justice, and despair of God. But this time will never come.

One of the most awful spectacles I ever saw, was this : A vast multitude attempting, at an orator's suggestion, to howl down the " Higher law ;" and when he said, " Will you have this to rule over you?" they answered, "Never!" and treated the " Higher law " to a laugh and a howl ! It

* This took place at a meeting in Faneuil Hall to welcome Mr. George Thompson.

was done in Faneuil Hall;* under the eyes of the three
Adamses, Hancock, and Washington; and the howl rung
round the venerable arches of that hall! I could not but
ask, " Why do the heathen rage, and the people imagine
a vain thing? the rulers of the earth set themselves, and
kings take counsel against the Lord and say, 'Let us
break his bands asunder, and cast off his yoke from us.'"
Then I could not but remember that it was written, "He
that sitteth in the heavens shall laugh; the Lord shall
have them in derision. He taketh up the isles as a very
little thing, and the inhabitants of the earth are as grass-
hoppers before him." Howl down the law of God at a
magistrate's command! Do this in Boston! Let us
remember this—but with charity.

Men say there is danger of disunion, of our losing fealty
for the Constitution. I do not believe it yet! Suppose it
be so. The Constitution is the machinery of the national
mill; and suppose we agree to take it out and put in new;
we might get worse, very true, but we might get better.
There have been some modern improvements; we might
introduce them to the State as well as the mill. But I do
not believe there is this danger. I do not believe the
people of Massachusetts think so. I think they are strongly
attached to the Union yet, and if they thought "the
Union was in peril—this day," and everything the nation
prizes was likely to be destroyed, we should not have had
a meeting of a few thousands in Faneuil Hall, but the
people would have filled up the city of Worcester with a
hundred thousand men, if need be; and they would have
come with the cartridge-box at their side, and the firelock
on their shoulder. That is the way the people of Massachusetts would assemble if they thought there was real
danger.

I do not believe the South will withdraw from the
Union, with five million free men, and three million slaves.
I think Massachusetts would be no loser, I think the
North would be no loser; but I doubt if the North will
yet allow them to go, if so disposed. Do you think the
South is so mad as to wish it?

But I think I know of one cause which may dissolve the

* At the "Union meeting," two days before the delivery of this
sermon.

Union—one which ought to dissolve it, if put in action: that is, a serious attempt to execute the fugitive slave law, here and in all the North. I mean an attempt to recover and take back all the fugitive slaves in the North, and to punish, with fine and imprisonment, all who aid or conceal them. The South has browbeat us again and again. She has smitten us on the one cheek with "Protection," and we have turned the other, kissing the rod; she has smitten that with "Free trade." She has imprisoned our citizens; driven off, with scorn and loathing, our officers sent to ask constitutional justice. She has spit upon us. Let her come to take back the fugitives—and trust me, she "will wake up the lion."

In my humble opinion, this law is a wedge—sharp at one end, but wide at the other—put in between the lower planks of our Ship of State. If it be driven home; we go to pieces. But I have no thought that that will be done quite yet. I believe the great politicians, who threatened to drive it through the gaping seams of our argosy, will think twice before they strike again. Nay, that they will soon be very glad to bury the wedge "where the tide ebbs and flows four times a day." I do not expect this of their courage, but of their fears; not of their justice— I am too old for that—but of their concern for property, which it is the "great object of government" to protect.

I know how some men talk in public, and how they act at home. I heard a man the other day, at Faneuil Hall, declare the law must be kept, and denounce, not very gently, all who preached or prayed against it, as enemies of "all law." But that was all talk, for this very man, on that very day, had violated the law; had furnished the golden wheels on which fugitives rode out of the reach of the arms which the marshal would have been sorry to lift. I could tell things more surprising—but it is not wise just now!*

I do not believe there is more than one of the New England men who publicly helped the law into being, but would violate its provisions; conceal a fugitive; share his loaf with a runaway; furnish him golden wings to fly with. Nay, I think it would be difficult to find a magistrate in New England, willing to take the public odium of

* Nor even yet. November 24, 1851.

doing the official duty.* I believe it is not possible to find a regular jury, who will punish a man for harbouring a slave, for helping his escape, or fine a marshal or commissioner for being a little slow to catch a slave.† Men will talk loud in public meetings, but they have some conscience after all, at home. And though they howl down the "Higher law" in a crowd, yet conscience will make cowards of them all, when they come to lay hands on a Christian man, more innocent than they, and send him into slavery for ever! One of the commissioners of Boston talked loud and long, last Tuesday, in favour of keeping the law. When he read his litany against the law of God, and asked if men would keep the "Higher law," and got "Never" as the welcome, and amen for response—it seemed as if the law might be kept, at least by that commissioner, and such as gave the responses to his creed. But slave-hunting Mr. Hughes, who came here for two of our fellow-worshippers,‡ in his Georgia newspaper, tells a different story. Here it is, from the "Georgia Telegraph," of last Friday. "I called at eleven o'clock at night, at his [the commissioner's] residence, and stated to him my business, and asked him for a warrant, saying that if I could get a warrant, I could have the negroes [William and Ellen Craft] arrested. He said the law did not authorize a warrant to be issued: that it was my duty to go and arrest the negro without a warrant, and bring him before him!" This is more than I expected. "Is Saul among the prophets?" The men who tell us that the law must be kept, God willing, or against his will—there are Puritan fathers behind them also; Bibles in their houses; a Christ crucified, whom they think of; and a God even in their world, who slumbers not, neither is weary, and is as little a respecter of parchments as of persons! They know there is a people, as well as politicians, a posterity not yet assembled, and they would not like to have certain words writ on their tombstone. "Traitor to the rights of mankind," is

---

* Subsequent events have shown the folly of this statement. Clergymen, it is said, are wont to err, by overrating the moral principle of men.

† Recent experiments fortunately confirm this, and, spite of all the unjust efforts to pack a jury, none has yet been found to punish a man for such a "Crime."

‡ Mr. William Craft, and Mrs. Ellen Craft.

no pleasant epitaph. They, too, remember there is a day after to-day; ay, a for ever; and, "Inasmuch as ye have not done it unto one of the least of these my brethren, ye have not done it unto me," is a sentence they would not like to hear at the day of judgment.*

Much danger is feared from the "political agitation" of this matter. Great principles have never been discussed without great passions, and will not be, for some time, I suppose. But men fear to have this despotic idea become a subject of discussion. Last spring, Mr. Webster said here in Boston, "We shall not see the legislation of the country proceed in the old harmonious way, until the discussion in Congress and out of Congress, upon the subject [of slavery], shall be in some manner suppressed. Take that truth home with you!" We have lately been told that political agitation on the subject must be stopped. So it seems this law, like that which Daniel would not keep, is one that may not be changed, and must not be talked of.

Now there are three modes in which attempts may be made to stop the agitation.

1. By sending

> "—— troops, with guns and banners,
> Cut short our speeches and our necks,
> And break our heads to mend our manners."

That is the Austrian way, which has not yet been tried here, and will not be.

2. By sending lecturers throughout the land, to stir up the people to be quiet, and agitate them till they are still; to make them sign the pledge of total abstinence from the discussion of this subject. That is not likely to effect the object.

3. For the friends of silence to keep their own counsel —and this seems as little likely to be tried, as the others to succeed.

Strange is it to ask us to forbear to talk on a subject which involves the welfare of twenty million men! As well ask a man in a fever not to be heated, and a consumptive person not to cough, to pine away and turn pale.

---

* This also appears to have been a mistake. Still I let the passage stand, though it is apparently not at all true.

Miserable counsellors are ye all, who give such advice. But we have seen lately the lion of the democrats, and the lamb of the whigs, lie down together, joined by this opinion, so gentle and so loving, all at once, that a little child could lead them, and so " fulfil the sure prophetic word." Yes, we have seen the Herod of one party, and the Pilate of the other, made friends for the sake of crucifying the freedom of mankind.

But there is one way in which, I would modestly hint, that we might stop all this talk " in Congress and out of Congress," that is, to " discuss" the matter till we had got at the truth, and the whole truth; then to " agitate" politically, till we had enacted justice into law, and carried it out all over the North, and all over the South. After that there would be no more discussion about the fugitive slave bill, than about the " Boston port bill;" no more agitation about American slavery, than there is about the condition of the people of Babylon before the flood. I think there is no other way in which we are likely to get rid of this discussion.

Such is our condition, such its causes, such our dangers. Now, for the lesson, look a moment elsewhere. Look at continental Europe, at Rome, Austria, Prussia, and the German States—at France. How uncertain is every government! France—the stablest of them all! Remember the revolution which two years ago shook those States so terribly, when all the royalty of France was wheeled out of Paris in a street cab. Why are those States so tottering? Whence those revolutions? They tried to make iniquity their law, and would not give over the attempt! Why are the armies of France five hundred thousand strong, though the nation is at peace with all the world? Because they tried to make injustice law! Why do the Austrian and German monarchs fear an earthquake of the people? Because they tread the people down with wicked laws! Whence came the crushing debts of France, Austria, England? From the same cause: from the injustice of men who made mischief by law!

It is not for men long to hinder the march of human freedom. I have no fear for that, ultimately,—none at all, simply for this reason, that I believe in the Infinite

God. You may make your statutes; an appeal always lies to the higher law, and decisions adverse to that get set aside in the ages. Your statutes cannot hold Him. You may gather all the dried grass and all the straw in both continents; you may braid it into ropes to bind down the sea; while it is calm, you may laugh, and say, "Lo, I have chained the ocean!" and howl down the law of Him who holds the universe as a rosebud in his hand— its every ocean but a drop of dew. "How the waters suppress their agitation," you may say. But when the winds blow their trumpets, the sea rises in its strength, snaps asunder the bonds that had confined his mighty limbs, and the world is littered with the idle hay! Stop the human race in its development and march to freedom? As well might the boys of Boston, some lustrous night, mounting the steeples of this town, call on the stars to stay their course! Gently, but irresistibly, the Greater and the Lesser Bear move round the pole; Orion, in his mighty mail, comes up the sky; the Bull, the Ram, the Heavenly Twins, the Crab, the Lion, the Maid, the Scales, and all that shining company, pursue their march all night, and the new day discovers the idle urchins in their lofty places, all tired, and sleepy, and ashamed.

It is not possible to suppress the idea of freedom, or for ever hold down its institutions. But it is possible to destroy a State; a political party with geographical bounds may easily be rent asunder. It is not impossible to shiver this American Union. But how? What clove asunder the great British party, one nation once in America and England? Did not our fathers love their fatherland? Ay. They called it home, and were loyal with abundant fealty; there was no lack of piety for home. It was the attempt to make old English injustice New England law! Who did it,—the British people? Never. Their hand did no such sacrilege! It was the merchants of London, with the "Navigation Act;" the politicians of Westminster with the "Stamp Act;" the tories of America, who did not die without issue, that for office and its gold would keep a king's unjust commands. It was they, who drove our fathers into disunion against their will. Is here no lesson? We love law, all of us love it; but a true man loves it only as the Safeguard of the Rights of Man.

If it destroys these rights, he spurns it with his feet. Is here no lesson? Look further, then.

Do you know how empires find their end? Yes, the great States eat up the little. As with fish, so with nations. Ay, but how do the great States come to an end? By their own injustice, and no other cause. They would make unrighteousness their law, and God wills not that it be so. Thus they fall; thus they die. Look at these ancient States, the queenliest queens of earth. There is Rome, the widow of two civilizations, — the Pagan and the Catholic. They both had her, and unto both she bore daughters and fair sons. But, the Niobe of Nations, she boasted that her children were holier and more fair than all the pure ideas of justice, truth, and love, the offspring of the eternal God. And now she sits there, transformed into stone, amid the ruins of her children's bones. At midnight I have heard the owl hoot in the coliseum and the forum, giving voice to desolation; and at midday I have seen the fox in the palace where Augustus gathered the wealth, the wit, the beauty, and the wisdom of a conquered world; and the fox and the owl interpreted to me the voice of many ages, which came to tell this age, that though hand joined in hand, the wicked shall not prosper.

Come with me, my friends, a moment more, pass over this Golgotha of human history, treading reverent as you go, for our feet are on our mothers' grave, and our shoes defile our fathers' hallowed bones. Let us not talk of them; go further on, look and pass by. Come with me into the Inferno of the nations, with such poor guidance as my lamp can lend. Let us disquiet and bring up the awful shadows of empires buried long ago, and learn a lesson from the tomb.

Come, old Assyria, with the Ninevitish dove upon thy emerald crown! What laid thee low? "I fell by own injustice. Thereby Nineveh and Babylon came, with me, also, to the ground."

Oh, queenly Persia, flame of the nations, wherefore art thou so fallen, who troddest the people under thee, bridgedst the Hellespont with ships, and pouredst thy temple-wasting millions on the western world? "Because I trod the people under me, and bridged the Hellespont with ships, and poured my temple-wasting millions on the western world. I fell by own misdeeds."

Thou muse-like, Grecian queen, fairest of all thy classic sisterhood of States, enchanting yet the world with thy sweet witchery, speaking in art, and most seductive song, why liest thou there with beauteous yet dishonoured brow, reposing on thy broken harp? "I scorned the law of God; banished and poisoned wisest, justest men; I loved the loveliness of flesh, embalmed it in the Parian stone; I loved the loveliness of thought, and treasured that in more than Parian speech. But the beauty of justice, the loveliness of love, I trod them down to earth! Lo, therefore, have I become as those Barbarian States— as one of them!"

Oh, manly and majestic Rome, thy sevenfold mural crown, all broken at thy feet, why art thou here? It was not injustice brought thee low; for thy great book of law is prefaced with these words, justice is the unchanging, everlasting will to give each man his right! "It was not the saint's ideal: it was the hypocrite's pretence! I made iniquity my law. I trod the nations under me. Their wealth gilded my palaces,—where thou mayst see the fox and hear the owl,—it fed my courtiers and my courtesans. Wicked men were my cabinet-counsellors, the flatterer breathed his poison in my ear. Millions of bondmen wet the soil with tears and blood. Do you not hear it crying yet to God? Lo, here have I my recompense, tormented with such downfall as you see! Go back and tell the new-born child, who sitteth on the Alleghanies, laying his either hand upon a tributary sea, a crown of thirty stars about his youthful brow—tell him that there are rights which States must keep, or they shall suffer wrongs! Tell him there is a God who keeps the black man and the white, and hurls to earth the loftiest realm that breaks His just, eternal law! Warn the young Empire that he come not down dim and dishonoured to my shameful tomb! Tell him that justice is the unchanging, everlasting will to give each man his right. I knew it, broke it, and am lost. Bid him to know it, keep it, and be safe!"

"God save the Commonwealth!" proclaims the Go-

vernor. God will do his part,—doubt not of that. But
you and I must help Him save the State. What can we
do? Next Sunday I will ask you for your charity; to-day
I ask a greater gift, more than the abundance of the rich,
or the poor widow's long-remembered mite. I ask you
for your justice. Give that to your native land. Do you
not love your country? I know you do. Here are our
homes and the graves of our fathers; the bones of our
mothers are under the sod. The memory of past deeds is
fresh with us; many a farmer's and mechanic's son
inherits from his sires some cup of manna gathered in the
wilderness, and kept in memory of our exodus; some
stones from the Jordan, which our fathers passed over
sorely bested and hunted after; some Aaron's rod, green
and blossoming with fragrant memories of the day of small
things, when the Lord led us—and all these attach us to
our land, our native land. We love the great ideas of the
North, the institutions which they founded, the righteous
laws, the schools, the churches, too—do we not love all
these? Ay. I know well you do. Then by all these,
and more than all, by the dear love of God, let us swear
that we will keep the justice of the Eternal Law. Then
are we all safe. We know not what a day may bring
forth, but we know that Eternity will bring everlasting
peace. High in the heavens, the pole-star of the world,
shines Justice; placed within us, as our guide thereto, is
Conscience. Let us be faithful to that—

> "Which though it trembles as it lowly lies,
> Points to the light that changes not in heaven."

X.

THE ASPECT OF FREEDOM IN AMERICA. A SPEECH AT THE MASS. ANTI-SLAVERY CELEBRATION OF INDEPENDENCE, AT ABINGTON, JULY 5, 1852.

MR. PRESIDENT, LADIES, AND GENTLEMEN,—This is one of the anniversaries which mark four great movements in the progressive development of mankind; whereof each makes an Epoch in the history of the human race.

The first is the Twenty-fifth of December, the date agreed upon as the anniversary of the Birth of Jesus of Nazareth, marking the Epoch of Christianity.

The next is the First of November, the day when, in 1517, Martin Luther nailed the ninety-five theses on the church-door at Wittenberg, the noise of his hammer startling the indolence, the despotism, and the licentiousness of the Pope, and his concubines, and his court far off at Rome. That denotes the Epoch of Protestantism, the greatest movement of mankind after the teaching of Jesus.

The third is the Twenty-second of December, the day when our Forefathers, in 1620, first set their feet on Plymouth Rock, coming, though unconsciously, to build up a Church without a Bishop, a State without a King, a Community without a Lord, and a Family without a Slave. This begins the Epoch of New England.

The last is the Fourth of July, when our Fathers, in 1776, brought distinctly to national consciousness what I call the American Idea; the Idea, namely, that all men have natural rights to life, liberty, and the pursuit of happiness; that all men are equal in their natural rights; that these rights can only be alienated by the possessor thereof; and that it is the undeniable function of government to preserve their rights to each and all. This day marks the Epoch of the United States of America—an Epoch indissolubly connected with the three preceding. The Idea was Christian, was Protestant, was of New England. Plymouth was becoming national, Protestantism going into politics; and the Sentiments and Ideas of Christianity getting an expression on a national scale. The Declaration of Independence was the American profession of faith in political Christianity.

This day is consecrated to freedom; let us look, therefore, at the Aspect of Freedom just now in America.

In 1776, there were less than three million persons in the United States. Now, more than three million voters. But, alas! there are also more than three million slaves. Seventy-six years ago, slavery existed in all the thirteen colonies; but New England was never quite satisfied with it; only the cupidity of the Puritan assented thereto, not his conscience. Soon it retreated from New England, from all the North, but strengthened itself in the South, and spread Westward and Southward, till now it has crossed the Cordilleras, and the Pacific Ocean is witness to the gigantic wrong of the American People.

But, spite of this growth of slavery, the American Idea has grown in favour with the American people, the North continually becoming more and more democratic in the best sense of the word. True, in all the great cities of the North, the love of slavery has also grown strong, in none stronger than in Boston. The Mother city of the Puritans is now the metropolis of the Hunkers. Slavery also has entered the churches of the North, and some of them, we see, when called on to choose betwixt Christianity and slavery, openly and boldly decide against the Law of God, and in favour of this great crime against man. But simultaneously with this growth of Hunkerism in the cities and the churches of the North, at the same time with the spread of slavery from the Delaware to the Sacramento, the Spirit of Liberty has also spread, and taken a deep hold on the hearts of the people.

In the material world, nothing is done by leaps, all by gradual advance. The land slopes upward all the way from Abington to the White Mountains. If Mt. Washington rose a mile and a quarter of sheer ascent, with perpendicular sides from the level of the ocean, only the

eagle and the lightning could gain its top.   Now its easy
slope allows the girl to look down from its summit.

What is true in the world of matter holds also good in
the world of man.   There is no leap, a slope always;
never a spring.   The continuity of historical succession is
never broke.   Newtons and Shakspeares do not come up
among Hottentots and Esquimaux, but among young
nations inheriting the old culture.   Even the men of
genius, who brood like a cloud over the vulgar herd, have
their predecessors almost as high, and the continuity of
succession holds good in the Archimedes, the Gallileos, the
Keplers, the Newtons, and the La Places.   Christianity
would not have been possible in the time of Moses ; nor
Protestantism in the days of St. Augustine ; nor a New
England Plymouth in the days of Luther ; nor any
national recognition of the American Idea in 1620.   That
Idea could not become a national Fact in 1776.   No, not
yet is it a fact.

First comes the Sentiment—the feeling of liberty ; next
the Idea—the distinct notion thereof ; then the Fact—the
thought become a thing.   Buds in March, blossoms in
May, apples in September—that is the law of historical
succession.

The Puritans enslaved the Indians.   In 1675, the
Indian apostle petitioned the " Honourable Governor and
Council sitting at Boston, this 13th of the 6th, '75," that
they would not allow Indians to be sold into slavery.
But John Eliot stood well-nigh alone in that matter.   For
three months later, I find the Governor, Leveret, gives a
bill of sale of seven Indians, " to be sold for slaves," and
affixes thereto the " Publique Seale of the Colony."

Well, there has been a great progress from that day to
the 12th of April, 1851, when the merchants of Boston
had to break the laws of Massachusetts, and put the
court house in chains, and get the chains over the neck of
the Chief Justice, and call out the Sims brigade, before
they could kidnap and enslave a single fugitive from
Georgia.

But it would not be historical to expect a nation to
realize its own Idea at once, and allow all men to be
" equal " in the enjoyment of their " natural and unalienable rights."   Still, there has been a great progress

towards that in the last seventy-six years, spite of the steps taken backward in some parts of the land. It is not a hundred and ten years since slaves were advertised for sale in Boston, as now in Norfolk; not eighty years since they were property in Massachusetts, and appraised in the inventories of deceased "Republicans." So then the cause of African freedom has a more auspicious look on the 4th of July, 1852, than it had on the 4th of July, 1776. We do not always think so, because we look at the present evil, not at the greater evils of the past. So much for the GENERAL aspect of this matter.

Look now at the present position of the Political Parties. There are two great parties in America — only two. I. One is the PRO-SLAVERY PARTY. This has not yet attained a distinct consciousness of its idea and consequent function; so there is contradiction in its opinions, vacillation in its conduct, and heterogeneous elements in its ranks. This has two divisions, namely: the Whigs and the Democrats. The two are one great national party— they are one in slavery, as all sects are "one in Christ." Yet they still keep up their distinctive banners, and shout their hostile war-cry; but when they come to action, they both form column under the same leader, and fight for the same end—the promotion, the extension, and the perpetuation of slavery.

Once the Whig Party wanted a Bank. Democracy trod it to the earth. Then the Whigs clamoured for a protective Tariff. That also seems now an obsolete idea, and a revenue tariff is a fact accomplished. The old issues between Whig and Democrat are out of date. Shall it be said the Whigs want a strong central government, and the Democrats are still anti-federal, and opposed to the centralization of power? It is not so. I can see no difference in the two parties in this matter; both are ready to sacrifice the individual conscience to the brute power of arbitrary law; each to crush the individual rights of the separate States before the central power of the federal government. In passing the Fugitive Slave Bill, which aims at both these enormities, the Democrats outvied the Whigs; in executing it, the Whigs outdo the Democrats, and kidnap with a more malignant relish. I believe the official kidnappers are all Whigs, in Boston, New York, Philadelphia, and Buffalo.

Both parties have now laid down their Platforms, and nominated their candidates for the Presidency, and hoisted them thereon. Their platforms are erected on slave soil, and made of slave timber. Both express the same devo-tion to slavery, the same acquiescence in the Fugitive Slave Bill. The Whig Party says, we "will *discounte-nance* all efforts at the renewal or continuance of such agitation [on the subject of slavery] in Congress or out of it—whenever, wherever, or however the attempt may be made." The Democrats say they "will *resist* all attempts at reviving, in Congress or out of it, the agitation of the slavery question, under whatever shape or colour the attempt may be made." There is the difference; one will *discountenance*, and the other *resist* all agitation of the question which concerns the freedom of three million American citizens. Slavery is their point of agreement.

Both have nominated their champions—each a "Gene-ral." They have passed by the eminent politicians, and selected men whose political experience is insignificant. The Democratic champion from New Hampshire jumps upon one platform, the Whig champion from New Jersey jumps upon the other, and each seems to like that "bad eminence" very well. But I believe that at what old politicians have left of a heart, both dislike slavery—per-haps about equally. General Pierce, in a public meeting, I am told, declared that the Fugitive Slave Bill was against the principles of the common law, and against natural moral right. General Scott, I am told, in a private conversation, observed, that if he were elected President, he would never appoint a slave-holder as Judge in any territory of the United States. Their letters accepting the nomination show the value of such public or private ejacu-lations.

It is a little remarkable that War and Slavery should be the *sine qua non* in the Chief Magistrate of the United States, and of no other country. A woman may be Queen of England, and rule one hundred millions of men, and yet not favour the selling of Christians. A man may be "Prince President" of the mock republic of France, and hate slavery; he may be Emperor of Austria, or Autocrat of all the Russias, and think kidnapping is a sin; yes, he may be Sultan of Turkey, and believe it self-evident that all men are created equal, with a natural, inherent, and unalienable right to life, liberty, and the pursuit of happiness! But, to be President of the United States, a man must be devoted to slavery, and believe in the "finality of the compromise measures," and promise to discountenance or to resist all agitation of the subject of slavery, whenever, wherever, or however! Truly, "it is a great country."

That is the aspect of the great Pro-Slavery Party of America. But I must say a word of the late Whig convention. It resulted in one of the most signal defeats that ever happened to an American statesman. Even Aaron Burr did not fall so suddenly and deep into the ground, at his first downfall, as Daniel Webster.

If I am rightly informed, Mr. Mason, in 1850, brought forward the Fugitive Slave Bill, with no expectation that it would pass; perhaps with no desire that it should pass. If it were rejected, then there was what seemed a tangible grievance, which the disunionists would lay hold of, as they cried for "secession." I do not know that it was so; I am told so. He introduced the Bill. Mr. Webster seized it, made it his "thunder" on the 7th of March, 1850. It seemed a tangible thing for him to hold on by, while he pushed from under him his old platform of liberty, made of such timbers as his orations at Plymouth, at Bunker Hill, at Faneuil Hall—his speech for the Greeks, and his speech against General Taylor. He held on to it for two years, and three months, and fourteen days;—a long time for him. He took hold on the 7th of March, 1850; and on the 21st of June, 1852, his hands slipped off, and the Fugitive Slave Bill took flight towards the Presidency, without Daniel Webster, but with General Pierce at one end of it, and General Scott at the other.

> "The fiery pomp ascending left the view;
> The prophet gazed—*and wished to follow too.*"

The downfall of Daniel Webster is terrible:—it was sudden, complete, and final. He has fallen "like Lucifer —never to hope again."

His giant strength was never so severely tasked as in

the support of slavery. What pains he took—up early and down late! What speeches he made,—at Boston, New York, Albany, Syracuse, Rochester, Buffalo, at Philadelphia, and I know not at how many other places! What letters he wrote! And it was all to end in this! What a fee for what a pleading! He was never so paid before.

The pride of Boston—its Hunkerism—ten hundred strong, went to Baltimore to see him rise. They came back amazed at the totality of his downfall!

I think this was at first the plan of some of the most skilful of the Northern leaders of the Whigs, to nominate General Scott without a platform—not committed to slavery or to freedom; then to represent him as opposed to slavery, and so on that ground to commend him to the North, and carry the election; for any day when the North rallies, it can outvote the South. But some violent pro-slavery men framed the present platform, and brought it forward. The policy of Mr. Webster's friends would have been to say—"We need no platform for Mr. Webster. The speech of March 7th is his platform. Mr. Fillmore needs none. General Scott needs a platform, for you don't know his opinions." But, "it is enough for the servant that he be as his master." As Mr. Webster had caught at Mason's Bill, so the "Retainers" caught at the Northern platform, and one who has a great genius for oratory enlarged on its excellence, and whitewashed it all over with his peculiar rhetoric. The platform was set up by the Convention, to the great joy of the "Retainers" from New England; when all at once, the image of General Scott appeared upon it! He as well as Fillmore or Webster can stand there. This was the weight that pulled them down; for after Scott had signified his willingness to accept the platform, the great objection to him on the part of the South was destroyed.

The defeat of Mr. Webster is complete and awful. In fifty-three ballotings, he never went beyond 32 votes out of 293. Fifty-three times was the vote taken, and fifty-three times the whole South voted against him. When it became apparent that the vote would fall to General Scott, Mr. Webster's friends went and begged the Southerners to give him a few votes, which could then do Mr. Fillmore no good; but the South answered—*not a vote!* They went with tears in their eyes; still the South answered—*not a vote!* That is a remarkable "chapter in History!"

Now that the great man has fallen,—utterly and terribly fallen,—a warning for many an age to come, I feel inclined to remember not only the justice of the judgment, but the great powers and the great services of the victim. I wish something may be done to comfort him in his failure, and am glad that his friends now seek an opportunity to express their esteem. Words of endearment are worth something when deeds of succour fail, and when words of consolation awake no hope. I think the anti-slavery men have dared to be just towards Mr. Webster, when he thundered from the seat of his power; now let us be generous. I hope no needless word of delight at his fall will be spoken by any one of us. If we fought against the lion in his pride, and withstood his rage and his roar, let us now remember that he was a LION, and not insult the prostrate majesty of mighty power. "It was a grievous fault, and grievously hath *Webster* answered it." But there was greatness, even nobleness in the man; and much to excuse so monstrous a departure from the true and right. He was a bankrupt politician, and fancied that he saw within his grasp the scope and goal of all his life; he represented a city whose controlling inhabitants prize gold and power above all things, and are not very scrupulous about the means to obtain either; men that run their taxes, let shops for drunkeries and houses for brothels, and bribe a senator of the nation! The New England doctors of divinity, in the name of God, justified his greatest crime. Do you expect more piety in the bear-garden of politics, than in the pulpit of the Christian church? Let us remember these things when the mighty is fallen. Let us pity the lion now that his mane is draggled in the dust, and his mouth filled with Southern dirt. Blame there must be indeed; but pity for fallen greatness should yet prevail—not the pity of contempt, but the pity of compassion, the pity of love. Let us gather up the white ashes of him who perished at the political stake, and do loving honour to any good thing in his character and his life. If we err at all, let it be on the side of charity. We all need that.

If General Scott is President, I take it we shall have a moderate pro-slavery administration, fussy and feathery; that we shall take a large slice from Mexico during the next four years. General Scott is a military man, of an unblemished character, I believe—that is, with no unpopular vices—but with the prejudices of a military man. He proposes to confer citizenship on any foreigner who has served a year in the army or navy of the United States, and seems to think a year of work at fighting is as good a qualification for American citizenship as five years industrious life on a farm, or in a shop. This is a little too military for the American taste, but will suit the military gentlemen who like to magnify their calling.

If General Pierce is chosen, I take it we shall have a strong pro-slavery administration; shall get the slice of Mexico, and Cuba besides, in the next four years. "Manifest destiny" will probably point that way.

I do not know that it will not be better for the cause of freedom that Pierce should succeed. Perhaps the sooner this whole matter is brought to a crisis, the better. In each party there is a large body of Hunkers,—men who care little or nothing for the natural rights of man; mean, selfish men, who seek only their own gratification, and care not at what cost to mankind this is procured. If the Whig Party is defeated, I take it the majority of these Hunkers will gradually fall in with the Democrats; that the Whig Party will not rally again under its old name; that the party of Hunkers will hoist the flag of slavery, and the whole hosts of noble, honest, and religious men in both parties will flee out from under that flag, and go over to the Party of Freedom. Now the sooner this separation of the elements takes place, the better. Then we shall know who are our friends, who our foes. Men will have the real issue set before them. But, until the separation is effected, many good men will cling to their old party organization, with the delusive hope of opposing slavery thereby. Thus we see two such valuable newspapers as the New York *Evening Post* and the *Tribune*, with strong anti-slavery feelings, at work for the Democrats or the Whigs. I think this is the last Presidential election in which such journals will defend such a platform.

II. Look at the ANTI-SLAVERY PARTY. Here also are two great divisions: one is political, the other moral. A word of each—of the political party first.

This is formed of three sections. One is the Free Soil party, which has come mainly from the Whigs; the next is the Free Democracy, the Barnburners, who have come mainly from the Democrats. Each of these has the prejudices of its own historical tradition—Whig prejudices or Democratic prejudices; it has also the excellences of its primal source. I include the Liberty party in this Free Soil, Free Democratic division. They differ from the other in this—a denial that the Constitution of the United States authorizes or allows slavery; a denial that slavery is constitutional in the nation, or even legal in any State.

But all these agree in a strong feeling against slavery. They are one in freedom, as the Whigs and Democrats are one in slavery. Part of this feeling they have translated into an Idea. To express it in their most general terms— Slavery is sectional, not national; belongs to the State, and not the Federal Government. Hence they aim to cut the nation free from slavery altogether, but will leave it to the individual States.

This political Anti-Slavery party is a very strong party. It is considerable by its numbers—powerful enough to hold the balance of power in several of the States. Four years ago, it cast three hundred thousand votes. This year I think it will go up to four hundred thousand.

But it is stronger in the talent and character of its eminent men, than in the force of its numbers. You know those men. I need not speak of Chase and Hale, of Giddings and of Mann, with their coadjutors in Congress and out of it. Look at names not so well known as yet in our national debates. Here is a noble speech from Mr. Townshend, one new ally in the field from the good State of Ohio. This is the first speech of his that I have ever read; it is full of promise. There is conscience in this man; there is power of work in him.

Mr. Rantoul has done honourably—done nobly, indeed. What he will say to-day, I shall not pretend to calculate. He is a politician, like others, and in a very dangerous position; but I have much faith in him; and, at any rate,

T 2

I thank God for what he has done already. He is a man of a good deal of ability, and may be trusted yet to do us good service, not in your way or my way, but in his own way.

I ought to say a word of Mr. Sumner. I know that he has disappointed the expectations of his best friends by keeping silent so long. But Mr. Sumner's whole life shows him to be an honest man, not a selfish man at all—a man eminently sincere, and eminently trustworthy, eminently just. He has a right to choose his own time to speak. I wish he had spoken long ago, and I doubt if this long delay is wholly wise for him. But it is for him to decide, not for us. "A fool's bolt is soon shot," while a wise man often reserves his fire. He should not be taunted with his remarks made when he had no thought of an election to the Senate. A man often thinks a thing easy, which he finds difficult when he comes up to the spot. But this winter past, Mr. Sumner has not been idle. I have a letter from an eminent gentleman at Washington—a man bred in kings' courts abroad—who assures me that Sumner has carried the ideas of freedom where they have never been carried before, and when he speaks, will be listened to with much more interest than if he had uttered his speech at his first entrance to Congress. Depend upon it, we shall hear the right word from Charles Sumner yet. I do not believe that he has waited to make it easy for him to speak, but that it may be better for his Idea, and the cause of Freedom he was sent there to represent.

Then there is another man of great mark on the same side. I mean Mr. Seward. He is nominally with the Whigs, but he is really of the political Anti-Slavery Party, the chief man in it. Just now he has more influence than any man in the Northern States, and is the only prominent Whig politician of whom we might wisely predict a brilliant future. General Scott, I take it, owes his nomination to Senator Seward. In the Convention, he seems to have wished for three things :—1. To defeat Mr. Webster at all events. 2. To defeat Mr. Fillmore, if possible. 3. To have the nomination of General Scott, without a platform, if possible, but if not, with a platform, even with the present platform. Had General Scott been nominated without a slavery platform, I think Mr. Seward, and many other leading Free Soilers, would have stood by to help his election—would have taken office had he succeeded, and I think his chance of success would not have been a bad one then. But now Mr. Seward stands out for a more distant day. He will not accept office under General Scott. He sees that Scott is a compromise candidate, conceded by the fears of the South; that his administration must be a compromise administration, and he that succeeds on that basis now is sure to be overtaken by political ruin at no distant day. He reserves his fire till he is nearer the mark! I think we may yet see him the candidate of a great Northern Party for the Presidency: see him elected.

Such is the aspect of the Political Anti-Slavery Party. It defeated the strongest pro-slavery section of the Whigs in their convention, defeated them of their candidate, sent the one thousand Hunkers of Boston home from Baltimore, in a rather melancholy state of mind. We shall soon see what it will do in its national convention at Pittsburgh, on the 11th of August.

Now a word on the MORAL division of the Anti-Slavery Party. I use the word Moral merely as opposed to Political. It is a party not organized to get votes, but to kindle a Sentiment and diffuse an Idea. Its Sentiment is that of Universal Philanthropy, specially directed towards the African race in America. Its Idea is the American Idea, of which it has a quite distinct consciousness—the Idea of the Declaration of Independence. It does not limit itself by constitutional, but only by moral restrictions.

The function of this party is to kindle the Sentiment and diffuse the Idea of Universal Freedom. It is about this work to-day. These four thousand faces before me at this moment are lit with this Idea; the other thousands beyond the reach of my voice are not without it. It will not be satisfied till there is not a slave in America—not a slave in the world.

This party is powerful by its Sentiments, its Ideas, and its Eminent Men; not yet by its numbers. Here is one indication of its power—the absolute hatred in which it is held by all the Hunkers of the land. How Mr. Webster speaks of this party; with the intense malignity of affected scorn. Men do not thus hate a mouse in the wall. Then the abuse which we receive from all the gnats and mosquitoes of the political penny press is a sign also of our power. There are Hunkers who know that our Ideas are just—that they will be triumphant; hence their hate of our Ideas, and their hate of us.

Well, gentlemen, the cause of freedom looks very auspicious to-day: it never looked better. Every apparent national triumph of slavery is only a step to its defeat. The annexation of Texas, the Fugitive Slave Bill, are measures that ultimately will help the cause of freedom. At first, if a man is threatened with a fever, the doctor tries to "throw it off." If that is impossible, he hastens the crisis—knowing that the sooner that comes, the sooner will the man be well again. I think General Pierce will hasten the crisis, when a Northern party shall get founded, with the American Idea for its motto. The recent action of Congress, the recent decisions of the Supreme Court, the recent action of the Executive, have *de facto* established this: that Slavery in the States is subject to the control of the Federal Government. True, they apply this only to the Northern States; but if the Federal Government can interfere with Slavery in Massachusetts, to the extent of kidnapping a man in Boston, and keeping him in duresse by force of armed soldiers, then the principle is established, that the Federal Government may interfere with Slavery in South Carolina; and when we get the spirit of the North aroused, and the numbers of the North on the side of freedom, it will take but a whiff of breath to annihilate human bondage from the Delaware to the Sacramento.

Even the course of Politics is in our favour. The spirit of this Teutonic family of men is hostile to Slavery. We alone preserve slavery which all the other tribes have cast off. We cannot keep it long. The Ideas of America, the Ideas of Christianity, are against it. The spirit of the age is hostile—ay, the spirit of mankind and the Nature of the Infinite God!

XI.

A NEW LESSON FOR THE DAY: A SERMON PREACHED AT THE MUSIC HALL, IN BOSTON, ON SUNDAY, MAY 25, 1856.

PSALM XII. 8.

"The wicked walk on every side, when the vilest men are exalted."

ON the last Sunday of May, 1854, which was also the beginning of Anniversary Week, I stood here to preach a Sermon of War. In 1846, at the beginning of the Mexican trouble, I spoke of that national wickedness, and again, at the end of the strife, warned the country of that evil deed, begun without the People's consent. When the next great quarrel broke out, in 1854, and Russia, Turkey, England, and France, were engaged in a war which threatened to set all Europe in a flame, I prepared an elaborate sermon on the causes and most obvious consequences of that great feud, an account of the forces then in the field or on the flood, and tried to picture forth the awful spectacle of Christian Europe in the hour of war. I spent many days in collecting the facts and studying their significance. But, while I was computing the cost and the consequence of foreign wickedness, a crime even more atrocious was getting committed under our own eyes, in the streets of Boston; and, when I came to preach on the Russian attack against the independence of a sister state, I found the sermon wholly out of time: for the Boston Judge of Probate had assaulted a brother man, innocent of all offence, poor, unprotected, and apparently friendless. The guardian of orphans—a man not marked by birth for such a deed, but spurred thereto by cruel goads—had kidnapped an American in our streets, clapped him into an unlawful gaol, watched him with ruffians, the offscouring of the town, and guarded him with foreign soldiers, hired to rend and kill whomsoever our masters set them on. Without hearing the evidence, this swift judge had already decided to destroy his victim, and told the counsel, Put no "obstacles in the way of his going back, as he probably will." The whole Commonwealth was in confusion. Boston was in a state of siege. A hundred and eighty foreign soldiers filled up the Court House. There had been an extemporaneous meeting at Faneuil Hall, an attempt to rescue the kidnapper's victim, an attack on the Court House, then unlawfully made a barracoon for our Southern masters to keep their slaves in. One of the volunteers in man-stealing had been slain, and ten or twelve citizens were in gaol on charge of murder. So, when I stood here, and looked into the eyes of the great crowd which filled up these aisles, I saw it was no time to treat of the Russian war against liberty; and my discourse of that wickedness turned into a "Lesson for the Day," touching the new Crime against Humanity. Since then, no occasion has offered for treating of that dreadful conflict of the European nations.

Now, when the Russian war is all over, the treaty of peace definitely settled, I thought it would be worth while to examine that matter : for the cloud of battle has lifted up, and we can look back, and learn the causes of the conflict; look round, and see the dead bodies, the remnants of cities burned, of navies sunk; can look forward, and calculate what loss or gain thence accrues to mankind; and so get possibly a little guidance, and a great deal of warning, for our own conduct. So, to-day, I had intended to preach a calm and philosophical Sermon of the Late War in Europe; examining at length its Cause, Process, and Results, for the present and the future, and its Relation to the Progress and Welfare of Mankind. I meant to look at that transaction in the light of modern philosophy, and of that religion which is alike human and Christian. But now, as before, a new Crime against Humanity has been committed. I must therefore lay by my speculations on that distant evil, and speak of what touches the sin at our own doors. So, this morning, I shall ask your attention to A NEW LESSON FOR THE DAY, in which I shall say a little about the Russian war and European affairs,—yet enough to give a tone of warning, and so likewise of guidance,—and shall have much to offer touching affairs in our country; a little of the Russian war, much of the American. This discourse·may be profitable; it is not pleasant to speak or hear.

When an important event occurs, I have felt it my duty, as a minister and public speaker, to look for its Causes,—which often lie far behind us, wholly out of sight,—and also for its Consequences, that are equally hidden in the distance before us. Accordingly, to some, who only look round them in haste, not far back or forth, what I say often seems improper and out of season. Thus, in 1846, when I treated of the Mexican war, many critics said, You must wait till we have done fighting, before you preach against its wrong! And when I reviewed the Life and Conduct of Mr. Webster,—the greatest understanding New England has borne in her bosom for a whole generation,—they said again, *De mortuis nil nisi bonum,*—You had better put off your criticism for fifty years! But at that time both you and I will not be here to make or profit by it. Some men will also doubtless condemn what I offer now. Wait a little, before you judge. A few years, perhaps a few days, will justify the saddest things I have to say. I wish to mount a great Lesson on this fleet occasion.

The events of the last week at Washington have caused a great heat in this community, not excessive at all; it is too little, rather than too much. They have not heated me in the smallest; my pulse has not beat quicker than before; and, though a tear may sometimes spring to my eye, my judgment is as calm and cool as before: for this assault on Mr. Sumner is no new thing. I have often talked such matters over with him, and said, I know you are prepared to meet the reasoning of the South when it is tendered in words; but her chief argument is bludgeons and bullets; are you ready for that? And our Senator was as cool about it as I am: he also had looked the matter in the face. It excites no surprise in him, none in me. When the iron is hot, it is just as well that the blacksmith should be cool.

First look at the Russian matter, then at the American.

Look at the Amount of Evil in that Russian war.
It did not last two years; yet see what vast sums of money it has cost! Here are the figures: they are partly conjectural, but wholly moderate; they are the estimates of some of the great European journals. France and England have paid four hundred and eighty millions of dollars, Turkey a hundred and forty millions, Austria a hundred millions, Russia three hundred millions. Here, then, ten hundred and twenty millions of dollars have been eaten up in a war not twenty-four months long. Now, that sum of money is more than seven times as great as the entire property, real and personal, of "the great State of South Carolina." That is the direct cost to the governments of the Five Nations: it does not include the damage done to their forts and ships (and, in a single night, Russia destroyed a larger navy of her own vessels than the United States owns,—burnt and sunk it in the harbour of Sebastopol); it does not embrace the diminution of military and naval supplies, or the pensions hereafter to be paid; it makes no account of the injury to individuals whose property has been consumed, or the great cost to the other powers of Europe. When all the bills are in, as they will be a hundred and fifty years hence, then I think it will appear that that two years' fight cost Europe two thousand millions of dollars. That is the amount of the personal and real estate of Massachusetts and Pennsylvania.

Here are the figures representing the deaths of soldiers. England has lost fifty thousand soldiers, France a hundred and seventy thousand, Turkey eighty thousand, and Russia four hundred thousand; making seven hundred thousand men, who have perished in the prime of life. This does not include those who will yet die of their wounds, nor such as perish by the worst of deaths,—the slow heart-break of orphans and widows, or those who meant to be wives, but are widows, though never married. Put it all together, and the two years' war has cost at least a million of lives. Such a spendthrift is war, both of money and men.

Now look at the Causes of this amount of evil, which are quite various. Some of them lie on the top.

First, there is the despotism of the Russian governors, who rule their subjects with an iron rod. There is no freedom of industry in Russia, none of religion; and freedom of speech is also cut off. They attack and despoil other nations more civilized than themselves. The Russian Government has long been the great filibuster of Christendom. Turkey was feeble, Russia strong; each was despotic ; and the big despot would eat up the little. Russia was Christian,—theologically Christian, not morally,—Turkey was Mahometan ; and the Christian wished to tread the Mahometan under foot. The Emperor said, "Turkey is a sick man; let us kill him, that the inheritance may be ours." This was the first obvious cause, the despotism of Russia, the initiating cause.

But other rulers had a kindred spirit. The other great powers of Europe are Prussia, Austria, France, and England. Prussia and Austria are despotic governments. A small class of oligarchs domineer over the people. They are closely joined to Russia by nature and aim; by alliances, matrimonial or diplomatic. The governments of Russia, Austria, and Prussia, are a national brotherhood of thieves. In the eighteenth century, they plundered Poland; in the nineteenth, other nations ; and their own subjects continually. This judgment seems rather harsh. I do not speak of the People, only of the oligarchy which rules the hundred and twenty millions who make up these three nations.

France has established a military despotism, with the picture of "universal suffrage" painted on the cannon. The farce of a Republic is every year enacted by soldiers and government officers,—administration officials. She also longs for conquest,—witness Algiers and Rome,— and in idle vanities consumes the people's wealth,—spends eighty thousand dollars to christen a little baby, an imperial doll.

Alone of all these great powers, England respects the rights of the people, and has institutions progressively democratic. She purposely advances towards freedom. But she, too, shares the instinct to conquer, and, after Russia, is the most invasive power in Europe. Witness her conquests all round the world.   She owns a sixth part of the earth's surface,—controls a fifth part of the population.   Besides that, this noble Anglo-Saxon nation is ruled by an hereditary aristocracy of kings, nobles, and priests, who, though the best perhaps in Europe, yet tread the people down, though far less than anywhere else in Europe.   Certainly, for the last three hundred years, England has been the great bulwark of human freedom; and, just now, she is the only European nation that allows liberty of speech on matters of religion, politics, science, everything.   In Europe, freedom can only be defended in the English tongue.

Now, in common with Austria, Russia, and France, the English Government had longed for the spoils of Turkey;—also counting the Sultan a sick man, and wanting his inheritance.   But these great powers could not agree as to the share that each should take; otherwise the Sultan had died twenty years ago.

All Europe is ruled by an affiliated oligarchy of kings, nobles, and priests, who have unity of idea and aim, to develop the power of the strong and to keep the people down, and unity of action in all great matters.   But in England there is such a mass of thoughtful men, men of property too, such a stern love of individual liberty, that the foot of despotism is never secure, nor its print is ever very deep, on that firm Saxon soil.   Just now the Anglo-Saxon nation in Europe presents a very grand spectacle.   She opens her arms to the exile from every land : despots find a home there, with none to molest nor make them afraid; and patriots are welcome to the generous bosom of England, which bore our fathers.   Though she once, and wickedly, fought against us, she respects and loves her sons, perhaps not the least noble portion of herself.

The spirit of despotism in the other governments of Europe, kindred to the invasive despotism of Russia, was the next cause of that war,—the cause co-operative.

The reputation of France and England for ancient mutual hate, led the Russian Emperor to believe they would not oppose his rapacity.   Neither was strong enough alone; and they could not join.   So he reached out his hand to snatch the glittering prize.   Of course, he began the robbery with a pious pretence : he did not wish for

Turkish soil, only "to protect the Christians," to "have access to the holy places where our blessed Lord was born and slain, and buried too;" so that all Christian people might fulfil the prophecy, and " go up to the mountain of the Lord." The Latin proverb says well, "All evil begins in the name of the Lord." This was no exception.

This brief quarrel, which costs mankind two thousand million dollars and ten hundred thousand lives, was a War of Politicians, not at all of the People. It began only with despots: there was no ill-blood between the nations. Had Nicholas asked the Russians, "Will you go and plunder Turkey in the name of Jesus of Nazareth?" the People would have said, "Not so; but we will stay at home." The war came from no sudden heat. Nicholas had foreseen it, planned it, and in secret made ready at Sebastopol the vast array of means for this wicked enterprise; had laid his gunpowder plot long years before; and, at the right time, this imperial Guy Faux fired the train which was to blow up an ancient empire, and open his way to the conquest of the Western World. No more liberty, if that scheme succeed! Yet the statesmen of France, Austria, Prussia, England, were privy to the intentions of this re-actionary, who sought to put back the march of human-kind: they were accessory to the purpose, though they knew not the hidden means. The war was the result of causes long in action, which produced this waste of life and its material—the "proximate formation " of men—as certainly as grass-seed comes up grass.

Here are the practical maxims of all despotism: No Higher Law of God above the selfish force of the strong; no natural rights of the weak; all belongs to the violence of power !

In open daylight, two things went before this European waste of life: (1.) The corruptions of the Ruling class: one of the most learned men in Christendom declares, that, since the downfall of the Roman State in the fourth and fifth centuries, Europe's controlling men have never been so corrupt, so mean and selfish, as are now the kings, nobles, and priesthood. (2.) The servility of the class next below the high aristocracy, who tolerate and encourage the inflicted wrong, hoping themselves to share the profit that it brings.

Still more, all this wickedness is the work of very few men. If a hundred politicians in Europe had said, " There shall be no war," there would have been no war ; nay, if ten men in Europe had distinctly said, " There shall be no war against Turkey," there would have been none ; if two men in the cabinets of each of the five great powers had said so, all this immense outlay would have been spared.

Such are the Causes. On so narrow a hinge turns the dreadful gate of war !

Look now at the Results. Some are good. The intervention of France and England has shown that national hatred can be overcome ; that difference of religion does not separate the Turk from Christian sympathy. The bloody valour of France and England has checked the Westward and Southward progress of Russian despotism for the next fifty years ; and that fillibustering nation is weakened in her purse, her army, and her navy, and restrained from immediate encroachment on other European States. She will now turn her immense power to develop the material resources of her own territory. And let me say, that the Russian People have grand and magnificent qualities ; and whoso stands here three hundred years hence will tell a history of them which few sanguine scholars would dare prophesy at this day. The Russian Government is another matter ; of that I do not wish to say anything. That is the first good that has been done ; it was done wholly by France and England. You do not forget the " perfidious " conduct of Austria.

Then, the war has led Russia to open her ports, and establish free trade with all the world ; and that will not only increase the material riches of Russia, but it will be in some measure a guaranty against future wars between her and other nations. For those fortresses which at this day most effectually keep war from a nation are not built of stone and earth : they are the warehouses in the great commercial streets, bales of goods, boxes of sugar, money on deposit in the great cities of the world. Free trade will help that.

Again, Turkey is delivered from her worst foe ; and a secret treaty between Austria, England, and France, guarantees the independence of that State. It seems the Allies stole a march on the Russian, and negotiated this treaty in the dark.

Besides, Turkey agrees to respect the Christians who have delivered her from the enemy. She has agreed to set a lesson of toleration ; and it is a little striking to see, that, just at the time when Turkey offered freedom of religion to the Christians and all others, California was doubting whether she should allow the Chinese to set up a temple to Buddha, which even Americans think should not be suffered. But I thank God that every form of Religion, old as the Buddhistic or new as the Mormon, can find a place in our land. I would not ask the Chinese to let our missionaries into their country, and refuse the Chinese missionary a corresponding privilege. Just now, Christianity is more free in Turkey than in Russia, Austria, or the Home of the Reformation itself. Another Arius or Athanasius might teach at Constantinople ; while neither would be allowed in a pulpit at Vienna, Moscow, or Wittenberg.

Moreover, the treaty makes a desirable change in the law of nations. Privateering is abolished ; a neutral flag protects enemy's goods, while the hostile flag does not imperil neutral goods ; there can be no paper blockades. This is a great step in civilization.

But all those things might have been done without drawing a sword or shedding a drop of blood. Had the controlling class been humane men ; nay, had the ten I speak of insisted on these few things,—the whole would have been done, and not a bullet shot. But the People must have leaders ; and the hereditary rulers in Europe seem hardly wiser than the elected in America. A born deceiver is no better than a deceiver chosen and sworn in ; and, if the wicked lead the ignorant, the latter are sure to fall into the ditch. The crimes of statesmen are written in the People's blood.

Some of the effects are only evil. There is a great debt entailed on the nations, to be paid by millions not yet born. The yoke of bondage is more firmly fixed than before, for the standing armies are increased all over Europe : and they are the tools of tyrants.

France and England have become stronger by their

union. To balance that increase of power, the Austrian Emperor has made a Concordat with the Pope; and those two are likewise at one. In all the Austrian territory, the Romish Priest controls the public worship, the public education, the printing and selling and reading of books. Thus a long step is taken backwards towards the dark ages.

Besides, there has been a considerable demoralization of the people in the greater part of Europe, caused by those deeds of violence, the spectacle and report of such national murder, which it will take years to overcome.

All the good, it seems to me, might have been effected with no war; all the evil saved, had only the leading statesmen of Europe had noble hearts, as well as able heads and high political rank. That vast sum of misery is to be set down to the account of a small number of men. Nicholas of Russia seems most of all to blame; next, mankind must charge this waste of property and life on the corruption and selfishness of the ruling class in Europe, and the servility of those next below them in social rank and public power. Remember all this when you come to think of America; and this old Hebrew oracle not less: "Righteousness exalteth a nation; but sin is the ruin of any people." The sin of the ruler is the destruction of the people.

So much for Europe. Now a word of our own country.

America is now in a state of incipient civil war: houses are burned, others are plundered; blood is shed. A few months ago, two worthy men from Kansas, Judge Conway and Gen. Pomeroy, were worshipping here with us. They were often at my house. They have violated no constitutional law, no legal statute. But the newspapers report that both are in gaol: if they are at large, it is through their skill in escaping from lawless foes. Governor Robinson, who was also here but a few weeks ago, is now in gaol, on the charge of Treason. The Border Ruffians will hang him, if they dare. His crime is obedience to the law of his land, and hatred to Slavery. Mr. Tappan, a young man known to many of you, a member of this congregation, went to Kansas with the first company of emigrants: a worthy man, but guilty of respect for the self-evident truths of the Declaration of Independence. If he is not in gaol, his freedom is due to his own adroitness, not the justice of the "Authorities." The usurping Government strikes at those men because they love justice. Lawrence has been sacked; property destroyed, one states to the amount of a hundred and thirty thousand dollars; and I know not how many men have been murdered. I shall not speak of the violence to women. These are acts for which the General Government is responsible, committed by its creatures, who have been set upon the honest inhabitants of Kansas.

We also have a Despotic Power in the United States. There is a Russia in America, a privileged class of three hundred and fifty thousand slaveholders, who own three million five hundred thousand slaves, and control four million poor whites in the South. This despotism is more barbarous than Russia; more insolent, more unscrupulous, more invasive. It has long controlled all the great offices in America. The President is only its tool. It directs the national policy, foreign and domestic; sympathizes with every foreign tyrant; and, at home, wages war on all the best institutions of the country. Impudent and consolidated, it governs the American Church and State. It says to the Tract Society, "Not a word against Slavery;" and the Tract Society bends its knees,—so limber to men, so stiff against God,—and answers, "Not a word against Slavery: we will take a South-side view of all popular wickedness. It is true, the North pays us the money; and so it is proper that the South should tell how it must be spent. Not a word against Slavery." It comes up to the Bible Society, and thunders forth, "Don't give the New Testament to the slaves!" And the Bible Society says, "Not a New Testament. Slavery is Christian. If Jesus of Nazareth were on earth, he would open a commissioner's office in Boston, and kidnap men. Judas is the beloved disciple. We never will disturb Slavery." It tells the Northern courts, legislatures, governors, "Steal men for us; kidnap your own fellow-citizens of New England, and deliver them up to be our bondsmen for ever, and then yourselves pay the costs!" And the Northern courts, legislatures, governors, citizen-soldiers, are ready: they volunteer to steal men, and then

pay the price, not only of blood, but of money, and that
"with alacrity."

In Kansas, on a large scale, this Russia in America, this
Privileged Class of despots in a democracy, wages war
against freedom. It burns houses, destroys printing-presses,
shoots men. There it was Missouri Ruffians, some of them
members of Congress, an Ex-Senator or so, United-States
soldiers, Southern immigrants, whom it furnishes with weapons, adorns with a legal collar, and then sets upon the people.
Just now, the House of Representatives asks what force the
Government has in Kansas, and what instructions have been
given. The answer is, There is only a Lieutenant-Colonel's
command there,—half a Regiment; the officer is ordered
not to enforce the laws of the territorial legislature. This
does not tell the whole story. The United-States Marshal does the bidding of the unlawful legislature which the
Missourians elected: he calls out his *posse comitatus*, and
the United-States Government furnishes them with weapons
and authority. They are the provisional army in this
civil war which the Government wages against the people.
Look at this fact: slaveholders have hired immigrants
to go from Alabama and South Carolina to Kansas, and
fight the battle of Slavery. When Col. Beaufort's party,
three or four hundred strong, arrived at Lawrence, they
were too poor to pay for their first breakfast. What shall
be done with them? They are draughted into the *posse*
of the sheriff; and in the service of the Government,
they burn the property and shoot the sons of New England: I need not dwell on these things. Every mail
brings tidings of fresh wickedness committed in that ill-
fated territory.

At Washington, on a small scale, this despotic power
wages war against freedom. There it uses an arm of a
different form,—the arm of an Honourable Ruffian, a member
of Congress, a (Southern) "gentleman," a "man of property and standing," born of one of the "first families
of South Carolina," a nephew (by marriage) of Senator
Butler. He skulks about the purlieus of the Capitol, and
twice seeks to waylay his victim, honourable, and suspecting
no dishonour. But, failing of that meanness, the assassin,
a bludgeon in his hand, pistols in his pocket, attended
by his five friends, armed also with daggers and pistols,

watches in the Senate Chamber till his enemy is alone, then steals up behind him as he sits writing, when his arms are pinioned in his heavy chair and his other limbs are under the desk, and on his naked head strikes him with a club loaded with lead, until he falls, stunned and bleeding, to the floor, and then continues his coward blows. South Carolina is very chivalrous! If an Irishman in Cove Place should strike another Irishman after he was down, it would be thought a very heinous offence amongst Irishmen. If Patrick had Michael down, and *then beat him*, (pardon me, forty thousand Irishmen in Boston, that I suppose it possible!) it would be thought a great outrage. Cove Place would hoot him forth with a shout of contemptuous rage. But when a son of South Carolina beats a defenceless man over the head, after he has stunned him and brought him to the ground, it is very chivalrous! South Carolina applauds it, and gets up a testimonial to do it honour. All the South will commend the mode as well as the matter of the deed.

This American oligarchy means to destroy all our democratic institutions. Russian despotism is not more hostile to liberty in Europe than the Slave Power to freedom here. But the slaveholders are not alone. American and Russian despotism have the same allies,—the corruption of many controlling men, such as direct the politics of the North, and to a great extent also its large commerce. Since the settlement of the country, the great mass of Northern men have never been so well educated and so moral. But the controlling class of men, who manage the high commerce and fill the political offices, have never been so corrupt, so unpatriotic, so mean and selfish. Will you say I am mistaken? Then the error is of long standing; a judgment formed after careful study of the past, and a wide knowledge of the present. Look at Massachusetts, the State officials, the United States officials, the United States Court in New England: can the past furnish a parallel since Andros was Commissioner, and Papal James II. was King? The Hutchinsons and the Olivers of revolutionary times would blush to be named with men whose brow no wickedness can shame. It would be cruel to Benedict Arnold to compare him with certain other sons of New England now in high official place.

Be not surprised at this attack on Mr. Sumner. It is no strange thing. It is the result of a long series of acts, each the child of its predecessor, and father of what followed, not exceptional, but instantial, in our history. Look with a little patience after the Cause of those outrages at Kansas and at Washington. You will not agree with me to-day; I cannot convince four thousand men, and carry them quite so far, all at once. Think of my words when you go home.

Look first at the obvious cause of the blows dealt that fair senatorial head by the Hon. Mr. Brooks, of South Carolina. It is the ferocious Disposition of the Slaveholder. I know the cruelty of that despotism only too well, and am not thought very sparing of my words. You know what I utter; God, what I withhold. Much, both of fact and feeling, I have always kept in reserve, and still keep it. What I give is quite as much as any audience can carry or will take.

This ferocious despotism has determined on two things:

First, Slavery shall spread all over the land, into the Territories, into the (so-called) free States.

Second, Freedom of speech against it shall not be allowed anywhere in the Territories, in the free States, or in the Capitol, any more than in South Carolina.

Proof of each is only too plentiful and plain. As a sign of the times, look at a single straw in the stream of slavery: it is a poison-weed in a muddy, fetid stream, but it shows which way its pestilential waters run. A few days since, a man, holding an important office under the United States Government in Boston, told one of my friends, " It won't be three years before a man will be punished for talking Nigger (speaking against slavery) in Boston, as surely as he now is in Charleston, S.C." This " unterrified democrat" has now gone to the Cincinnati Convention, whereof he is a worthy member, to organize means to attain that end. I shall not tell you his name,—that is hateful enough already; but turn your wrath against the ferocious despotism which uses him to bark and bite.

That is the obvious cause, the cause initiative, of which I have much more to tell, only not now.

Look next at the Secondary Causes, not quite so plain, but as fertile in results.

The North allows the South to steal black men, and men

not much darker than you and I, if born of swarthy mothers; it allows the South to sell them at will, brand them as cattle, mutilate them as oxen, beat them, not seldom to death, burn them alive with green fagots, for the sport of a mob of " very respectable gentlemen," a " minister of the Gospel" looking on and justifying the deed as " Christian." The North allows all this: it is only " an incident of Slavery," the shadow of the substance. New England allows it. Boston has no considerable horror at any of these things,—I mean a part of Boston. Up to this time Boston has defended slavery with her " educated intellect," and by means of many of her " citizens of eminent gravity." Hitherto the controlling men of Boston have been the defenders of slavery; this day they are not its foes.

Now, if the South may thus ruin one black man, so it may all white men whom it can master. Colour is an accident to man as to these roses; it determines neither genus nor species; it is of the dress, not the person. There is only one genus of man, one species,—the human genus, human species. The right to enslave one innocent man is the right to enslave all innocent men. One-seventh part of the Federal House is painted black, the rest white: do you believe you can set the black part on fire, and not burn down the white, not scorch it, not crack the boards, nor smoke the paint? You may say, "Thus far, but no farther:" will the fire heed you? I rather think not: I believe the experience of mankind tells another story. If you sustain the claim of South Carolina to beat black men at Charleston, you need not be surprised if she is logical enough to beat a white man at Washington, soon as she dares. And her daring will be just in proportion to your forbearance. It is a very courageous State, its chivalry bravely attacking defenceless persons.

A portion of the North—of New England, Massachusetts, Boston, those portions deemed best educated, and, in general, most " orthodox" and " Christian" in the church, most respectable in society—have all along made mouths at everybody who complained that slavery was wicked, was cruel, even that it was unprofitable. We were told, "It is none of your business; you have nothing to do with slavery: let it alone. Besides," they said, "it is not cruel nor unprofitable. It is true, we should not like it for ourselves;

but it is good enough for black men: it is a very Christian thing." You do not forget, surely, that there is a doctor of South-side Divinity in the city of Boston, a most thoroughly "respectable man." He has not lost a hair of "respectability" from his clerical head by perverting the Bible to the defence of slavery. When the United States Court opens its session, it asks him to come and pray for a blessing on the Court of Kidnappers in the city of Boston. It is very proper. And he represents the opinion of a large class of men, who are bottomed on money, who have a good intellectual education, and very high social standing.

When South Carolina shut up coloured sailors of Massachusetts in her gaols at Charleston, and made the merchants of Boston pay the bill, the State sent one of her eminent men to remonstrate, and take legal measures to secure the constitutional rights of her citizens. But Mr. Hoar was ignominiously driven out of the State; and it was only the handsome presence of his daughter that saved him from a fate far worse than what befell Mr. Sumner. Massachusetts bore it all. Boston capitalists were angry if a man complained above his breath at this indignity; but, when they came to be tired of paying the bills, they got up a petition to Congress, very numerously signed, asking Congress to abolish that nuisance, and secure the constitutional rights of Massachusetts men. The petition was put into the hands of the senator from Boston; but he "lost it:" he "put it into his hat, and, some way or other, it fell out." But the sagacious merchants had kept a duplicate, and the senator had an attested copy sent him. He lost that too. He never dared to offer the petition of Boston merchants against an outrage which had no colour of constitutional plea to stand under. Freedom of speech was struck dumb on the floor of the Senate more than ten years ago. Even the almighty dollar could not find a tongue. But, when Rufus Choate returned to Boston, his "respectability" was not harmed in the least: he was still the "Hon. Mr. Choate." Suppose it had been a petition to increase the duty on cottons and woollens fifty per cent. and he had "lost *that* out of his hat?" Why, when he returned to Boston—I will not say he would have lost his head from his shoulders, but it would have been worth very little upon them.

Long ago, the South said the North should not discuss the morality of slavery; that was their business. Well, the controlling men of Boston obeyed. They said, "No: the North shall not discuss the subject of slavery." The lips of yonder college were sewed up with Slavery's iron thread: I hope they will open now. Slavery put its thumbs into the ears, and its fingers over the eyes, of Boston respectability; and it sewed up the mouth of Commerce, Fashion, Politics, —I was going to say Religion; but it did not: it sewed up the mouth only of the *churches.*

It is not twenty-five years since the Governor of Virginia asked Mayor Otis, of Boston, to put a stop to the efforts of the Abolitionists; and, after three days' search, the police of Boston found the "Liberator," who was making all this mischief. His office was in a garret; and his "only visible auxiliary," quoth Mr. Otis, "was a negro boy." Mr. Otis wanted to ferret out antislavery, and put the heel of the Hartford Convention upon it.

It is not twenty-one years since a Governor of Massachusetts, in his annual message, recommended the Legislature to inquire if some law should not be made to suppress the freedom of speech. It is not yet quite twenty-one years since there was a meeting in Faneuil Hall to denounce the discussion of this very matter. Here is what a distinguished man said; he was not a young man then: "I would beseech them" [the Abolitionists] "to discard their dangerous abstractions," [the abstractions that *"all men are endowed with certain unalienable rights,* among which is the right to life, liberty, and the pursuit of happiness,"] "which they adopt as universal rules of conduct, . . *which darken the understanding, and mislead the judgment."* He would advise them to consider "the precepts and example of their Divine Master. He found slavery, Roman slavery, an institution of the country in which he lived. Did he denounce it? Did he attempt its immediate abolition? Did he do any thing, or say any thing, which could, in its remotest tendency, encourage resistance and violence? No: his precept was, SERVANTS (SLAVES), OBEY YOUR MASTERS! It was because he *would not interfere with the administration of the laws of the land."* If the "Divine Master" was Jesus of Nazareth, then no such word is given to us in this Bible. It was only the gospel according to Peleg Sprague. Boston honoured it. The hall rang with applause when he invented a Bible to suppress discussion. Since that time he has had his reward: he is a judge of the Court of the United States.

It is not twenty-one years since a mob of well-dressed "gentlemen of property and standing," in this very city, broke up a prayer-meeting of women, where a Quaker lady presided, because they came together to discuss slavery. It is not quite twenty-one years since the great advocate of freedom for all men was forced to take shelter in the stone gaol of Boston, to secure him from the fury of a mob,— the only place in Boston where he could be secure from the hands of the property, the education, the fashion, the respectability, of this town. It is not twenty-one years since, at night, a gallows was erected before his house, with an appropriate motto on it, meaning, "If you don't hold your peace, we will take your life!" You know what insults, private as well as public, were heaped upon Dr. Channing, as soon as he spoke in behalf of freedom. He lost his influence; he hurt his reputation. If a minister said a word in behalf of the slave, that minister was an object of scorn in his own parish, and in the whole town also. No man took an interest in promoting the cause of humanity but he lost all his "respectability." Personal qualities stood him in no stead; birth from a distinguished line was of no consequence; even money did not save him. "Decency" dropped him out of its ranks. Freedom of speech was assaulted with violence in Boston long before the experiment was tried on the senatorial head of Mr. Sumner. Mr. Brooks, in Washington, only does in 1856, what Mr. Sprague, in Boston, encouraged twenty years before,—puts down discussion.

When the Slave Power wanted Texas annexed, to spread bondage over two hundred and thirty-seven thousand square miles of land, the controlling men of Boston were anxious for that measure. Even the indignant voice of Mr. Webster could not make a public opinion against that extension of wickedness. "However bounded" was the cry!

When the Mexican War broke out, by the act of the slave despotism, how feebly did Boston oppose the crime! Nay, its representative voted for the war and the falsehood

which laid the blame on the feebler nation. How few
ministers dared speak against the evil deed! The Peace
Society turned its secretary out of office because he spoke
against that war. It struck its own flag as soon as Slavery
gave command.

Alas! how sad a gift is memory! You cannot forget
the year 1850, the Fugitive Slave Bill, the discussions on
it at Boston and at Washington. It is dreadful to bring
up the terrible speech in the Senate House on the 7th of
March, when that mighty power of eloquence shook the
land, so loud did it cry for the extension and perpetuation of
slavery!

You remember the nine hundred and eighty-seven
men of Boston, who thanked the recreant son of New
England for his treason to humanity, told him he had
pointed out " the path of duty, convinced the understanding, and touched the conscience, of a nation;" nay, expressed their " entire concurrence in the sentiments of that
speech," and gave him " their heartfelt thanks for the ines-
timable aid it afforded to the preservation of the Union."
You cannot forget the speech from the steps of the Revere
House on the 29th of April,—the declaration from those
senatorial lips that " discussion" on the subject of slavery,
in Congress and out of it, must " in some way be suppressed." You remember that Massachusetts was to " conquer her prejudices" in favour of justice and the law of God,
to " do a disagreeable duty," and kidnap her own citizens.
How many controlling men of Boston said " Ay," we will
conquer those " prejudices," do that " disagreeable duty!"
Political and commercial journals, ministers in their pulpits,
—they went for the Fugitive Slave Bill! I wish I could
forget it all. May God forgive them for the atheism
they preached, and the dreadful woe springing up in our
future path from the seed they cast abroad! But there
were honourable exceptions, commercial and ecclesiastical,
—a few !

Mr. Eliot voted for the bill (I had hoped better things
from a man with so much good in him, which no wickedness, past or future, shall blot from my book); and, when
he returned, the prominent citizens of Boston called upon
him, and one by one, in public places, they grasped his
hand, and said, " We thank you for all this; it was just

what we wanted you to do ; you have represented the feel
ing, not of all Boston, but of the property, the talent, the
piety, of Boston."

When the first kidnappers came here, you will easily call
to mind the indignation of the controlling men, because
William and Ellen Craft could not be taken and made
slaves. You will not forget the Union meeting in Faneuil
Hall, the resolutions, the speeches of Mr. Hallett and
Mr. Curtis. From the senator who had lost the petition
out of his hat came the triple admonition, "REMEMBER,
REMEMBER, REMEMBER." Let us keep it in recollection.

When the country towns, like Lynn and Worcester, said,
"We will not kidnap men," what did the great political
and commercial journals say ? "We will cut off their trade;
we will starve them out. If they do not mean to sustain
that law, Boston will not deal with them : it won't sell
West-India goods and calicoes to Lynn and Worcester."
You know what the most distinguished men of Boston said
of the Free Soilers about that time. Some men of high social
standing, large talent, great character, inherent nobleness of
spirit, said, "We will have nothing to do with slave-hunting.
That bill is a bill of abominations : we tread it under our
feet." One of the most conspicuous men of Boston called
these men " a nest of vipers,"—said they " broke their teeth
gnawing a file :" how many echoed the word all around the
town ! Charles Sumner belonged to this " nest of vipers"
in 1851.

When Shadrach was rescued, you know how the newspapers mourned over it, and the ministers of Boston
made public lamentation.

When the Mayor of Boston was kidnapping Thomas
Sims, to gratify the desire of a certain family of Boston,
Marshal Tukey drilled the police in Court Square, teaching
them " military duty." A man laughed at the evolutions
of the " awkward squad," and, for that offence, was imprisoned in the lockup. A woman was threatened with the
same punishment, for the same offence ; but the Quakeress
laughed it down. "Fifteen hundred gentlemen of property
and standing" volunteered their armed help to deliver the
poor boy into the bondage which now wears his wretched
life away. What respectable and affluent joy lit up both
the parlours and the churches of commerce and politics when

Boston bore the first-fruits of the Fugitive Slave Bill! How blessed was the brig " Acorn," which cradled Thomas Sims in its shell!

Men of shortest memory can reach back to Anniversary Week, 1854, and recollect Anthony Burns, a Baptist minister, " ordained" a slave by Commissioner Loring,—fore-ordained, as the sentence was given without waiting for the " trial." I hope you remember the kidnapper's counsel on that occasion. I know you will recall the soldiers in Court Square, who loaded their muskets with powder and ball. I think you have not forgotten the cannon, filled with canister-shot at that time, in Court Square. I am sure some of you remember the charge of the United States Judge on the 7th of June, 1854; the indictment, in October, 1854, against Wendell Phillips. He had made a fatal mistake; he did not know that freedom of speech was " to be crushed out" of Massachusetts. So, in the Cradle of Liberty, he had spoken such words as he always speaks, straight out from the heart of Humanity, and with a tongue of such persuasion as never before his time has rung through New England; and, depend upon it, when that ceases to be mortal, God will not create such eloquent lips again in any haste. He had spoken, at Faneuil Hall, against kidnapping. Messrs. Hallett and Curtis had him indicted for a misdemeanor; and he was held to bail in fifteen hundred dollars. The punishment was to be a fine of three hundred dollars, and imprisonment in gaol for twelve months. That was the state of things at that time. Look at Boston now. The Judge of Probate, who sent Anthony Burns into bondage, is still the guardian of orphans. He holds the same office he held before, though a law of Massachusetts has been made expressly forbidding it. That law of Massachusetts is trodden under foot; the Governor treads it under his feet; the Judge of Probate, the House of Representatives, the Senate, the press of Boston, tread it under their feet. The City Authorities of Boston must have some one to deliver an oration on the birthday of American independence. Do they invite Mr. Sumner? Not at all. Mr. Phillips? They would sink the State rather than have him. No: it must be one of the kidnapper's counsel in 1854. A very proper man to preach a sermon to the people on the Fourth of July, with the Declaration of Independence for a text! He can go back two years, and find an illustration of it. The argument he used in the kidnapper's court, in May, 1854, would be very convenient for him to introduce on the Fourth of July, 1856. The Declaration of Independence must be read. I suppose that will be done by George Ticknor Curtis, Benjamin Franklin Hallett, or some other of that excellent fraternity of kidnappers who are appointed to rule over us.

The Legislature of last winter (1855) was the greenest Legislature we ever had : it had less legislative experience than any other. It was the poorest in point of property: none ever represented so small a ratio of the wealth of Massachusetts. It was the most uneducated : none ever had so little of the superior education which falls to the lot of lawyers, doctors, and ministers. But no Legislature, since I have known lawmakers, ever showed so much honesty, humanity, and justice. It cleared the Massachusetts statute-book of obnoxious laws, and passed an excellent law, making kidnapping impossible on the soil of Massachusetts. That was a Legislature which contained the better portion of what is called the "American party." The present Legislature contains a large portion of that other part of the American party, which is more properly called *Know Nothing*, which required no inauguration for membership; and you know what this Legislature proposes to do. It would repeal the Personal Liberty Law. Nothing but the assault on freedom in Washington will save it. It is laid over until next Tuesday, when it receives its final judgment. What that judgment shall be, I will not now say.

Now, put all these six or seven things together, and see what they amount to. The slaveholders understand this perfectly well. They know, that, when they strike at the head of Charles Sumner in the Senate of the United States, they attack a man whom the respectability of Boston called one of a "brood of vipers," whom it seeks to put down.

Put all these things together, and you see the Secondary Cause of this wickedness,—the cause co-operative. Corrupt men at the North, in New England, in Boston, have betrayed the People. They struck at freedom before South Carolina dared lift an arm. The slaveholders know these things,—that, as often as they have demanded wickedness, Boston has answered the demand: they piece out their small bit of lion's skin with the pelt of many a Northern fox. They are in earnest for slavery: they think New England is not in earnest for freedom. Do you blame them for their inference? A few years ago, Mr. Sumner spoke in Boston, on "the True Grandeur of Nations," a lofty word before the City Fathers, on the Fourth of July, 1845. An Argument against War, a Plea for Peace. As two of our most distinguished citizens came from listening, one said to the other, "Well, if that young man is going to talk in that way, he cannot expect Boston to hold him up." Since then, that young man has spoken even nobler words. Boston has not held him up; nay, the controlling part of it has sought to strike him down,—counted him one of "a nest of vipers,"—done nothing to support, all to overthrow him. Why? Because he was the continual defender of the unalienable rights of man. Slaveholders are not fools: they know all this. The South never struck a Northern advocate of a tariff, or a defender of the Union. She knew the North would "hold up" the champions of the Union and the tariff. It attacks only the Soldiers of Freedom, knowing that the controlling power of the North also hates them. I know men in Boston to-day, who would long since have struck Mr. Sumner, had they only dared, —nor him alone.

Last week, there were two remarkable spectacles in the United States. One at the State House, in Boston: it was the Legislature, stimulated by the enemies of freedom, proceeding to repeal the Personal Liberty Law, and seeking to restore kidnapping to Massachusetts. I need not tell here who it was—a very few men—that plotted the wickedness, nor how much they expected to gain by it. On the same day, not far from the same hour, in the Nation House at Washington, there was another spectacle. A Representative of slavery, with a bludgeon, knocks our Senator to the ground,—strikes him twenty or thirty blows after he is down. They are two scenes in the same tragedy. Both blows were dealt by the same arm,—the Slave Power; both aimed at the same mark,—the Head of Freedom; each came from the same motive, which I need not name.

My friends, I am not sorry to see you thus excited. I am too old to look on such scenes with astonishment. I entertain no sudden heat. Pardon me that I am cool to-day.

To me, Massachusetts is the twelve hundred thousand persons in it; or, more emphatically, it is the thoughtful, it is the moral, it is the religious, people of Massachusetts. To me, Boston is the one hundred and sixty thousand men within her limits; or, more properly speaking, it is the moral and religious part of them. I am proud of Massachusetts: it is the grandest State in the world, I think. I am proud also of Boston. I respect and venerate her manifold excellence. I know her past history, and look for a future far more glorious than the deeds of Pilgrim or Patriot Fathers have rendered days gone by. For this reason, I tell Boston her faults; whereof the noble city is not conscious, else had she never done those deeds of shame. I do not hesitate to expose this wickedness to you, who easily understand it all; and even to men not familiar with such thoughts, whose disapproval was most grateful unto me,—such men could not believe that our Boston was an accomplice with Carolina in this foul work. I say I am proud of Boston,—not of those controlling men, who darkly misrule its politics, whose Machiavelian craft is like the Venetian poisons of old time, which destroyed sight, hearing, feeling, every noblest sense, and only left the vegetative life : I am ashamed of them. I do not hate them; I shall never belittle their excellence; I do not scorn them. I may be allowed to have pity for them,—not the pity of contempt, but the pity of charity and love. I am not proud of them; but of the sober, moral part of Boston, I am proud,—thereof is New England proud. It is the grandest city in this world; it is the humanest city, the most thoughtful city, on this continent; it is the furthest advanced in its humanity.

But the Boston which the South knows, listens to, and respects, is a very different city. It is a Boston that consists of some twenty or thirty persons, perhaps a hundred, "men of property and standing;" and some two or three thousand flunkies,—I do not know exactly how numerous they are. That is the Boston which the South knows. Now, that Boston, which the South knows, hates freedom, hates democracy, hates religion. In 1835, it put down a woman's prayer-meeting. In 1844, it annexed Texas. In 1846, it liked the Mexican War. In 1850, it indorsed the Fugitive Slave Bill. In 1851, it sent back Thomas Sims to bondage. In 1854, it "restored" Anthony Burns. In 1856, it pays the kidnapper's counsel to discourse to the people on the Fourth of July. The South understands that that Boston hates Mr. Sumner,—hates him because he loves liberty; hates Mr. Wilson and Mr. Banks; and hates the memory of Washington, and, whenever it mentions him, it disembowels him of his noblest humanity before it dares to praise. Last night, at Faneuil Hall, there was much official talk about freedom of speech. Some of it was honest; but how much of it was only "sound and fury, signifying nothing?" Study the history of the speakers,—it is not a long task,—and then judge.

The ghastly evils which Southern despotism has brought on us in ten years' time are to be charged to a few persons. I could mention ten men in Boston who might have saved us all this woe. In 1844, if they had said, No such annexation of Texas,—her hand red with Mexican blood, her breath foul with Slavery,—the Slave Power would have yielded before us. In 1850, had they said, There shall be no Fugitive Slave Act, Mr. Mason's Bill had slept the sleep of death. Even after Mr. Webster had spoken against the best instincts of his nature, which I still love to think was generous, they might have forbid the evil which came. Had they said the word, no kidnappers had profaned the grave of Hancock and Adams. In April, 1851, if they had said, Mr. Sims is not to be a slave henceforth, the family of man-stealers would suddenly have "caved in." In the winter of 1854, when Mr. Douglas wished to spread Slavery into Nebraska, had these men heartily said, It shall not be, it would not be. In the May of that year, if they had declared, We have had enough of man-stealing for Boston; nay, if only four of them had entered the Court House, and spoken to Mr. Burns, given him the public sign of their sympathy,—depend upon it, we should not have been a second time tormented with that hideous sin. Commissioner Loring was not born for a kidnapper: that once kindly and now suffering heart took such wickedness by collateral infection, not hereditary taint. But those ten men wanted this iniquity brought about, wanted slave-ridden Texas in '44, wanted the Fugitive Slave Bill in '50, kidnapping in '51, and again in '54. They protested against the " abrogation of the Missouri Compromise," but in such language that the South knew it meant, " Do as you like; we will not prevent you." So it has been continually, " On the side of the Oppressor there was Power."

Where are such men.now? Recall the platform of last night. Where were the citizens of most " eminent gravity," where the great fortunes, the great offices, the judges of the courts, the great " reputations ?" Not one of them was there. Of the Boston which the South cares for, I saw not a man. Why not ? You shall answer that question.

In Boston, there are three men of senatorial dignity: they have been in the Senate of the United States, and have all left it. They are men of large talent, good education, high social standing. They are all public orators, and seek occasions on which to address the people ; and, to one of them, speech is as the breath of his nostrils. Last night, there was a meeting to express the indignation of Boston at the outrage on Mr. Sumner. These three men were asked to go and speak : not one of them was there. *Twice* the Committee waited on Mr. Winthrop and Mr. Everett, and *twice solicited* the ex-senators to come and speak ; and twice was the labour thrown away. Did Mr. Everett, once a minister of this city, remember that he refused to present in the Senate the petition of three thousand New-England ministers against the enslavement of Kansas ? Did he recollect, that, a whole generation since, he volunteered to shoulder his musket, and march from Bunker Hill to Virginia to put down any attempt of the slaves to regain their natural and unalienable Right to Liberty ? At a generous word, Massachusetts, who never forgets, would have rejoiced anew in the bounteous talents, in the splendid scholarship, of the man,—would have recalled every public service he has done, and dropped a tear on his failures and evil deeds. But it was not in him. Mr. Winthrop inherits a name dear to all New England,—connected with her earliest history, stitched into the cradle-clothes of American liberty. Could not he add a personal leaf to the ancestral bough,—a merit to an accident? Or did he, who called Mr. Sumner one of a "nest of vipers," think Mr. Brooks was that prophetic "seed of the woman," who was to "bruise the serpent's head?" Let us honour every public service of such men with generous gratitude, but not forget how they fail us in an hour of need,—never, till they repent: then let the dead bury their dead, and let us manfully forgive.

There is great talk about the freedom of speech: how much of it is sincere? Last night, at the indignation meeting,—which had a low platform,—there were two speakers, who, as a hearer said, "had got the hang of the school-house," and knew what to say; but, with these exceptions, the speaking was rather dull, and did not meet the feelings of the people. Towards the end, the audience, seeing the well-known face of that man whose eloquence never fails him, because it is eloquence that comes out of so brave a heart, called for him: "Phillips! *Phillips!* PHILLIPS! PHILLIPS!" What said the platform? "Phillips shan't be heard;" and they dismissed the meeting,—a meeting called to vindicate freedom of speech in Massachusetts; and the one speaker of Massachusetts—who would have gathered that audience, as I hold up in my hand these sweet Lilies of the Valley, and have raised them towards heaven, and then brought them down for common duty — must not speak, though the audience calls for him! The South understands us perfectly well.

Blame me as much as you please for what I say: ten years hence you will say that I am right. But, ere I go further on, let me do an act of gratitude and justice. In all those dark days behind us, there have been found faithful men, who risked their political prospects, the desires of honourable ambition, their social standing, nay, the esteem of their nearest relatives, and were faithful to Truth and Justice. What treatment have they met with in the Parlour, in the Forum, in the Market, in the Church? One day, their history must be writ; and some names now hated will appear like those which were the watch-words of the Revolution, and are now the heavenly sounds that cheer the young patriot in this night of storms. In such men, no city is so rich as this. Daughter of Nobleness, she is its Mother too. I hope to live long enough to do public honour to their high worth.

Be not surprised at the attack on our Senator. Violence at Washington is no new thing. You have not forgot the threat to assassinate John Quincy Adams. I knew men in Boston who said they wished it might be executed. But, not to go back so far, see what has happened this present year. Mr. William Smith, formerly Governor of Virginia (Extra Billy), knocked down an editor in the House of Representatives. Mr. Rusk, of Arkansas, with equal cowardliness, attacked another editor in the street,— Mr. Greeley. Some Boston newspapers justified the outrage: a man who ventures to say a word against a distinguished slaveholder must expect to be knocked down. Alabamian Mr. Herbert shoots a waiter; the House takes the matter into consideration, and will not expel him: the Democratic party vote against it; not a Southern Democrat, and but one Northern Democrat, I think, saying otherwise. The Know-nothing part of the American party go in the same direction: all the South justify the deed. It is a country in which there is only one class of men, and freedom of religion is secure! But it is of no consequence if an Irish Catholic, who is a waiter, is shot down by an Alabamian!

Charles Sumner is the next victim. One thing I must tell you, which you do not understand. There was a plot laid among these " chivalrous gentlemen " to do the deed. When the Senate adjourned, several distinguished Southern Senators staid: it was noticed by some persons, and one said, "I wonder what is in the wind now." Mr. Wilson has not the reputation of a non-resistant; he is a mechanic, and a soldier,—a general. He carried his pistols to Washington, and caused it to be distinctly understood that he had not the common New-England prejudice against shooting a scoundrel. He has not been insulted, and he will not be. That day he had some business with Mr. Sumner. He came and spoke a word to him as he sat and wrote at his desk. Those ruffians, Mr. Brooks and Mr. Keitt, had come into the Senate; they did not advance, but sat down and waited until Mr. Wilson had withdrawn. The only ally of Mr. Sumner was then gone; not a friend stood near him. Then the Southern "chivalry" gathered around, and Mr. Brooks came and assaulted him.

Now, do you know the seed whence came the bludgeon which struck that handsome and noble head? It was the "ACORN," in whose shell Boston carried back Thomas Sims in 1851; and on the 19th of April, on the seventy-sixth anniversary of the battle of Lexington, she took him out of that shell and put him in a gaol at Savannah, where he was scourged till a doctor said, "You will kill him if you strike him again!" and the master said, "Let him die!" That was the Acorn whence grew the bludgeon which struck Charles Sumner.

Here is a letter from him, written but a day before beginning his speech: "Alas! alas!" he says, "the tyranny over us is complete! Will the people submit? When you read this, I shall be saying in the Senate, they will not. I shall pronounce the most thorough Philippic [against Slavery] ever uttered in a legislative body." He kept his word; it was the most thorough Philippic against Slavery ever uttered in an American Parliament. Nay, Wilberforce and Brougham, and their famous peers, never surpassed it in the British House. The talent, the learning, the eloquence of Mr. Sumner never went further. The composure, the respectful dignity, of this man, who is a gentleman amongst gentlemen, was never more decorous and manly than at that time. He gave an argument: the South has answered it with a bludgeon cut from a tree whose seed was sown in Boston,—Mr. Pearson's Acorn. Two years before this assault, Judge Loring was kidnapping Mr. Burns. That very day, the Know-nothing Legislature, stimulated thereto by men well known, was attempting to re-establish kidnapping in Boston, by destroying the Personal Liberty Law. It was not my Boston that wanted such wickedness; it was the slave-hunter's Boston that wanted it,—a few men, idiotic in conscience, heart, and soul.

I keep the coat of Thomas Sims; it is rent to tatters. I wish I had also the bloody garment of Charles Sumner, that I might show it to you; and I would ask Boston,

"Knowest thou whether this be thy son's coat or no?"
And Boston would answer, "It is my son's coat: an evil
beast hath devoured him." And I would say, "The evil
beast is of your own training."

When Mr. Phillips was indicted for freedom of speech,
the bail was fixed at fifteen hundred dollars. Mr. Brooks
is arrested for beating a man to an extent which may
cause his death: the bail was fixed at five hundred dollars.
The crime is only one-third so great. In 1851, when a
Pennsylvania Quaker, a miller with a felt hat, rides to his
neighbour's house on his sorrel horse, and the coloured
people, resisting a kidnapper, cheer him, he is indicted for
high treason against the United States, and spends months
in gaol; but Mr. Brooks goes at large. Passmore Wil-
liamson was charged with contempt,—not for the United
States, not for its laws, but only for Judge Kane; and he
spends months in gaol; and Mr. Representative Brooks
goes at large all this time.

Now, I am not surprised at this. They who sow the
wind must expect to see the whirlwind come up in time.
It is very pretty work sowing the wind broadcast; light
and clean to the hand, very respectable: but when you
come to eat the harvest of whirlwinds, when the bread of
storms is broke on your table, then you remember that
"righteousness exalteth a nation, and sin is the ruin of
any people." When the vilest of men are exalted, you
must expect the wicked will "walk on every side." Remember the Cause of this wickedness in Washington,
Kansas, all over the land,—the ferocious disposition of the
slaveholders, their fixed determination to spread bondage
over the whole country, to "crush out" all freedom of
speech. Remember the allies of that ferocity,—corrupt
men in the midst of us who have promoted this wickedness, who still encourage it. Remember the general
servility of the Northern people, who tread down the
black man that the white might gain money from the
oppressor.

Do not think this is the act of a single person. Mr.
Brooks is a representative man, more decorous and well-
mannered than most men of his section or his State. He
was but the agent of the Slave Power: all the South will
justify his deed. Already South Carolina sends him a

"testimonial" of its gratitude,—a pitcher and a cane. Of course there are honourable men in the South, who abhor this cowardly violence; but they will not dare to speak aloud.

Do not think the blow was struck at Mr. Sumner alone. It was at you and me and all of us,—a blow at freedom of speech. Violence must begin somewhere, and he happened to be there. Now threats are uttered against all others who oppose the enslavement of the people : your masters say that Seward, Wilson, Wade, and Hale shall next take their turn.

It is encouraging to see the effect of this outrage on the people at the North. Nothing has so stirred men before. Each new stroke of the slave-driver's whip startles some one. Whenever Slavery is driven through our Northern cities, it breaks up the pavement a little; the stones are never replaced : by and by, the street will be impassable for that tumbril. The Fugitive Slave Bill opened some Northern eyes; others were unstopped by its enforcement here. Some recovered their conscience when the Nebraska iniquity was first proposed; the blows in the Senate House waken yet more; the fall of the buildings at Lawrence startle other men from deadly sleep. "Let bygones be bygones :" if a man comes into the field at the eleventh hour, to honest work, let not those who have borne the burthen and heat of the day grudge him his place and his penny. If a man stand with his back leaning against the public whipping-post in Charleston, S.C., but looks northward, and loves freedom, and will do anything for it, let us give him our thanks and our help.

The crime which the slaveholders have now committed against our senator is very small compared to the sin of Boston against two of its inhabitants. Which is worse, for Mr. Brooks at Washington to beat an unarmed senator with a heavy bludgeon, taking him unawares, or for Commissioner Curtis and Commissioner Loring to steal Mr. Sims and Mr. Burns ? What are a few blows, to slavery for life? what the Southern "testimonial," compared to the "fifteen hundred *gentlemen*" who volunteered for the first kidnapping, and the citizen soldiers who so eagerly took part in the last one ? Will Massachusetts ask the House of Representatives to expel the assassin ? Who is Judge of Probate in Suffolk County? Two years ago, with the sword of Boston, the slaveholders cut and wounded peaceful citizens of our own town, and in vain do they besiege the courts of our own State for redress! Mr. Brooks obeys the law of honour among ruffians, Messrs. Curtis and Loring the Fugitive Slave Bill: which is the better of the two, — the law of bullies, or of kidnappers? If Mayor Smith had a right to tread down the laws of Massachusetts, and smite and stab men with the sword, that he might steal a negro, why may not Mr. Brooks beat a senator who speaks against the great crime of the nation?

I rejoice in the indignation which this outrage has caused. Boston is stirred as never before. Does she know that Mr. Sumner was wounded for *her* transgression, and bruised for *her* iniquity? Let us lay these things sorrowfully to heart. The past cannot be recalled; but we may do better in the future,—remove the causes of this evil; may root slavery out of the land, " peaceably if we can, forcibly if we must."

In the country, I expect great good from this wickedness. New-England farmers cover the corn they plant with a prayer for God's blessing : this year they will *stamp* it also with a curse on Slavery. The matter will be talked over by the shoemakers, and in every carpenter's and trader's shop. The blacksmith, holding the horse's hoof between his legs, will pause over the inserted nail, and his brow grow darker while the human fire burns within. Meetings will be held in fifty towns of Massachusetts, nowhere with a platform so tame as that last night.

There is a war before us worse than Russian. It has already begun : when shall it end? " Not till Slavery has put freedom down," say your masters at the South. "Not till Freedom has driven slavery from the continent," let us say and determine.

I have four things to propose : First, Ask Mr. Sumner to come to Boston on the 4th of July, and, in this place, give us an oration worthy of the day, worthy of Boston, and worthy of himself. If he is too sick, ask Wendell Phillips ; and, depend upon it, he will be well. Second, Make Mr. Sumner senator next time, and let those men who talk about a "nest of vipers" understand that Massachusetts knows who has got poison on his tongue. Third, Make a man President who is not a knave, not a dunce. Fourth, Reverence the higher law of God in politics and in everything else ; be not afraid of men ; do not be *afraid* of God, but afraid to violate any law which he has writ on your soul ; and then his blessing will be upon you, and his peace will be with us for ever and ever.

LONDON :

WILLIAM STEVENS, PRINTER, 37, BELL YARD,

TEMPLE BAR.

Printed in the United States
52105LVS00006B/28

9 781417 946907